4 All-Star

Linda Lee

Kristin Sherman ★ **Stephen Sloan**

Grace Tanaka ★ **Shirley Velasco**

All-Star 4 Student Book, 1st Edition

Published by McGraw-Hill ESL/ELT, a business unit of The McGraw-Hill Companies, Inc. 1221 Avenue of the Americas, New York, NY 10020. Copyright © 2006 by The McGraw-Hill Companies, Inc. All rights reserved. No part of this publication may be reproduced or distributed in any form or by any means, or stored in a database or retrieval system, without the prior written consent of The McGraw-Hill Companies, Inc., including, but not limited to, in any network or other electronic storage or transmission, or broadcast for distance learning.

ISBN 0-07-284687-9 (Student Book)
1 2 3 4 5 6 7 8 9   QPD/QPD   11 10 09 08 07 06 05

ISBN 0-07-321855-3 (Student Book with Audio Highlights)
1 2 3 4 5 6 7 8 9   QPD/QPD   11 10 09 08 07 06 05

ISBN 0-07-111546-3 (International Student Edition)
1 2 3 4 5 6 7 8 9   QPD/QPD   11 10 09 08 07 06 05

Editorial director: Tina B. Carver
Executive editor: Erik Gundersen
Developmental editor: Terre Passero
Production manager: Juanita Thompson
Interior designer: Wee Design Group
Cover designer: Wee Design Group
Illustrators: Burgundy Beam, Andrew Lange, Rich Stergulz, Carlotta Tormey
Photo research: David Averbach
Photo credits: see page 193

ACKNOWLEDGEMENTS

The authors and publisher would like to thank the following individuals who reviewed the *All-Star* program at various stages of development and whose comments, reviews, and field-testing were instrumental in helping us shape the series:

Carol Antunano • The English Center; Miami, FL

Feliciano Atienza • YMCA Elesair Project; New York, NY

Nancy Baxer • Lutheran Social Ministries of New Jersey Refugee Resettlement Program; Trenton, NJ

Jeffrey P. Bright • Albany Park Community Center; Chicago, IL

Enzo Caserta • Miami Palmetto Adult Education Center; Miami, FL

Allison Freiman • YMCA Elesair Project; New York, NY

Susan Gaer • Santa Ana College School of Continuing Education; Santa Ana, CA

Toni Galaviz • Reseda Community Adult School; Reseda, CA

Maria Hegarty • SCALE; Somerville, MA

Virginia Hernandez • Miami Palmetto Adult Education Center; Miami, FL

Giang Hoang • Evans Community Adult School; Los Angeles, CA

Edwina Hoffman • Miami-Dade County Adult Schools; Miami, FL

Ionela Istrate • YMCA of Greater Boston International Learning Center; Boston, MA

Janice Jensen • Santa Ana College School of Continuing Education; Santa Ana, CA

Jan Jerrell • San Diego Community College District; San Diego, CA

Margaret Kirkpatrick • Berkeley Adult School; Berkeley, CA

LaRanda Marr • Oakland Unified School District; Office of Adult Education; Oakland, CA

Patricia Mooney-Gonzalez • New York State Department of Education; Albany, NY

Paula Orias • Piper Community School; Broward County Public Schools; Sunrise, FL

Linda O'Roke • City College of San Francisco; San Francisco, CA

Betsy Parrish • Hamline University; St. Paul, MN

Mary Pierce • Xavier Adult School; New York, NY

Marta Pitt • Lindsey Hopkins Technical Education Center; Miami, FL

Donna Price-Machado • San Diego Community College District; San Diego, CA

Sylvia Ramirez • Community Learning Center • MiraCosta College; Oceanside, CA

Inna Reydel • YMCA of Greater Boston International Learning Center; Boston, MA

Leslie Shimazaki • San Diego Community College District; San Diego, CA

Betty Stone • SCALE; Somerville, MA

Theresa Suslov • SCALE; Somerville, MA

Dave VanLew • Simi Valley Adult & Career Institute; Simi Valley, CA

Scope and Sequence

	Life Skills				
Unit	**Listening and Speaking**	**Reading and Writing**	**Critical Thinking**	**Vocabulary**	**Grammar**
Pre-Unit **Getting Started** *page 2*	• Express opinions • Introduce yourself • Interview your classmates	• Write about your classmates • Preview the book	• Evaluate • Choose the best alternative • Preview	• Introductions • Information questions	
1 **Skills and Abilities** *page 4*	• Talk about continuing education • Talk about personal and professional goals • Listen to telephone conversations and messages • Talk about telephone behavior • Talk about job interviews • Talk about importance of writing skills • Discuss success **Focus on Pronunciation:** Blending words in questions with *you*	• Complete a class registration form • Read about types of skills • Write about types of skills • Write telephone messages • Read a success story • Read about career plans • Preview a reading **Spotlight: Reading** Make inferences **Spotlight: Writing** Write business letters	• Evaluate • Apply knowledge • Analyze	• Types of courses • Educational and professional goals • Word forms	• Direct and indirect *yes/no* and *wh-* questions
2 **Getting Around** *page 22*	• Talk about types of transportation • Talk about solving transportation problems • Talk about automobile insurance • Listen to conversations regarding a traffic accident and car repair • Listen to conversations about making car and travel reservations • Get information about travel schedules **Focus on Pronunciation:** Reduction of past modals	• Read an insurance policy • Read automobile insurance terms • Read a bus schedule • Read about travel options • Take notes on transportation issues • Write synonyms • Fill out accident reports **Spotlight: Reading** Identify the topic and main idea **Spotlight: Writing** compound subjects, verbs, and objects	• Make inferences • Compare information • Analyze • Interpret	• Automobile insurance terms • Parts of an automobile • Synonyms • Car accident checklist	• Past form of *should* • Past form of *could*

		Correlations to National Standards			
Civics Concepts	**Math Skills**	**CASAS Life Skill Competencies**	**SCANS Competencies (Workplace)**	**EFF Content Standards**	**Literacy Completion Points (LCPs)**
		• 0.1.2, 0.1.4, 0.2.1, 0.2.4, 7.2.3, 7.4.6, 7.5.6	• Decision making • Sociability • Knowing how to learn	• Communicate so that others understand • Reflect on and reevaluate your opinions and ideas	• 83.03, 83.11
• Identify educational opportunities • Recognize personal and professional goals • Recognize personal job skill abilities • Recognize appropriate interviewing behavior • Ability to take and interpret telephone messages • Recognize do's and don'ts of phone use • Recognize behavior that leads to promotion		• **1:** 0.2.2, 2.5.5, 4.4.5, 6.7.3, 7.1.1, 7.26, 7.5.1 • **2:** 7.2.1, 7.2.4, 7.31, 7.32, 7.5.1, 7.5.6 • **3:** 0.1.2, 0.1.3, 2.1.7, 4.5.4, 7.2.1, 7.2.2 • **4:** 4.4.2, 4.6.2, 4.6.5, 7.2.4, 7.2.5, 7.2.6 • **5:** 0.1.2, 7.2.2 • **6:** 4.1.5, 4.1.7, 4.4.1, 7.2.1, 7.2.2, 7.2.3, 7.2.5 • **7:** 0.1.2, 7.1.4, 7.2.4, 7.4.7 • **RS:** 7.2.4, 7.2.5 • **WS:** 0.1.2, 0.1.4, 4.6.2, 7.2.2, 7.2.3	Emphasized are the following: • Understand systems • Reasoning • Organize and maintain information • Problem solving • Self-management • Decision making • Work well with others	Emphasized are the following: • Create vision of future • Plan and renew career goals • Pursue personal self-improvement • Reflect on and reevaluate your opinions and ideas • Develop a sense of self that reflects your values	• **1:** 71.01, 83.13 • **2:** 70.01, 70.02, 83.06 • **3:** 74.01, 74.02, 83.02, 83.04 • **4:** 83.05, 83.10, 83.14 • **5:** 83.16 • **6:** 69.04, 70.01 • **7:** 83.02, 83.18 • **RS:** 83.05, 83.12, 83.14 • **WS:** 83.15
• Compare travel schedule and cost • Interpret information about automobile insurance • Understand what to do in case of an accident • Identify basic travel signs • Interpret highway and traffic signs		• **1:** 0.1.2, 1.9.1, 1.9.7, 2.2.3, 7.1.1, 7.2.4, 7.3.1, 7.3.2 • **2:** 0.1.2, 1.9.7, 1.9.8, 7.2.1, 7.2.3 • **3:** 0.1.2, 1.1.3, 1.9.4, 1.9.6, 1.9.7, 1.9.8, 2.2.2, 2.2.4, 2.2.5, 7.2.2, 7.2.4, 7.2.5 • **4:** 0.1.2, 1.2.2, 1.9.1, 1.9.3, 1.9.4, 2.2.3, 2.2.4, 2.2.5, 5.2.4, 7.2.1, 7.2.2, 7.2.3, 7.2.5, 7.4.2 • **5:** 0.1.3, 7.2.2, 7.2.4, 7.2.5 • **6:** 0.1.3, 1.9.7, 1.9.8, 2.1.2, 7.2.1, 7.2.5 • **7:** 0.1.2, 7.1.4, 7.2.1, 7.4.7 • **RS:** 0.1.2, 1.9.2, 7.2.2 • **WS:** 1.9.2, 1.9.7, 7.2.2	Emphasized are the following: • Participate as a member of a team • Acquire and evaluate information • Understand systems • Know how to learn • Organize and maintain information • Creative thinking • Interpret and communicate information	Emphasized are the following: • Reflect on and reevaluate opinions and ideas • Find and use community resources and services • Communicate so that others understand • Participate in group processes and decision making	• **1:** 77.03, 77.04, 83.12 • **2:** 77.02, 83.06 • **3:** 77.01, 77.04, 83.04, 83.13 • **4:** 77.01 • **5:** 84.02, 83.18 • **6:** 77.04, 83.13, 85.02 • **7:** 66.01, 66.19 • **RS:** 83.05 • **WS:** 83.16

CASAS and LCP standards: Numbers in bold indicate lesson numbers.   •   **RS:** Reading Strategy Spotlight   •   **WS:** Writing Spotlight

v

Scope and Sequence

Unit	Life Skills				
	Listening and Speaking	Reading and Writing	Critical Thinking	Vocabulary	Grammar
3 **Your Health** *page 40*	• Talk about a health emergency • Talk about types of health care professionals and specialties • Listen to phone conversations between patients and doctors' offices • Role-play phone conversations between patients and doctors' offices • Clarify information • Talk about food labels and nutrition • Talk about immunizations • Talk about healthy and unhealthy diets	• Read about health care professionals and specialties • Read nutrition labels • Read an online schedule book • Write appointments in a schedule book • Read about immunizations • Read a graph • Take notes **Spotlight: Reading** Use context clues **Spotlight: Writing** Punctuation marks	• Classify • Analyze • Make inferences • Use context clues • Prioritize	• Types of health care professionals and specialties • Nutritional labels • Words about immunization • Synonyms	• Adverb clauses of time • Adverb clauses of reason and contrast
4 **Rights and Responsibilities** *page 58*	• Talk about Washington D.C. • Talk about marches and protests • Talk about rights and responsibilities • Discuss social issues • Listen to conversations about educational system • Express agreement and disagreement • Talk about government agencies • Talk about unions	• Read about marches and protests • Read and take notes on rights and responsibilities • Read charts about education in the U.S. • Read about government agencies • Write initials of agencies to contact in emergencies • Read about acronyms vs. initials • Read and write about work unions • Scan a reading **Spotlight: Reading** Adjust your reading speed **Spotlight: Writing** Identify purpose for writing business letters	• Analyze • Rank information • Summarize • Predict • Apply knowledge to new situations	• U.S. constitutional rights and responsibilities • Educational system • Homonyms • Government agencies • Workers' rights • Unions	• Active and passive verbs • Forming the passive

Civics Concepts	Math Skills	CASAS Life Skill Competencies	SCANS Competencies (Workplace)	EFF Content Standards	Literacy Completion Points (LCPs)
• Understand when to call 911 • Understand types of health care professionals • Determine who to see for different health issues • Understand and analyze food labels • Analyze personal health habits	**Focus on Math:** Convert numbers to percentages	• **1:** 0.1.2, 2.5.1, 7.2.1, 7.2.2, 7.2.6, 7.5.1 • **2:** 0.1.2, 3.1.3, 7.2.1, 7.2.3, 7.2.5, 7.4.2 • **3:** 0.1.2, 0.1.6, 2.1.8, 3.1.2, 3.1.3, 3.2.4, 7.2.1, 7.4.2 • **4:** 0.1.2, 1.6.1, 3.5.1, 3.5.2, 6.1.1, 6.1.3, 6.1.4, 6.4.2, 7.2.3, 7.2.5, 7.3.2, 7.3.3 • **5:** 0.1.2, 7.2.2 • **6:** 1.1.3, 3.2.2, 6.4.2, 6.4.3, 6.7.1 • **7:** 0.1.2, 7.1.4, 7.2.4, 7.4.7 • **RS:** 7.2.1, 7.2.4, 7.4.1 • **WS:** 7.2.2, 7.4.1	Emphasized are the following: • Decision making • See things in the mind's eye • Self-management • Acquire and evaluate information • Organize and maintain information • Know how to learn • Reasoning • Creative thinking • Problem solving	Emphasized are the following: • Provide for physical needs • Participate in group processes and decision making • Organize and maintain information • Communicate so that others understand • Reflect on and reevaluate opinions and ideas • Find, interpret, and analyze diverse sources of information • Give and receive support outside the immediate family • Help self and others	• **1:** 75.01, 83.13 • **2:** 75.01, 83.06, 83.14 • **3:** 74.01, 83.02, 83.04, 83.13 • **4:** 75.03 • **5:** 83.16 • **6:** 75.01, 75.05 • **7:** 83.02, 83.18 • **RS:** 83.06 • **WS:** 78.01
• Identify U.S. constitutional rights and responsibilities • Understand the U.S. educational system • Identify which government agencies to use for different needs • Understand educational rights and options • Understand protests and marches	**Focus on Math:** Understand bar and line graphs	• **1:** 0.1.2, 2.7.3, 5.3.1, 5.3.2, 7.2.2, 7.5.1 • **2:** 0.1.2, 5.2.2, 5.3.2, 5.6.3, 7.2.1 • **3:** 0.1.2, 1.1.3, 6.7.2, 7.2.1, 7.2.3, 7.2.5, 7.4.2 • **4:** 1.6.2, 1.6.3, 5.3.2, 5.6.2, 7.2.1, 7.2.4 • **5:** 0.1.2, 7.2.2 • **6:** 1.1.3, 4.2.2, 4.2.3, 6.7.1, 6.7.2, 6.7.4, 7.2.1, 7.2.2 • **7:** 0.1.2, 7.1.4, 7.2.4, 7.4.7 • **RS:** 7.2.1, 7.2.2, 7.2.5, 7.4.1, 7.4.3 • **WS:** 4.6.2, 7.2.1	Emphasized are the following: • Participate as a member of a team • See things in the mind's eye • Know how to learn • Reasoning • Acquire and evaluate information • Organize and maintain information • Problem solve • Understand how systems work • Work within the system • Interpret and communicate information	Emphasized are the following: • Reflect on and reevaluate opinions and ideas • Find and use community resources and services • Recognize and understand your human and legal rights and civic responsibilities • Communicate so that others understand • Participate in group processes and decision making • Figure out how systems work	• **1:** 80.01, 83.12 • **2:** 80.01, 83.05, 83.06 • **3:** 82.01, 82.03, 83.04, 83.13 • **4:** 70.05, 80.02, 83.10, 83.14 • **5:** 84.03, 83.18 • **6:** 70.04, 83.05, 83.13 • **7:** 83.02, 83.18 • **RS:** 70.04, 83.14 • **WS:** 83.05, 83.08

CASAS and LCP standards: Numbers in bold indicate lesson numbers. • **RS:** Reading Strategy Spotlight • **WS:** Writing Spotlight

vii

Scope and Sequence

	Life Skills				
Unit	**Listening and Speaking**	**Reading and Writing**	**Critical Thinking**	**Vocabulary**	**Grammar**
5 **Consumer News and Views** *page 76*	• Discuss advertising • Talk about shopping and comparison shopping • Listen to conversations between customers and salespeople • Role-play conversations between customers and salespeople • Discuss food shopping tips • Talk about finding housing • Express doubt **Focus on Pronunciation:** Intonation in tag questions	• Read advertisements • Read tips for consumers and means of credit • Write definitions from context • Write a shopping list and compare ads • Read tips for food shopping • Read housing ads **Spotlight: Reading** Use a dictionary **Spotlight: Writing** Write a letter of complaint	• Analyze advertisements • Use context clues • Compare • Evaluate	• Advertisements • Shopping terms • Food shopping tips • Housing ads	• Tag questions
6 **Rules and Laws** *page 94*	• Talk about courtrooms and people in them • Summarize • Talk about a bar graph • Talk about types of crime and common laws • Listen to recorded messages • Listen to information about getting a marriage and driver's license • Talk about getting a marriage and driver's license • Paraphrase • Talk about traffic tickets • Talk about neighborhood problems **Focus on Pronunciation:** Changing stress on *that*	• Read roles of people in a courtroom • Read journal entries • Read a bar graph • Read checklists about getting a marriage and driver's license • Take notes on prerecorded instructions • Read about traffic citations • Write details about traffic citations • Read about community involvement **Spotlight: Reading** Recognize cause and effect **Spotlight: Writing** Use graphic organizers for writing	• Sequence • Summarize • Compare • Paraphrase • Interpret	• Courtroom language • Types of crimes • Word forms • Instructions to obtain a marriage license • Instructions to obtain a driver's license • Citations	• Adjective clauses

Correlations to National Standards

Civics Concepts	Math Skills	CASAS Life Skill Competencies	SCANS Competencies (Workplace)	EFF Content Standards	Literacy Completion Points (LCPs)
• Engage in comparison shopping • Understand impulse buying • Analyze advertisements • Analyze personal shopping behavior • Identify financial service options for making purchases		• **1**: 0.1.2, 1.2.1, 7.1.1, 7.2.3, 7.2.5 • **2**: 0.1.2, 1.3.1, 1.3.3, 1.6.3, 7.2.1, 7.2.3, 7.2.4 • **3**: 0.1.2, 1.3.3, 7.2.1, 7.2.4, 7.2.6 • **4**: 1.1.7, 1.2.1, 1.2.2, 1.2.3, 1.2.4, 7.2.3 • **5**: 7.2.2, 7.2.5, 7.2.6 • **6**: 1.4.2, 7.2.3, 7.2.6 • **7**: 0.1.2, 7.1.4, 7.2.4, 7.4.7 • **RS**: 7.2.2, 7.2.4, 7.4.5 • **WS**: 0.1.2, 1.6.3	Emphasized are the following: • See things in the mind's eye • Understand systems • Analyze and communicate information • Creative thinking • Decision making • Acquire and evaluate information • Organize and maintain information • Problem solving • Participate as a member of a team • Reasoning • Use resources wisely	Emphasized are the following: • Participate in group processes and decision making • Provide for physical needs • Identify and monitor problems • Listen to and learn from others' experiences and ideas • Communicate with others inside and outside the organization • Find and use community resources and services • Put ideas and directions into action • Teach children	• **1**: 79.03, 83.04 • **2**: 79.03, 83.06 • **3**: 83.02, 83.04 • **4**: 79.03 • **5**: 83.16 • **6**: 79.01, 83.01, 85.01 • **7**: 83.02, 83.18 • **RS**: 83.09 • **WS**: 83.14, 83.15
• Interpret basic court procedures • Understand requirements for obtaining licenses • Understand different types of crimes • Understand information about traffic tickets		• **1**: 0.1.2, 5.3.3, 5.5.3, 5.6.3, 7.2.1, 7.2.2, 7.2.3, 7.4.2, 7.4.3 • **2**: 1.1.3, 5.3.1, 5.3.7, 6.7.2, 7.2.3 • **3**: 1.9.2, 2.1.7, 2.5.7, 5.3.1, 7.2.1, 7.4.2 • **4**: 1.9.1, 5.3.5, 5.3.7, 7.2.1, 7.4.2, 7.4.3 • **5**: 0.1.2, 7.2.2, 7.2.5, 7.2.6 • **6**: 5.6.1, 5.6.2, 7.2.5 • **7**: 0.1.2, 7.1.4, 7.2.4, 7.4.7 • **RS**: 7.2.1, 7.2.4, 7.4.2 • **WS**: 7.2.3, 7.4.1, 7.4.2	Emphasized are the following: • Know how to learn • See things in the mind's eye • Analyze and communicate information • Decision making • Responsibility • Integrity and honesty • Acquire and evaluate information • Organize and maintain information • Problem solving • Work well with others	Emphasized are the following: • Participate in group processes and decision making • Identify and monitor problems, community needs, strengths, and resources • Develop a sense of self that reflects your history, values, beliefs, and roles in the larger community • Reflect on and reevaluate your opinions and ideas • Get involved in the community and get others involved • Define common values and goals and resolve conflict • Listen to and learn from others' experiences and ideas • Use technology • Recognize and understand your human and legal rights and civic responsibilities	• **1**: 80.04, 83.07 • **2**: 80.01, 83.06, 83.13 • **3**: 74.01, 77.02, 83.01, 83.02, 83.04 • **4**: 77.02, 77.03, 83.05 • **5**: 83.16, 84.02 • **6**: 80.02, 85.01 • **7**: 83.02, 83.18 • **RS**: 83.05, 83.15 • **WS**: 83.13, 83.14, 83.15

CASAS and LCP standards: Numbers in bold indicate lesson numbers. • **RS**: Reading Strategy Spotlight • **WS**: Writing Spotlight

Scope and Sequence

Unit	Life Skills				
	Listening and Speaking	Reading and Writing	Critical Thinking	Vocabulary	Grammar
7 **Career Paths** *page 112*	• Talk about workplace situations • Talk about workplace responsibilities and behavior • Talk about interviews • Listen to job interviews • Roleplay job interviews • Discuss ideal employees and employers • Describe workplace tasks • Expand responses to questions	• Read work rules • Read online job postings • Write a job description • Write job tasks • Read an employment application • Read a company profile **Spotlight: Reading** Identify a sequence of events **Spotlight: Writing** Understand the writing process	• Solve problems • Analyze • Evaluate • Rank job benefits • Solve problems based on new information	• Workplace skills and behavior • Prefixes • Word forms • Classified job postings	• Past perfect • Past unreal conditional
8 **Money Matters** *page 130*	• Talk about household budgets • Talk about expenses • Listen to conversations about banking • Talk about protecting your money • Talk about financial terms • Give advice	• Read questions about money issues • Read about credit cards • Read about ways to save and invest • Take notes • Write a budget **Spotlight: Reading** Compare and contrast **Spotlight: Writing** Use transition words	• Evaluate • Analyze • Apply knowledge • Compare banking alternatives	• Expenses and budgeting • Banking • Credit cards	• Quoted speech • Reported speech

Appendices

Grammar Reference Guide *page 148*

Audio Script *page 157*

Vocabulary List *page 171*

Glossary *page 173*

Skills Index *page 182*

Authentic Materials *page 187*

Map of the United States *page 192*

Correlations to National Standards

Civics Concepts	Math Skills	CASAS Life Skill Competencies	SCANS Competencies (Workplace)	EFF Content Standards	Literacy Completion Points (LCPs)
• Understand and analyze appropriate workplace behavior • Understand how to interview effectively • Understand and rank job benefits • Identify job perfomance in an employee evaluation form	**Focus on Math:** Compute averages	• **1:** 0.1.3, 4.4.1, 4.8.2, 7.2.5, 7.2.7, 7.3.2 • **2:** 4.1.3, 4.1.6, 7.2.1, 7.2.3 • **3:** 0.1.2, 0.2.4, 4.1.2, 4.1.5, 4.1.7, 7.2.2, 7.2.5 • **4:** 0.1.3, 4.4.2, 4.4.4, 7.2.3, 7.2.4, 7.2.5, 7.2.6 • **5:** 7.2.2, 7.2.6 • **6:** 1.1.8, 4.2.1, 6.7.5, 7.2.1, 7.2.2, 7.2.4, 7.2.7 • **7:** 0.1.2, 7.1.4, 7.4.7 • **RS:** 7.2.3, 7.2.5, 7.4.2 • **WS:** 7.2.3, 7.2.6, 7.4.2	Emphasized are the following: • Interpret and communicate information • See things in the mind's eye • Reasoning • Work well with others • Know how to learn • Acquire and evaluate information • Organize and maintain information • Self-management • Creative thinking • Use resources wisely • Self esteem	Emphasized are the following: • Participate in group processes and decision making • Pursue personal self-improvement • Create a vision of the future • Plan and renew career goals • Balance and support work, career, and personal goals • Organize, plan, and prioritize work and use resources • Reflect on and reevaluate your opinions and ideas • Find and get a job • Communicate with others inside and outside the organization	• **1:** 69.01, 70.01, 70.02 • **2:** 69.01, 69.02, 83.06 • **3:** 69.03, 70.01, 83.02, 83.04 • **4:** 69.01, 70.01, 71.02, 83.14 • **5:** 83.16, 83.18, 84.01 • **6:** 71.01, 83.05, 83.14 • **7:** 83.02, 83.18 • **RS:** 83.07, 83.17 • **WS:** 83.13, 83.15
• Interpret credit card applications • Understand the use of credit • Understand a budget • Understand interest rates • Understand banking services	**Focus on Math:** Understand rates	• **1:** 1.5.1, 6.0.3, 6.0.4, 6.4.3, 7.1.1, 7.2.6, 7.4.3 • **2:** 1.3.2, 1.8.3, 6.7.2, 7.2.1, 7.2.5, 7.3.2 • **3:** 0.1.6, 1.2.2, 1.8.1, 1.8.5, 7.2.3, 7.2.5 • **4:** 1.6.2, 7.2.5, 7.3.2 • **5:** 0.1.2, 7.2.2 • **6:** 1.2.4, 4.2.1, 6.1.3 • **7:** 0.1.2, 7.1.4, 7.2.4, 7.4.7 • **RS:** 7.2.3, 7.4.2 • **WS:** 7.2.2, 7.2.6	Emphasized are the following: • See things in the mind's eye • Acquire and evaluate information • Reasoning • Problem solving • Analyze and communicate information • Use resources wisely • Understand how systems work	Emphasized are the following: • Manage resources • Provide for physical needs • Educate self and others	• **1:** 76.02, 83.13 • **2:** 76.01, 83.06, 83.13, 83.14 • **3:** 76.01, 83.02, 83.04 • **4:** 83.05, 83.06, 83.14 • **5:** 83.02, 83.04, 83.18 • **6:** 69.05, 83.13 • **7:** 83.02, 83.18 • **RS:** 83.05, 83.13, 83.14 • **WS:** 83.16, 83.18

CASAS and LCP standards: Numbers in bold indicate lesson numbers. • **RS:** Reading Strategy Spotlight • **WS:** Writing Spotlight

xi

TO THE TEACHER

All-Star is a four-level, standards-based series for English learners featuring a picture-dictionary approach to vocabulary building. "Big picture" scenes in each unit provide springboards to a wealth of activities developing all of the language skills.

An accessible and predictable sequence of lessons in each unit systematically builds language and math skills around life-skill topics. *All-Star* presents family, work, and community topics in each unit, and provides alternate application lessons in its Workbooks, giving teachers the flexibility to customize the series for a variety of student needs and curricular objectives. *All-Star* is tightly correlated to all of the major national and state standards for adult instruction.

Features

★ **Accessible "big picture" scenes** present life-skills vocabulary, activities, and discussion, and provide engaging contexts for all-skills language development.

★ **Predictable sequence of nine, two-page lessons** in each unit reduces prep time for teachers and helps students get comfortable with the pattern of each lesson type.

★ **Flexible structure** allows teachers to customize each unit to meet a variety of student needs and curricular objectives, with application lessons addressing family, work, and community topics in both the Student Book and Workbook.

★ **Comprehensive coverage of key standards, such as CASAS, SCANS, EFF, and LCPs,** prepares students to master a broad range of critical competencies.

★ **Multiple assessment measures** like CASAS-style tests and performance-based assessment offer a broad range of options for monitoring and assessing learner progress.

★ **Dynamic, Interactive CD-ROM program** in Levels 1 and 2 integrates language, literacy, and numeracy skill building with computer practice.

The Complete *All-Star* Program

★ The **Student Book** features eight, 18-page units, integrating listening, speaking, reading, writing, grammar, math, and pronunciation skills with life-skill topics, critical thinking activities, and civics concepts. As in levels 1, 2, and 3, Student Book 4 addresses the themes central to the lives of adult ESL learners, making it easy to use the *All-Star* series in multi-level classrooms.

★ The **Student Book with Audio Highlights** provides students with audio recordings of all of the conversations and example dialogues in the Student Book.

★ The **Teacher's Edition with Tests** provides:
  • Step-by-step procedural notes for each Student Book activity
  • More than 200 expansion activities for Student Book 4,

many of which offer creative tasks tied to the "big picture" scenes in each unit
  • Culture, Grammar, Pronunciation, and Academic Notes
  • Two-page written test for each unit (*Note:* Listening passages for the tests are available on the Student Book Audiocassettes and Audio CDs.)
  • Audio scripts for all audio program materials
  • Answer keys for Student Book, Workbook, and Tests

★ The **Interactive CD-ROM** included in Levels 1 and 2 incorporates and extends the learning goals of the Student Book by integrating language, literacy, and numeracy skill building with multimedia practice on the computer. A flexible set of activities correlated to each unit builds vocabulary, listening, reading, writing, and test-taking skills.

★ The **Color Overhead Transparencies** encourage teachers to present new vocabulary and concepts in fun and meaningful ways. This component provides a full-color overhead transparency for each of the "big picture" scenes.

★ The **Workbook** includes supplementary practice activities correlated systematically to the Student Book. As a bonus feature, the Workbook also includes alternate application lessons addressing the learner's role as worker, family member, and/or community member. These additional, optional lessons may be used in addition to, or as substitutes for, the application lessons found in Lesson 6 of each Student Book unit.

★ The **Audiocassettes** and **Audio CDs** contain recordings for all listening activities in the Student Book. Listening passages for each unit test are provided at the end of the audio section for that unit.

Overview of the *All-Star* Program

UNIT STRUCTURE

Consult the *Welcome to All-Star* guide on pages xvi–xix. This guide offers teachers and administrators a visual tour of one Student Book unit.

All-Star is designed to maximize accessibility and flexibility. Each unit contains the following sequence of nine, two-page lessons that develop vocabulary and build language, grammar, and math skills around life-skill topics:

★ Lesson 1: Talk about It

★ Lesson 2: Vocabulary in Context

★ Lesson 3: Listening and Speaking

★ Lesson 4: Reading and Critical Thinking

★ Lesson 5: Grammar

★ Lesson 6: Application

★ Lesson 7: Review and Assessment

★ Spotlight: Reading Strategy

★ Spotlight: Writing Strategy

Each lesson addresses a key adult standard, and these standards are indicated in the upper right-hand corner of each lesson in a yellow bar.

SPECIAL FEATURES OF EACH UNIT

★ *Warm-Up.* These activities activate students' background knowledge, access their personal experience, and generate their interest in the topic of the lesson. They serve to introduce students to the lesson topic and prompt classroom discussion.

★ *Try This Strategy.* This feature presents students with learning strategies (such as identifying goals), vocabulary strategies (such as learning synonyms), and academic learning strategies (such as evaluating texts) towards the beginning of each unit so they can apply them as they proceed through the lessons. These strategies allow students to build skills to continue their lifelong learning.

★ *Communication Strategy.* This feature presents students with communication strategies that will improve their ability to communicate effectively and help them become more fluid, natural speakers. Communication strategies, such as disagreeing politely, are introduced and then practiced in real-life role-play activities called *Use the Communication Strategy.*

★ *Grammar Lessons.* Grammar is presented and practiced in Lesson 5 of each unit. These two-page lessons offer students more in-depth grammar practice than at the lower levels of the series. The essential grammar content is correlated to a variety of national and state standards. A comprehensive *Grammar Reference Guide* at the back of the book summarizes all of the structures and functions presented.

★ *Window on Math.* Learning basic math skills is critically important for success in school, on the job, and at home. As such, national and state standards for adult education mandate instruction in basic math skills. In half of the units, a blue box called *Window on Math* is dedicated to helping students develop the functional numeracy skills they need for basic math work in everyday math applications such as payroll deductions.

★ *Window on Pronunciation.* Improving pronunciation skills can greatly improve students' ability to understand others and to be understood. In half of the units, a blue box called *Window on Pronunciation* is dedicated to helping students achieve two major goals: (1) hearing and producing specific sounds, words, and minimal pairs of words so they become better listeners and speakers; and (2) addressing issues of stress, rhythm, and intonation so that the students' spoken English becomes more comprehensible.

★ *Spotlight: Reading Strategy.* After the *Review and Assessment* lesson in each unit, students and teachers will find

a *Spotlight* dedicated to presenting students with academic reading strategies. These are optional, two-page lessons that offer a supplementary focus on reading skill development.

★ *Spotlight: Writing Strategy.* At the end of each unit, students and teachers will find a *Spotlight* dedicated to presenting students with academic and professional writing strategies. These are optional, two-page lessons that offer a supplementary focus on writing skill development.

TWO-PAGE LESSON FORMAT

The lessons in *All-Star* are designed as two-page spreads. Lessons 5–7 and the Spotlights employ a standard textbook layout, but Lessons 1–4 follow an innovative format with a list of activities on the left-hand page of the spread and rich textual input supporting these activities on the right-hand page. The textual input includes authentic and adapted newspaper articles, letters, and official forms and applications. The list of activities, entitled *Things To Do*, allows students and teachers to take full advantage of the visuals in each lesson, inviting students to achieve a variety of learning, by evaluating, synthesizing, and analyzing.

As in previous levels, Lessons 1–4 provide learners with the input necessary to facilitate comprehension. Student Books 3 and 4 include much of the rich visual input found in Student Books 1 and 2, but also has greater textual input in keeping with the students' more advanced abilities.

"BIG PICTURE" SCENES

Each unit includes one "big picture" scene. In Student Books 3 and 4, the "big picture" scene begins each unit in Lesson 1. This scene is the visual centerpiece of each unit, and serves as a springboard to a variety of activities provided in the Student Book, Teacher's Edition, Color Overhead Transparencies package, and the Interactive CD-ROM program in Levels 1 and 2. The "big picture" activates background knowledge, accesses students' personal experience, increases their motivation, and serves as a prompt for classroom discussion.

The Teacher's Edition includes a variety of all-skills "Big Picture Expansion" activities that are tied to the Student Book scenes. For each unit, these expansion activities address listening, speaking, reading, writing, and grammar skill development, and allow teachers to customize their instruction to meet the language learning needs of each group of students.

In the Color Overhead Transparencies package, teachers will find transparencies of each "big picture" scene, which they can use to introduce the vocabulary and life-skill concepts in each unit. They can also use these transparencies to facilitate the "Big Picture Expansion" activities in the Teacher's Edition.

Finally, the Interactive CD-ROM program in Levels 1 and 2 highlights an additional aspect of the "big picture" scenes in its listening activities. Students working with the CD-ROM program listen to a series of new conversations taking place between characters in the "big picture" scenes. They then work through a series of interactive activities based on these conversations and receive immediate feedback on their work.

CIVICS CONCEPTS

Many institutions focus direct attention on the importance of civics instruction for English language learners. Civics instruction encourages students to become active and informed community members. *Application* lessons provide activities that help students develop their roles as workers, parents, and community members. Those lessons targeting the students' role as a community member encourage learners to become more active and informed members of their communities.

CASAS, SCANS, EFF, LCPs, AND OTHER STANDARDS

Teachers and administrators benchmark student progress against national and/or state standards for adult instruction. With this in mind, *All-Star* carefully integrates instructional elements from a wide range of standards including CASAS, SCANS, EFF, and the Literacy Completion Points (LCPs). Unit-by-unit correlations of these standards appear in the scope and sequence on pages iv–xi. Here is a brief overview of our approach to meeting the key national and state standards:

★ **CASAS.** Many U.S. states, including California, tie funding for adult education programs to student performance on the Comprehensive Adult Student Assessment System (CASAS). The CASAS (www.casas.org) competencies identify more than 300 essential skills that adults need in order to succeed in the classroom, workplace, and community. Examples of these skills include identifying or using appropriate non-verbal behavior in a variety of settings, responding appropriately to common personal information questions, and comparing price or quality to determine the best buys. *All-Star* comprehensively integrates all of the CASAS Life Skill Competencies throughout the four levels of the series. Level 4 addresses the CASAS Level C Life Skills test items on CASAS Test Forms 35, 36, 55, and 56.

★ **SCANS.** Developed by the United States Department of Labor, SCANS is an acronym for the Secretary's Commission on Achieving Necessary Skills (www.doleta.gov/SCANS/). SCANS competencies are workplace skills that help people compete more effectively in today's global economy. The following are examples of SCANS competencies: works well with others, acquires and evaluates information, and teaches others new skills. A variety of SCANS competencies are threaded throughout the activities in each unit of *All-Star*. The incorporation of these competencies recognizes both the intrinsic importance of teaching workplace skills and the fact that many adult students are already working members of their communities.

★ **EFF.** Equipped for the Future (EFF) is a set of standards for adult literacy and lifelong learning, developed by The National Institute for Literacy (www.nifl.gov). The organizing principle of EFF is that adults assume responsibilities in three major areas of life—as workers, as parents, and as citizens. These three areas of focus are called "role maps" in the EFF

documentation. In the parent role map, for example, EFF highlights these and other responsibilities: participating in children's formal education, and forming and maintaining supportive family relationships. Each *All-Star* unit addresses all three of the EFF role maps in its *Application* lessons. Lesson 6 in each Student Book unit includes one of the three application lessons for that unit. The remaining two application lessons are found in the corresponding Workbook unit.

★ **LCPs.** Florida and Texas document the advancement of learners in an adult program through their system of Literacy Completion Points (LCPs). Community college and school districts earn an LCP each time an adult student advances to a higher proficiency level or completes a program. *All-Star* Level 4 incorporates into its instruction the vast majority of standards at LCP Level E.

NUMBER OF HOURS OF INSTRUCTION

The *All-Star* program has been designed to accommodate the needs of adult classes with 70–180 hours of classroom instruction. Here are three recommended ways in which various components in the *All-Star* program can be combined to meet student and teacher needs.

★ **70–100 hours.** Teachers are encouraged to work through all of the Student Book materials, incorporating the *Reading* and *Writing Spotlights* as time permits. The Color Overhead Transparencies can be used to introduce and/or review materials in each unit. Teachers should also look to the Teacher's Edition for teaching suggestions and testing materials as necessary.

Time per unit: 9–13 hours.

★ **100–140 hours.** In addition to working through all of the Student Book materials, teachers are encouraged to incorporate the Workbook for supplementary practice.

Time per unit: 13–18 hours.

★ **140–180 hours.** Teachers and students working in an intensive instructional setting can take advantage of the wealth of expansion activities threaded through the Teacher's Edition to supplement the Student Book and the Workbook.

Time per unit: 18–22 hours.

ASSESSMENT

The *All-Star* program offers teachers, students, and administrators the following wealth of resources for monitoring and assessing student progress and achievement:

★ **Standardized testing formats.** *All-Star* is correlated to the CASAS competencies and many other national and state standards for adult learning. Students have the opportunity to practice answering CASAS-style listening and reading questions in Lesson 7 of each unit (*What do you know?*) and in Lesson 7 of the Workbook (*Practice Test*). Students practice with the same item types and bubble-in answer sheets they encounter on CASAS and other standardized tests.

★ **Achievement tests.** The *All-Star* Teacher's Edition includes end-of-unit tests. These paper-and-pencil tests help students demonstrate how well they have learned the instructional content of the unit. Adult learners often show incremental increases in learning that are not always measured on standardized tests. The achievement tests may demonstrate learning even in a short amount of instructional time. Twenty percent of each test includes questions that encourage students to apply more academic skills such as determining meaning from context, making inferences, and understanding main ideas. Practice with these question types will help prepare students who may want to enroll in academic classes.

★ **Performance-based assessment.** *All-Star* provides several ways to measure students' performance on productive tasks. The Teacher's Edition suggests writing and speaking prompts and rubrics that teachers can use for performance-based assessment. These prompts derive from the "big picture" scene in each unit and provide rich visual input as the basis for the speaking and writing tasks asked of the students.

★ **Portfolio assessment.** A portfolio is a collection of student work that can be used to show progress. Examples of work that the instructor or the student may submit in the portfolio include writing samples, speaking rubrics, audiotapes, videotapes, or projects. The Teacher's Edition identifies activities that require critical thinking and small group project work which may be included, as well as those that may be used as documentation for the secondary standards defined by the National Reporting System.

★ **Self-assessment.** Self-assessment is an important part of the overall assessment picture, as it promotes student involvement and commitment to the learning process. When encouraged to assess themselves, students take more control of their learning and are better able to connect the instructional content with their own goals. The Student Book includes *Learning Logs* at the end of each unit, which allow students to check off the vocabulary they have learned, and the skills and strategies they have acquired. The Workbook provides a *Practice Test Performance Record* graph where students record their number of correct answers on each practice test, encouraging them to monitor their own progress as they advance through the book.

★ **Other linguistic and non-linguistic outcomes.** Traditional testing often does not account for the progress made by adult learners with limited educational experience or low literacy levels. Such learners tend to take longer to make smaller language gains, so the gains they make in other areas are often more significant. These gains may be in areas such as self-esteem, goal clarification, learning skills, and access to employment, community involvement and further academic studies. The SCANS and EFF standards identify areas of student growth that are not necessarily language based. *All-Star* is correlated with both SCANS and EFF standards. Every unit in the student book contains a lesson that focuses on one of the EFF role maps (worker, family member, community member), and the Workbook provides alternate lessons that address the other two role maps. Like the Student Book, the Workbook includes activities that may provide documentation that can be added to a student portfolio.

About the authors and series consultants

Linda Lee is lead author on the *All-Star* series. Linda has taught ESL/ELT in the United States, Iran, and China, and has authored or co-authored a variety of successful textbook series for English learners. As a classroom instructor, Linda's most satisfying teaching experiences have been with adult ESL students at Roxbury Community College in Boston, Massachusetts.

Kristin Sherman is a contributing author on *All-Star*, Student Book 2 and a co-author on Student Book 3. Kristin has 10 years of teaching experience in both credit and non-credit ESL programs. She has taught general ESL, as well as classes focusing on workplace skills and family literacy. She has authored a number of workbooks and teacher's editions for English learners. Her favorite project was the creation of a reading and writing workbook with her ESL students at the Mecklenburg County Jail.

Stephen Sloan is Title One Coordinator at James Monroe High School in the Los Angeles Unified School District. Steve has more than 25 years of teaching and administrative experience with both high school and adult ESL learners. Steve is also the author of McGraw-Hill's *Rights and Responsibilities: Reading and Communication for Civics.*

Grace Tanaka is professor and coordinator of ESL at the Santa Ana College School of Continuing Education, in Santa Ana, California, which serves more than 20,000 students per year. She is also a textbook co-author and series consultant. Grace has 23 years of teaching experience in both credit and non-credit ESL programs.

Shirley Velasco is assistant principal at Palmetto Adult Education Center in Miami, Florida. She has been a classroom instructor and administrator for the past 24 years. At Palmetto, Shirley has created a large adult ESOL program based on a curriculum she developed to help teachers implement the Florida LCPs (Literacy Completion Points).

Welcome to All-Star

All-Star is a four-level series featuring a "big picture" approach to meeting adult standards that systematically builds language and math skills around life-skill topics.

Accessible, two-page lesson format in Lessons 1–4 follows an innovative layout with a list of activities labeled "Things to Do" on the left and picture-dictionary visuals and readings on the right.

Predictable unit structure includes the same logical sequence of seven two-page lessons and two Spotlight lessons in each unit.

"Big picture" scenes are springboards to a wealth of life-skills vocabulary, activities, and discussions in the Student Book and all-skills expansion activities in the Teacher's Edition.

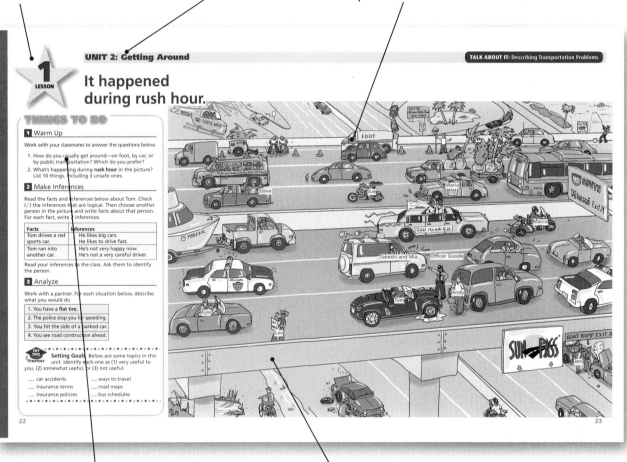

Warm Up activities activate students' background knowledge and interest in the topic, and prompt discussion.

Color overhead transparencies for the "big picture" scenes provide fun and meaningful ways to present new life-skills vocabulary and concepts, and to prompt classroom discussion.

Highlighted life-skills vocabulary is presented through compelling realia, illustrations, and in rich contextual environments. Highlighted vocabulary is defined in the glossary in the appendix.

Comprehensive coverage of key standards such as CASAS, SCANS, EFF, and LCPs prepares students to master critical competencies.

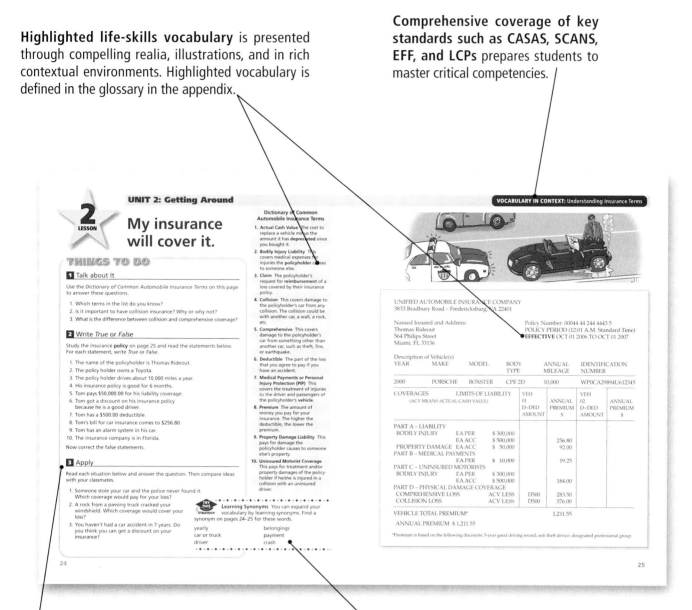

UNIT 2: Getting Around

2 LESSON

My insurance will cover it.

THINGS TO DO

1 Talk about It

Use the *Dictionary of Common Automobile Insurance Terms* on this page to answer these questions.

1. Which terms in the list do you know?
2. Is it important to have collision insurance? Why or why not?
3. What is the difference between collision and comprehensive coverage?

2 Write *True* or *False*

Study the insurance **policy** on page 25 and read the statements below. For each statement, write *True* or *False*.

1. The name of the policyholder is Thomas Rideout.
2. The policy holder owns a Toyota.
3. The policy holder drives about 10,000 miles a year.
4. His insurance policy is good for 6 months.
5. Tom pays $50,000.00 for his liability coverage.
6. Tom got a discount on his insurance policy because he is a good driver.
7. Tom has a $500.00 deductible.
8. Tom's bill for car insurance comes to $256.80.
9. Tom has an alarm system in his car.
10. The insurance company is in Florida.

Now correct the false statements.

3 Apply

Read each situation below and answer the question. Then compare ideas with your classmates.

1. Someone stole your car and the police never found it. Which coverage would pay for your loss?
2. A rock from a passing truck cracked your windshield. Which coverage would cover your loss?
3. You haven't had a car accident in 7 years. Do you think you can get a discount on your insurance?

Dictionary of Common Automobile Insurance Terms

1. **Actual Cash Value** The cost to replace a vehicle minus the amount it has **depreciated** since you bought it.
2. **Bodily Injury Liability** This covers medical expenses for injuries the **policyholder** causes to someone else.
3. **Claim** The policyholder's request for **reimbursement** of a loss covered by their insurance policy.
4. **Collision** This covers damage to the policyholder's car from any collision. The collision could be with another car, a wall, a rock, etc.
5. **Comprehensive** This covers damage to the policyholder's car from something other than another car, such as theft, fire, or earthquake.
6. **Deductible** The part of the loss that you agree to pay if you have an accident.
7. **Medical Payments or Personal Injury Protection (PIP)** This covers the treatment of injuries to the driver and passengers of the policyholder's **vehicle**.
8. **Premium** The amount of money you pay for your insurance. The higher the deductible, the lower the premium.
9. **Property Damage Liability** This pays for damage the policyholder causes to someone else's property.
10. **Uninsured Motorist Coverage** This pays for treatment and/or property damages of the policyholder if he/she is injured in a collision with an uninsured driver.

TRY THIS STRATEGY **Learning Synonyms** You can expand your vocabulary by learning synonyms. Find a synonym on pages 24–25 for these words.

yearly   belongings
car or truck   payment
driver   crash

24

VOCABULARY IN CONTEXT: Understanding Insurance Terms

UNIFIED AUTOMOBILE INSURANCE COMPANY
3833 Bradbury Road – Fredericksburg, VA 22401

Named Insured and Address: Policy Number: 00044 44 244 4443 5
Thomas Rideout   POLICY PERIOD (12:01 A.M. Standard Time)
564 Philips Street   **EFFECTIVE** OCT 01 2006 TO OCT 01 2007
Miami, FL 33136

Description of Vehicle(s)

YEAR	MAKE	MODEL	BODY TYPE	ANNUAL MILEAGE	IDENTIFICATION NUMBER
2000	PORSCHE	BOXSTER	CPE 2D	10,000	WP0CA29894U612345

COVERAGES	LIMITS OF LIABILITY (ACV MEANS ACTUAL CASH VALUE)		VEH 01 D=DED AMOUNT	ANNUAL PREMIUM $	VEH 02 D=DED AMOUNT	ANNUAL PREMIUM $
PART A – LIABILITY						
BODILY INJURY	EA PER	$ 300,000				
	EA ACC	$ 500,000		256.80		
PROPERTY DAMAGE	EA ACC	$ 50,000		92.00		
PART B – MEDICAL PAYMENTS						
	EA PER	$ 10,000		19.25		
PART C – UNINSURED MOTORISTS						
BODILY INJURY	EA PER	$ 300,000				
	EA ACC	$ 500,000		184.00		
PART D – PHYSICAL DAMAGE COVERAGE						
COMPREHENSIVE LOSS		ACV LESS	D500	283.50		
COLLISION LOSS		ACV LESS	D500	376.00		
VEHICLE TOTAL PREMIUM*				1,211.55		

ANNUAL PREMIUM $ 1,211.55

*Premium is based on the following discounts: 5-year good driving record; anti theft device; designated professional group.

25

Critical thinking activities such as evaluating and classifying, allow students to interact with the content in a meaningful way.

Try This Strategy activities present specific ways to help students learn vocabulary, understand their personal learning style, and approach academic tasks. These are included towards the beginning of each unit.

Listening activities include a rich variety of everyday personal, academic, and workplace conversations. Activities ask students to listen for important details as well as main ideas.

Realia-based readings and narrative selections like maps, advertisements, stories, graphs, and online articles provide the basis for developing reading skills and associating text with listening passages.

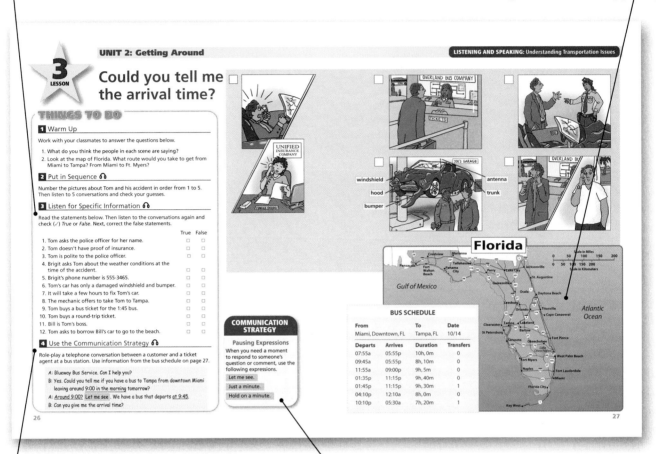

Use the Communication Strategy activities invite students to engage in everyday conversations with their classmates, using the vocabulary, grammar, and communication strategy they have learned.

Communication Strategy boxes present specific strategies that will improve students' ability to communicate effectively, helping them become more fluid, natural speakers.

WINDOW ON MATH
Converting numbers to percentages

A Read the information.

To convert numerical information to a percentage, you should divide the part by the whole and multiply by 100.

1. 130 calories (from fat) ÷ 170 calories × 100 = 76.5% total calories from fat

2. 5 calories (from protein) ÷ 14 calories (total) × 100 = 36% total calories from protein

B Calculate the percentages.

1. One package of peanut butter crackers contains 180 calories. Ninety calories come from fat. What percentage of the calories are from fat? _____

2. A serving of pasta has 42 grams of total carbohydrates. The recommended daily amount of carbohydrates is 300 grams. What percent of the recommended daily amount is the serving of pasta? _____

Windows on Math help students develop functional numeracy skills needed in everyday applications.

A grammar lesson is presented in each unit, offering in-depth grammar practice. The essential grammar content is correlated to a variety of national and state standards.

Grammar boxes describe the structure of the grammar and offers everyday examples to help students understand usage.

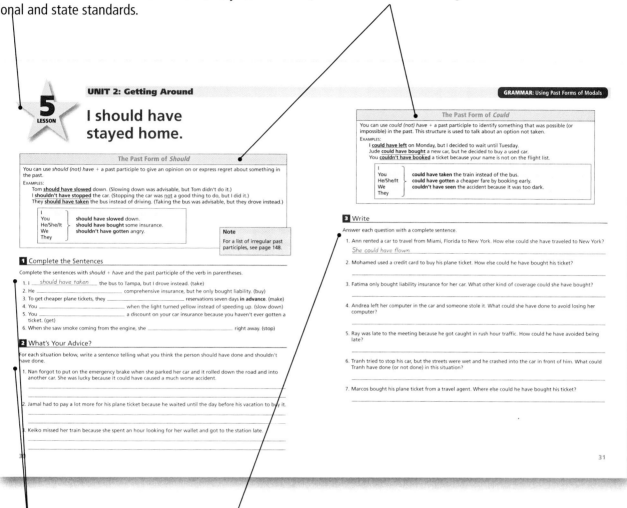

UNIT 2: Getting Around

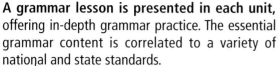

I should have stayed home.

GRAMMAR: Using Past Forms of Modals

The Past Form of *Should*

You can use *should (not) have* + a past participle to give an opinion on or express regret about something in the past.

EXAMPLES:
Tom **should have slowed** down. (Slowing down was advisable, but Tom didn't do it.)
I **shouldn't have stopped** the car. (Stopping the car was <u>not</u> a good thing to do, but I did it.)
They **should have taken** the bus instead of driving. (Taking the bus was advisable, but they drove instead.)

| I You He/She/It We They | **should have slowed** down. **should have bought** some insurance. **shouldn't have gotten** angry. |

Note
For a list of irregular past participles, see page 148.

1 Complete the Sentences

Complete the sentences with *should* + *have* and the past participle of the verb in parentheses.

1. I ___should have taken___ the bus to Tampa, but I drove instead. (take)
2. He _____ comprehensive insurance, but he only bought liability. (buy)
3. To get cheaper plane tickets, they _____ reservations seven days **in advance**. (make)
4. You _____ when the light turned yellow instead of speeding up. (slow down)
5. You _____ a discount on your car insurance because you haven't ever gotten a ticket. (get)
6. When she saw smoke coming from the engine, she _____ right away. (stop)

2 What's Your Advice?

For each situation below, write a sentence telling what you think the person should have done and shouldn't have done.

1. Nan forgot to put on the emergency brake when she parked her car and it rolled down the road and into another car. She was lucky because it could have caused a much worse accident.

2. Jamal had to pay a lot more for his plane ticket because he waited until the day before his vacation to buy it.

3. Keiko missed her train because she spent an hour looking for her wallet and got to the station late.

The Past Form of *Could*

You can use *could (not) have* + a past participle to identify something that was possible (or impossible) in the past. This structure is used to talk about an option not taken.

EXAMPLES:
I **could have left** on Monday, but I decided to wait until Tuesday.
Jude **could have bought** a new car, but he decided to buy a used car.
You **couldn't have booked** a ticket because your name is not on the flight list.

| I You He/She/It We They | **could have taken** the train instead of the bus. **could have gotten** a cheaper fare by booking early. **couldn't have seen** the accident because it was too dark. |

3 Write

Answer each question with a complete sentence.

1. Ann rented a car to travel from Miami, Florida to New York. How else could she have traveled to New York?
   She could have flown.

2. Mohamed used a credit card to buy his plane ticket. How else could he have bought his ticket?

3. Fatima only bought liability insurance for her car. What other kind of coverage could she have bought?

4. Andrea left her computer in the car and someone stole it. What could she have done to avoid losing her computer?

5. Ray was late to the meeting because he got caught in rush hour traffic. How could he have avoided being late?

6. Tranh tried to stop his car, but the streets were wet and he crashed into the car in front of him. What could Tranh have done (or not done) in this situation?

7. Marcos bought his plane ticket from a travel agent. Where else could he have bought his ticket?

31

Grammar practice activities guide students through structured and progressively more open-ended ways to use the target grammar.

Interactive CD-ROM program for **Levels 1 and 2** incorporates and extends the learning goals by integrating language, literacy, and numeracy skill building with computer practice.

Application lessons focus on developing the students' roles in life as workers, parents, and community members.

Real-world documents and situations are highlighted in the *Application* lessons, exposing students to critical concepts they encounter at work, at home, and in the community.

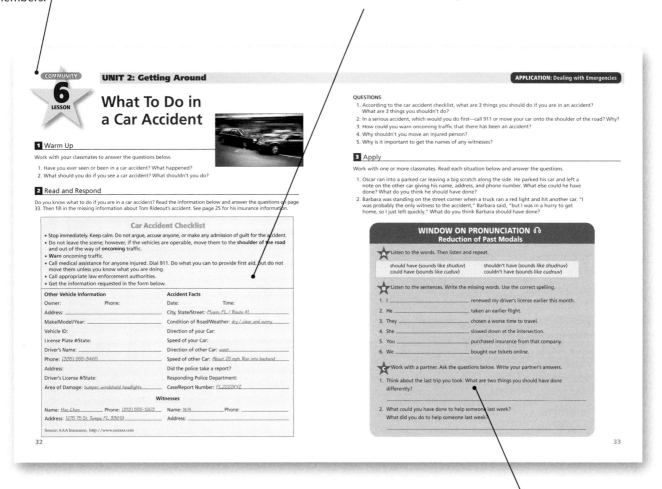

Windows on Pronunciation help students produce difficult sounds in English and address issues of stress, rhythm, and intonation.

Alternate application lessons in the Workbook provide a flexible approach to addressing family, work, and community topics in each unit.

Listening Reviews help teachers assess listening comprehension, while giving students practice with the item types and answer sheets they encounter on standardized tests.

Vocabulary Reviews provide engaging activities for students to review and assess their knowledge of the vocabulary they learned in each unit.

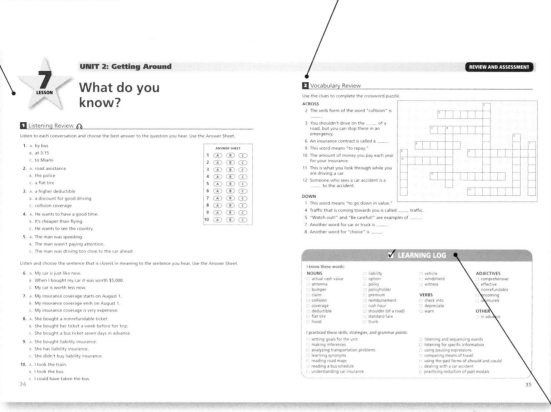

Spotlight: Reading and **Spotlight: Writing** lessons appear at the end of each unit, offering supplementary and targeted reading and writing skill development.

Learning Logs ask students to catalog the vocabulary, grammar, life-skills, and strategies they have learned, and determine which areas they need to review.

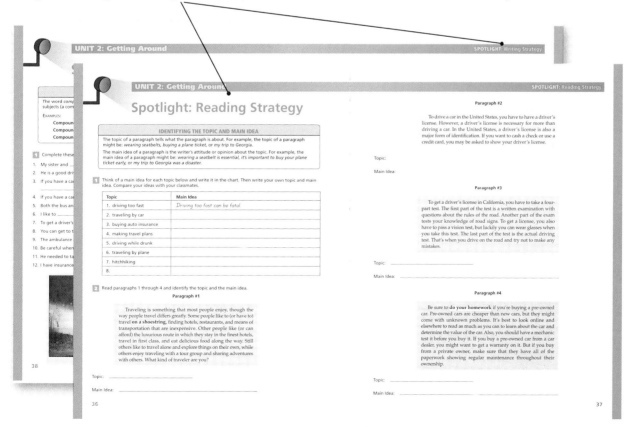

INTRODUCTION

Have we met before?

1 Evaluate

How can you start a conversation with someone you don't know? Read and evaluate the conversations below. Check (✓) *Good start* or *Not a good start*.

1

Nice weather today.

Sure is.

Do you live around here?

Yes, I do. I live on the East Side. What about you?

❏ Good start
❏ Not a good start

2

Hi. You look familiar. Have we met before?

No, I don't think so.

❏ Good start
❏ Not a good start

3

Hi, my name is Eva.

Hi, Eva. I'm Scott. Where are you from, Eva?

I'm from Mexico. And you?

❏ Good start
❏ Not a good start

4

Hi.

Hi. I'm Leo. Are you married?

Excuse me?

Are you married?

No, I'm not.

❏ Good start
❏ Not a good start

What did you like and dislike about each conversation? Share ideas with your classmates.

2 Talk about It 🎧

Talk to a classmate. Take turns asking and answering questions 1 to 4 in the chart below. Write your classmate's answers. Then repeat with 2 more classmates.

EXAMPLE: A: Hi. My name's Oscar.

B: Hi, Oscar. My name's Shirin. It's nice to meet you.

A: Nice to meet you, too. Where are you from, Shirin?

B: I'm from Iran. And you?

A: I'm from Mexico.

B: Oh, that's an interesting country. What languages do you speak?

A: I speak Spanish and English. What about you?

B: I speak French, Farsi, and English.

A: Wow! How long have you been here?

B: For about a year. And you?

A: I've been here for two years.

B: What classes are you taking?

A: I'm taking this class, a history class, and physics. What about you?

B: I'm just taking this class for now.

A: That's great. I think it will be a good class.

B: I think so, too. Well, nice talking with you.

A: Nice to talk to you, too.

Name	1. Where are you from?	2. What languages do you speak?	3. How long have you been here?	4. What classes are you taking?
1.				
2.				
3.				

3 Look It Over

What's in this book? Look at the Scope and Sequence, or Table of Contents, on pages iv–xi and answer the questions below.

1. Most textbooks are divided into chapters or units. How many units are there in this book? _____
2. What is the topic of Unit 5? _____
3. What page does Unit 3 begin on? _____
4. How many categories of things are there in the Appendices? _____
5. If you want to find the definition of a word, where in the Appendices can you look? _____
6. If you want to know what states border Nevada, where in this book can you find the answer? _____
7. If you have a question about grammar, where in the Appendices can you look for the answer? _____

1 LESSON

What skills do you want to learn?

Writing II

THINGS TO DO

1 Warm Up

Work with your classmates to answer the questions below.

1. What are 3 things you would like to learn to do for personal growth? For professional growth?
2. Which class in the picture would you like to take? Why?

2 Identify

What do you see people in the picture learning to do? List 6 activities below. Then check (✓) the things you know how to do or would like to learn to do.

Skills	I know how to	I would like to learn to
take photographs	☐	☐
	☐	☐
	☐	☐
	☐	☐
	☐	☐
	☐	☐
	☐	☐

Find a classmate who wants to learn something you want to learn. Discuss 3 ways to learn it.

EXAMPLE: I could learn Thai cooking by working in a Thai restaurant.

3 Write

Complete the registration form below with information about yourself. Choose 2 courses from the schedule.

Name _____

Address _____

City/State/Zip _____

Course #1 _____

Course #2 _____

Tuition total: $ _____

Continuing Education Course Schedule
Wednesday Evening Classes

COURSE	WKS	TIME	TUITION	
Auto Body Repair	12	6:30–9:30	$145	B3
Basic Computer Skills	10	7:00–9:00	$124	B307
Careers in Banking	8	6:30–9:00	$109	B223
Computer Repair	10	6:30–9:30	$149	B234
Defensive Driving	1	7:45–10:00	$45	PE22
Drawing Workshop	8	6:30–9:00	$124	W453
Interviewing Skills	12	6:00–9:00	$165	Th43
Italian Cooking	10	7:00–8:30	$89	B304
Keyboarding	8	7:00–8:00	$120	B231
Photography	8	6:45–9:45	$149	B303
Pottery I	10	6:00–8:30	$109	B308
Public Speaking	8	7:00–9:00	$109	B302
Small Engine Repair	12	7:00–9:00	$165	B306
Stress Management	12	4:00–5:00	$89	W233
Tai Chi	10	7:00–8:30	$75	B305
Writing II	10	7:00–9:00	$124	B301

Pottery I

Basic Computer Skills

OFFICE

Small Engine Repair

Public Speaking

Photography

303

Tai Chi

Italian Cooking

2 LESSON

What skills do you need?

See page 171 for a glossary of highlighted vocabulary.

THINGS TO DO

1 Warm Up

Work with your classmates to answer the questions below.

1. What skills do you need to be successful at work?
2. What skills do you need to be a good parent?
3. What skills do you see people using in the pictures?

2 Read and Respond

Read the information in boxes 1 to 6 and circle your answer to the question in each box. Then compare answers with a partner.

3 Evaluate

Read about the situations below and identify a skill each person has or doesn't have.

1. Laura made a presentation at work and at the end everyone looked confused and no one asked her any questions.
2. Charles and his neighbors are cleaning up the park down the street. One neighbor wants to plant flowers in the park, but Charles said that was a stupid idea.
3. Violet noticed that people are very formal at her new job, so she has started to be more formal, too.
4. Sean owns a coffee shop downtown. His new waitress is very slow and clumsy. As a result, many customers have stopped coming in the morning. Sean can't understand why business is slow.

What would you do in each situation? Talk with a classmate.

TRY THIS STRATEGY

* *

Setting Goals Below are some things you can do in this unit. Number them in order from most useful to you (1) to least useful (5).

___ interpret phone messages
___ read about common writing problems
___ write email messages
___ evaluate telephone skills
___ practice a job interview

* *

1 Listening Skills

Good listening skills are **essential** for success at work and in personal life. Good listeners **concentrate** on what the speaker is saying; they don't get **distracted** by their own thoughts or by other things going on. They also know how to show the speaker they are listening.

How good are your listening skills?

Very good	Good	OK	Not very good
1	2	3	4

4 Interpersonal Skills

Interpersonal skills are the **behaviors** people use when they **interact** with other people. To improve your interpersonal skills you must understand how your behavior **affects** other people.

How good are your interpersonal skills?

Very good	Good	OK	Not very good
1	2	3	4

JOB SKILLS

2 Oral Communication Skills

People with good speaking skills are able to express their ideas **clearly**. It is easy for their listeners to understand what they are saying. Good oral communicators can also express their ideas **concisely**. They are able to focus on the important information and **leave out** unnecessary details.

How good are your speaking skills?

Very good	Good	OK	Not very good
1	2	3	4

3 Writing Skills

Proficient writers are able to express their ideas clearly and concisely so that their writing is easy for others to **comprehend**.

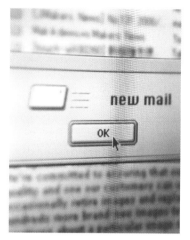

How good are your writing skills?

Very good	Good	OK	Not very good
1	2	3	4

5 Problem-Solving Skills

People with good problem-solving skills are able to identify a problem and then **come up with** possible solutions to the problem. They know how to evaluate the possible solutions and choose the best one.

How good are your problem-solving skills?

Very good	Good	OK	Not very good
1	2	3	4

6 Team Skills

People with good team skills are **cooperative** when they work with others. They **encourage** other team members by listening and responding to their ideas. They **resolve** differences for the benefit of the team. They also take **personal responsibility** for accomplishing the team's goals and they do their **share** of the work.

How good are your team skills?

Very good	Good	OK	Not very good
1	2	3	4

3 LESSON

Please leave a message.

THINGS TO DO

1 Warm Up

Work with your classmates to answer these questions.

1. Do you have a telephone answering machine or service? What does the message say?
2. Read the list of Telephone Do's and Don'ts. Add two more ideas to each list.

2 Listen for General Information 🎧

Listen to 6 telephone calls and number them in order from first (1) to last (6).

___ Someone calls to inquire about a job.

___ Someone calls to apologize for something.

_1_ Someone calls to ask a favor.

___ The caller hears a message about business hours.

___ Someone calls to invite someone to something.

___ The caller is returning a call.

3 Listen for Specific Information 🎧

Read the telephone messages on page 9 and listen to the 6 telephone calls again. Add the missing information to the messages.

4 Use the Communication Strategy 🎧

Choose a reason for calling a classmate. Practice leaving a message on his or her answering machine. Then ask your classmates to evaluate your message. Use the communication strategy on this page.

> A: You have reached the Li family. Please leave a message.
>
> B: Hi. This is Rick Martinez calling for Jim. Jim, I'm calling to get the homework assignment for English class. Could you please call me at 555-8933? Thanks. Bye.

Telephone Do's and Don'ts

Do

- speak clearly.
- identify yourself when you leave a telephone message.
- be concise when you leave a message.
- avoid using filler words such as "you know," "like," and "you guys."
- **speak softly** when you use a cell phone in a public place.
- _____
- _____

Don't

- use a cell phone in a restaurant.
- hang up without saying "Goodbye."
- keep anyone on hold for more than a few seconds.
- _____
- _____

COMMUNICATION STRATEGY

Stating Your Purpose

When you call someone on the phone, it helps to first state your name and purpose for calling.

I'm calling to . . .

My purpose for calling is to . . .

The reason I'm calling is to . . .

1

Pat,

Leila left a message. She wants to know if you can

Call her at 555-   .

Don

2

Redwood High School
Continuing Education Office

HOURS:

Monday through Friday
_____

Saturday _____

Sunday _____

3

WHILE YOU WERE OUT

FOR: Mr. Takase

DATE: June 15   TIME: 12:30

FROM: _____

OF: _____

PHONE: _____

EMAIL: _____

☐ Telephoned   ☒ Will Call Again
☒ Returned Call   ☐ Please See Me
☐ Please Call   ☐ Important

MESSAGE: Mr. Lee said he will
_____
_____
_____
_____ .

4

Jan,
Maria called to _____
_____
_____
              Mario
                7:30

5

FROM Betty

DATE June 12

TIME 2:30

TO _____

MESSAGE Called to _____
_____ on
[day] _____ at [time]
_____ . Her number is
555-   .

6

WHILE YOU WERE OUT

FOR: Ms. Parker

DATE: June 14   TIME: 10:30

FROM: Sam

OF: _____

PHONE: _____

EMAIL: _____

☐ Telephoned   ☐ Will Call Again
☐ Returned Call   ☐ Please See Me
☐ Please Call   ☐ Important

MESSAGE: Called to _____
_____
_____

Would like you to call back
when convenient.
_____

9

LESSON 4

Writing Skills

THINGS TO DO

1 Warm Up

Work with your classmates to answer the questions below.

1. In what jobs is it important to have good writing skills?
2. In your personal life, when is it useful to have good writing skills?
3. Skim, or read quickly, the article on page 11 to find the main ideas or facts. Then complete the chart below.

Title of the Article: _How well do you write_

Source (where it is from): _Metscape Network..._

Topic (what it is about): _____

How does important to employees write well

2 Read and Respond

Read the article on page 11 and answer these questions below.

1. According to the article, what do 33% of employees fail at?
2. Who is Susan Traiman and why does the writer **quote** her? _'expert_
3. Why are writing skills more important today than 20 years ago?
4. According to the article, why is it a good idea to improve your writing skills? _People who_
5. Of the six writing problems listed in the article, which is the most difficult for you? Why?

3 Evaluate

Read the email messages on page 11 and answer the questions below. Write *yes* or *no*. Circle the mistakes and underline the unclear portions. Then correct the mistakes.

	Email #1	Email #2
1. Are there any spelling mistakes?	yes	no
2. Is there any missing punctuation?	yes	yes
3. Are there any grammar mistakes?	yes	yes
4. Is it clear?	no	yes
5. Is it concise?	no	yes

4 Write

Write an email message to a classmate. Ask your classmate to evaluate your message by answering the 5 questions in Activity 3 above.

Sixty-six percent of salaried workers in the U.S. have jobs that require writing.

This community college student is drafting an essay.

This construction worker is writing a project report.

How Well Do You Write?

1   Whether it's an e-mail memo or a **complex** report, fully one-third of the U.S. workforce does not meet the minimum writing requirements of the jobs they currently hold, **according to** a survey by the College Board's National Commission on Writing.

2   "Businesses are really crying out. They need to have people who write better," College Board President Gaston Caperton told the Associated Press. The survey was done with 64 companies across six industries representing four million employees: mining, construction, manufacturing, transportation and utilities, services and finance, and insurance and real estate.

3   With a computer on every desk, writing is more important now than it has ever been. Fully 66 percent of all salaried workers in large U.S. companies have jobs that require at least some writing. Sadly, not everyone is **up to** the task.

4   The top writing problems for most employees:

- **Accuracy**
- Punctuation
- **Clarity**
- Grammar
- Spelling
- Conciseness

5   People who have mastered these writing skills are among the most **sought after** employees. "There's no way to say that writing has gotten worse," Susan Traiman, director of the education initiative for the Business Roundtable, told the Associated Press. Rather, "the **demand** has gotten greater."

6   That demand has spread to jobs that once were filled by employees who didn't have to know a verb from a noun, including electricians, engineers, and foremen or forewomen. Improving your writing skills is worth the time and effort. More than half the companies surveyed said they do **assess** writing skills when they make hiring and **promotion** decisions for salaried employees.

Source: Netscape Network, http://channels.netscape.com

Email #1

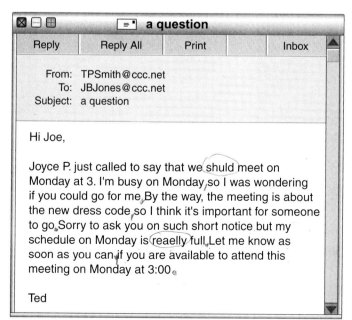

a question

| Reply | Reply All | Print | Inbox |

From: TPSmith@ccc.net
To: JBJones@ccc.net
Subject: a question

Hi Joe,

Joyce P. just called to say that we shuld meet on Monday at 3. I'm busy on Monday so I was wondering if you could go for me. By the way, the meeting is about the new dress code so I think it's important for someone to go. Sorry to ask you on such short notice but my schedule on Monday is reeally full. Let me know as soon as you can if you are available to attend this meeting on Monday at 3:00.

Ted

Email #2

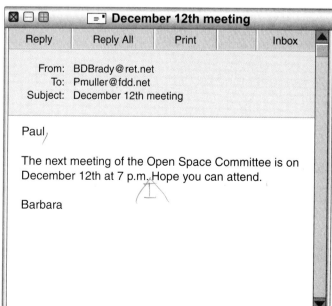

December 12th meeting

| Reply | Reply All | Print | Inbox |

From: BDBrady@ret.net
To: Pmuller@fdd.net
Subject: December 12th meeting

Paul,

The next meeting of the Open Space Committee is on December 12th at 7 p.m. Hope you can attend.

Barbara

11

5 LESSON

Do you know if Maria is married?

Indirect *Yes/No* Questions

It's common to ask a direct question when you think the other person probably knows the answer. However, when the other person might not know the answer, it's common to ask an indirect question. We also use indirect questions to ask politely for information. Indirect questions often begin with *Do you know,* or *Can you tell me.*

Direct question	Indirect questions
Is Maria married?	**Do you know** if Maria is married?
	Can you tell me if Maria is married?

To change a direct *yes/no* question to an indirect question, use *if* + noun + verb.

Direct questions	Indirect questions
Does Rita speak Spanish?	Do you know **if Rita speaks** Spanish?
Is Sam a good driver?	Can you tell me **if Sam is** a good driver?
Did Joe get the job?	Do you know **if Joe got** the job?

---

1 Write the Question

Change the direct questions to indirect questions.

1. Is Hanh a good writer?

   Indirect question: *Do you know if Hanh is a good writer?*

2. Does Tom have good problem-solving skills?

   Indirect question: _____

3. Is the President of the U.S. married?

   Indirect question: _____

4. Did Sam call?

   Indirect question: _____

5. Did Jan apologize to Chandra?

   Indirect question: _____

6. Did Lilia register for a computer class?

   Indirect question: _____

7. Does Miguel have good communication skills?

   Indirect question: _____

Indirect *Wh–* Questions	

You can also ask an indirect *wh-* question.

Direct question	Indirect questions
Where is Jack?	**Do you know** where Jack is? **Can you tell me** where Jack is?

To change a direct *wh-* question to an indirect question, put the subject before the verb.

Direct questions	Indirect questions
What time is it?	Do you know **what time it is**?
What are your greatest strengths?	Can you tell me **what your greatest strengths are**?
What did she say?	Do you know **what she said**?
Who teaches the writing class?	Can you tell me **who teaches the writing class**?

2 Write and Ask

Rewrite each direct question as an indirect question. Then ask a classmate the questions.

1. Who is the President of the United States?

   Do you know who the President of the United States is?

2. Where is San Diego?

   Do you know where San Diego is?

3. How old is the President of the U.S.?

4. What time is it?

   what time it is

5. What street is the post office on?

   Do you know

6. When is the teacher's birthday?

   when the teacher's birthday is?

7. Where is Arizona?

   where Arizona is

8. When did class start?

   when class started

9. Who wrote this book?

   who wrote this book

10. What did the teacher just say?

    what the teacher just said

UNIT 1: Skills and Abilities

Job Interview Questions

1 Warm Up

Work with your classmates to answer the questions below.

1. Have you ever had a job interview? What questions did the interviewer ask you?
2. What advice would you give someone who was going to a job interview?

2 Read and Respond

Read this article and complete the chart below. Then compare charts with your classmates.

Job Interview Questions

When you interview for a job, the interviewer is very likely to ask about your skills and abilities. Below are three common questions that interviewers ask:

1. Tell me about yourself.

This is a very general request and it can be difficult to know what to say and what not to say. Basically, the interviewer wants a quick **overview** of your work and educational background with a focus on your accomplishments. The interviewer is not interested in learning about your personal life or your personal problems. He or she wants to know about your skills and abilities. Don't be afraid to use strong adjectives such as dependable, creative, cooperative, competent, and determined to describe yourself.

2. What is your greatest strength?

You might be a very creative cook for your friends or an **incredibly** patient parent, but the interviewer probably doesn't want to hear about your strengths at home. Instead, identify one of your strengths and explain how it could be useful in a work situation. A creative cook might say that she enjoys coming up with new ways to do things. She should give an example showing how she's done that in a work environment. A patient parent could say that he is a good listener who likes to work with others to resolve problems.

3. What is your greatest weakness?

When you answer this question, focus on the positive not the negative. Identify a work-related weakness that could be viewed as a strength, and then immediately tell what you did or are now doing to **overcome** this weakness. For example, you might say that when you see a problem, you feel a responsibility to solve it. As a result, you sometimes have more to do than you can handle. You are resolving that by learning to distribute work more equally.

Interview Question	Do's	Don'ts
Tell me about yourself.	*give a summary of your work and school background.*	
What is your greatest strength?		
What is your greatest weakness?		

3 Apply

Read the answers to each job interview question. Check (✓) the answer you like best. Then tell a partner what you like and dislike about each answer.

1. Interviewer: Tell me about yourself.

☐ Answer #1: As you can see from my résumé, I'm a part-time student at Boxfield Community College, but I have also worked at a number of different part-time jobs since I moved here. My most interesting job so far was at the college library where I helped with the organization of their computer system. I enjoyed this work especially because it required a lot of attention to detail.

☐ Answer #2: Well, I'm married and I have 2 children and we just moved to this area because the schools here are good. I am hoping my children will get a better education than I got. Our schools were terrible. The classes were huge and we never did anything interesting.

2. Interviewer: What is your greatest strength?

☐ Answer #1: Well, you know, I think I make friends very easily. Wherever I go I meet new people and I keep in touch with them. At my last birthday party there were more than 50 friends at my house.

☐ Answer #2: I'd say my greatest strength is my ability to get to know people. Many people dislike meeting new people, but I love it. I seem to be able to make people feel comfortable right away. Maybe it's because I really enjoy listening to them.

3. Interviewer: What is your greatest weakness?

☐ Answer #1: I have trouble getting off the telephone. I just enjoy talking with my friends, but it takes up a lot of my time. Some days I spend hours on the phone.

☐ Answer #2: I enjoy talking to people and I know that in the past I spent too much time on the telephone. Now I watch the clock while I'm making business calls and I've cut my telephone time in half.

Work with a partner. Role-play a job interview. Ask the questions above.

WINDOW ON PRONUNCIATION 🎧
Blending Words in Questions with *You*

A Sometimes when two consonants are next to each other we blend the sounds together. Listen to the phrases below. Listen again and repeat.

can't you	did you	haven't you	shouldn't you
could you	don't you	should you	would you

B Write the phrases from Activity A in the correct column below.

Underlined letters sound like *j* (as in *juice*)	Underlined letters sound like *ch* (as in *chew*)
	can't you

C Listen to the sentences. Write the missing phrases from Activity A. Then take turns with a partner asking and answering the questions.

1. _____ have any supervisory experience in your last position?
2. _____ tell me what your greatest strength is?
3. _____ describe your duties in your last job?
4. _____ like to study something new?

7 LESSON

What do you know?

1 Listening Review 🎧

Listen and choose the statement that is closest in meaning to the statement you hear. Use the Answer Sheet.

1. A. Juanita didn't care about her work.
   B. Juanita did her part of the job.
   C. Juanita didn't share her work.

2. A. Bill solved the problem.
   B. Bill's problem doesn't have a solution.
   C. Bill needs a solution to his problem.

3. A. He can't concentrate.
   B. He is a skilled writer.
   C. He encouraged me to write.

4. A. John called me first.
   B. I returned John's call.
   C. John called me back.

5. A. I'm calling to inquire about the job.
   B. I'm calling to apologize.
   C. My purpose for calling is to invite you to the sale.

ANSWER SHEET			
1	A	B	C
2	A	B	C
3	A	B	C
4	A	B	C
5	A	B	C
6	A	B	C
7	A	B	C
8	A	B	C
9	A	B	C
10	A	B	C

Listen to each conversation and choose the best answer to the question you hear. Use the Answer Sheet.

6. A. He's a new employee.
   B. He's dependable.
   C. He has good team skills.

7. A. She writes well.
   B. She is a good speaker.
   C. She is good at solving problems.

8. A. Please call Mike Jones at 555-7793.
   B. Please call Mike Jones at 555-7993.
   C. Please call Mike Jones tonight at 555-7799.

9. A. Please call Jan Smith later.
   B. Jan Smith will meet you later.
   C. Jan Smith will call back later.

10. A. the time
    B. the day
    C. the date

2 Dictation 🎧

Listen and write the sentences you hear.

1. _____

_____

2. _____

_____

3. _____

_____

3 Vocabulary Review

Write the missing noun or verb form in Chart #1. Write the missing adjective or adverb form in Chart #2.

Chart #1

	NOUN	VERB
1.	*behavior*	behave
2.	comprehension	
3.	concentration	
4.		cooperate
5.	demand	
6.	encouragement	
7.	distraction	
8.	interaction	
9.		promote
10.	resolution	

Chart #2

	ADJECTIVE	ADVERB
11.	clear	*clearly*
12.	concise	
13.		cooperatively
14.		responsibly
15.		essentially
16.	proficient	
17.		personally
18.	accurate	
19.	soft	
20.	incredible	

Choose 6 words from the charts above and write 6 questions. Then ask your classmates your questions.

EXAMPLE: How can you improve your listening comprehension?

✔ LEARNING LOG

I know these words:

NOUNS	VERBS	ADJECTIVES	ADVERBS
☐ accuracy	☐ affect	☐ complex	☐ clearly
☐ behavior	☐ assess	☐ cooperative	☐ concisely
☐ clarity	☐ come up with	☐ distracted	☐ incredibly
☐ demand	☐ comprehend	☐ essential	
☐ overview	☐ concentrate	☐ interpersonal	**OTHER**
☐ responsibility	☐ encourage	☐ proficient	☐ according to
☐ personal	☐ interact	☐ sought after	☐ up to
☐ promotion	☐ leave out		
☐ share	☐ overcome		
	☐ quote		
	☐ resolve		
	☐ speak softly		

I practiced these skills, strategies, and grammar points:

☐ setting goals for the unit	☐ taking phone messages
☐ identifying skills to learn	☐ evaluating email messages
☐ evaluating work skills	☐ asking direct and indirect *yes/no* questions
☐ listening for general phone information	☐ asking direct and indirect *wh-* questions
☐ listening for specific phone information	☐ understanding job interviews
☐ stating your purpose on the phone	☐ applying job interview skills

Spotlight: Reading Strategy

MAKING INFERENCES

A fact is information that can be verified, or shown to be true. An inference is a logical conclusion based on factual information. An inference is an interpretation of a fact.

EXAMPLES:

Fact:	Oscar found the problem with my computer and fixed it.
Inference:	Oscar is a good problem solver.

Fact:	Oscar always gets to work on time.
Inference:	Oscar is dependable.

When you read, it's important to distinguish facts from inferences. It's also important to be able to make logical inferences from the facts you read.

---

1 Read each fact below. Then check (✓) the logical inference in each pair.

1. **Fact**: Everyone in the class failed the test.

   Inferences: ☐ The test was very difficult.
   ☐ Everyone in the class understood the material.

2. **Fact**: It's about 200 miles from Boston to New York.

   Inferences: ☐ You can't fly from Boston to New York.
   ☐ It takes about 4 hours to drive from Boston to New York.

3. **Fact**: Carlos spoke Spanish to his grandmother.

   Inferences: ☐ Carlos is bilingual.
   ☐ Carlos's grandmother understands Spanish.

4. **Fact**: Taka wants to take a computer course.

   Inferences: ☐ Taka has excellent computer skills.
   ☐ Taka wants to improve her computer skills.

5. **Fact**: Manuel stopped talking on his cell phone when he realized it disturbed his coworkers.

   Inferences: ☐ Manuel has good interpersonal skills.
   ☐ Manuel doesn't like to talk on the telephone.

2 Read the article and answer the questions below with facts from the article.

With Big Risks Come Big Rewards for Immigrant Family
by Christina Lima

In 1979, To and Hong Trieu arrived in Portland, Oregon from war-ravaged Vietnam. To was 30 and Hong was 22. Once in the United States, they married and dreamed of having children and getting good jobs. But finding work wasn't easy. They spoke little English, so their choices were limited to jobs such as washing dishes and cleaning floors.

Now, many years later, things have **turned around** for the Trieus. They own two successful Asian restaurants. "It's a dream come true. I feel **fulfilled**," Hong Trieu says. The Trieus' story reveals a sharp business sense. The couple blends Vietnamese and Chinese cuisines to reflect their Vietnamese birthplace and Chinese ancestry, and to capture a larger market. They've picked busy locations for their restaurants. And, perhaps more than anything, they've listened closely to their customers, many of whom insisted they expand both the dining space and the restaurants' hours.

Source: www.oregonlive.com

1. How long ago did To and Hong come to the United States?

   _____

2. What goals did they have when they came to the United States?

   _____

3. Why did they have trouble finding good jobs when they first came to the United States?

   _____

4. What do the Trieus do for work now?

   _____

5. What did their customers want them to do?

   _____

3 Give an inference about the Trieus based on the factual information below.

1. To and Hong didn't speak much English when they came to the U.S.
   To and Hong probably didn't study English for very long in Vietnam.

2. To and Hong own two successful Asian restaurants.

   _____

3. It was difficult for the Trieus to find work when they came to the U.S.

   _____

4. To and Hong listened to their customers and expanded the size of the dining area.

   _____

5. The Trieus have lived in the U.S. since 1979.

   _____

Spotlight: Writing Strategy

WRITING BUSINESS LETTERS	
A business letter has six main parts: *heading, inside address, salutation, body, closing,* and *signature*.	
Heading:	The heading includes the writer's complete address and the full date.
Inside Address:	The inside address should include the name and complete address of the person and/or the company to whom you are writing. The person's name is on the first line, then his or her title, then the company and address.
Salutation:	The salutation goes below the inside address. Some common salutations are: Dear Ms. Wong: / To Whom It May Concern: / Dear Mr. Hernandez: / Dear Sir or Madam:
Body:	The body of the letter gives your reason for writing. This information should be clear and brief.
Closing:	The closing is below the body of the letter. Common closings for a business letter are: *Very truly, Yours truly, Sincerely,* or *Sincerely yours*. Use a comma at the end of the closing.
Signature:	The writer's signature goes under the closing. In a typed letter, the writer's name is also typed below the signature.
The layout of a business letter is usually in semi-block style or full-block style.	

1 Label the parts of Letter A below and Letter B on page 21.

Letter A: Semi-block Style

4355 Bryson Avenue
Chicago, IL 60607
November 12, 2005

Mathew Chico
Director of the Americas Region
American Red Cross
P.O. Box 37243
Washington, DC 20013

Dear Sir or Madam:

   Enclosed please find my financial donation to help
the Red Cross with its relief services.

Sincerely,

Daisy Miller
Daisy Miller

Letter B: Full-block Style

4355 Bryson Avenue
Chicago, IL 60607
November 14, 2005

Ms. Anna Phillio
Director, Customer Service
Real Goods Company
4335 West Wilson Avenue
Chicago, IL 60625

Dear Ms. Phillio,

Thank you for the opportunity to interview for a position as sales associate. Talking with you yesterday strengthened my interest in working for Real Goods. I believe that with my educational and work background, I could carry out the responsibilities of a sales associate with both energy and confidence. I look forward to hearing from you.

Sincerely,

Daisy Miller

Daisy Miller

---

2 How is the semi-block style different from the full-block style? List 2 things.

EXAMPLE: The semi-block style has the heading in the upper right while the full-block style has the heading in the upper left.

_____

_____

3 Write a sample business letter to the Speedy English Language Program. Imagine that you want to take classes. Ask for specific information about their program. Use either the semi-block style or the full-block style for your business letter. Address your letter to:

Howard Smith, Director
Speedy English Language Program
1234 16th Street NW
Washington, DC 20036

It happened during rush hour.

THINGS TO DO

1 Warm Up

Work with your classmates to answer the questions below.

1. How do you usually get around—on foot, by car, or by public transportation? Which do you prefer?

2. What's happening during **rush hour** in the picture? List 10 things, including 3 unsafe ones.

2 Make Inferences

Read the facts and inferences below about Tom. Check (✓) the inferences that are logical. Then choose another person in the picture and write facts about that person. For each fact, write 2 inferences.

Facts	Inferences
Tom drives a red sports car.	__ He likes big cars. __ He likes to drive fast.
Tom ran into another car.	__ He's not very happy now. __ He's not a very careful driver.

Read your inferences to the class. Ask them to identify the person.

3 Analyze

Work with a partner. For each situation below, describe what you would do.

1. You have a **flat tire**.
2. The police stop you for speeding.
3. You hit the side of a parked car.
4. You see road construction ahead.

TRY THIS STRATEGY **Setting Goals** Below are some topics in this unit. Identify each one as (1) very useful to you, (2) somewhat useful, or (3) not useful.

__ car accidents   __ ways to travel

__ insurance terms   __ road maps

__ insurance policies   __ bus schedules

22

LESSON 2

My insurance will cover it.

THINGS TO DO

1 Talk about It

Use the *Dictionary of Common Automobile Insurance Terms* on this page to answer these questions.

1. Which terms in the list do you know?
2. Is it important to have collision insurance? Why or why not?
3. What is the difference between collision and comprehensive coverage?

2 Write *True* or *False*

Study the insurance **policy** on page 25 and read the statements below. For each statement, write *True* or *False*.

1. The name of the policyholder is Thomas Rideout. _____
2. The policy holder owns a Toyota. _____
3. The policy holder drives about 10,000 miles a year. _____
4. His insurance policy is good for 6 months. _____
5. Tom pays $50,000.00 for his liability coverage. _____
6. Tom got a discount on his insurance policy because he is a good driver. _____
7. Tom has a $500.00 deductible. _____
8. Tom's bill for car insurance comes to $256.80. _____
9. Tom has an alarm system in his car. _____
10. The insurance company is in Florida. _____

Now correct the false statements.

3 Apply

Read each situation below and answer the question. Then compare ideas with your classmates.

1. Someone stole your car and the police never found it. Which coverage would pay for your loss?
2. A rock from a passing truck cracked your windshield. Which coverage would cover your loss?
3. You haven't had a car accident in 7 years. Do you think you can get a discount on your insurance?

Dictionary of Common Automobile Insurance Terms

1. **Actual Cash Value** The cost to replace a vehicle minus the amount it has **depreciated** since you bought it.
2. **Bodily Injury Liability** This covers medical expenses for injuries the **policyholder** causes to someone else.
3. **Claim** The policyholder's request for **reimbursement** of a loss covered by their insurance policy.
4. **Collision** This covers damage to the policyholder's car from any collision. The collision could be with another car, a wall, a rock, etc.
5. **Comprehensive** This covers damage to the policyholder's car from something other than another car, such as theft, fire, or earthquake.
6. **Deductible** The part of the loss that you agree to pay if you have an accident.
7. **Medical Payments or Personal Injury Protection (PIP)** This covers the treatment of injuries to the driver and passengers of the policyholder's **vehicle**.
8. **Premium** The amount of money you pay for your insurance. The higher the deductible, the lower the premium.
9. **Property Damage Liability** This pays for damage the policyholder causes to someone else's property.
10. **Uninsured Motorist Coverage** This pays for treatment and/or property damages of the policyholder if he/she is injured in a collision with an uninsured driver.

TRY THIS STRATEGY

Learning Synonyms You can expand your vocabulary by learning synonyms. Find a synonym on pages 24–25 for these words.

yearly _____   belongings _____

car or truck _____   payment _____

driver _____   crash _____

UNIFIED AUTOMOBILE INSURANCE COMPANY
3833 Bradbury Road – Fredericksburg, VA 22401

Named Insured and Address:
Thomas Rideout
564 Philips Street
Miami, FL 33136

Policy Number: 00044 44 244 4443 5
POLICY PERIOD (12:01 A.M. Standard Time)
EFFECTIVE OCT 01 2006 TO OCT 01 2007

Description of Vehicle(s)

YEAR	MAKE	MODEL	BODY TYPE	ANNUAL MILEAGE	IDENTIFICATION NUMBER
2000	PORSCHE	BOXSTER	CPE 2D	10,000	WP0CA29894U612345

COVERAGES LIMITS OF LIABILITY (ACV MEANS ACTUAL CASH VALUE)		VEH 01 D=DED AMOUNT	ANNUAL PREMIUM $	VEH 02 D=DED AMOUNT	ANNUAL PREMIUM $
PART A – LIABILITY					
BODILY INJURY	EA PER $ 300,000				
	EA ACC $ 500,000		256.80		
PROPERTY DAMAGE EA ACC	$ 50,000		92.00		
PART B – MEDICAL PAYMENTS					
	EA PER $ 10,000		19.25		
PART C – UNINSURED MOTORISTS					
BODILY INJURY	EA PER $ 300,000				
	EA ACC $ 500,000		184.00		
PART D – PHYSICAL DAMAGE COVERAGE					
COMPREHENSIVE LOSS	ACV LESS	D500	283.50		
COLLISION LOSS	ACV LESS	D500	376.00		

VEHICLE TOTAL PREMIUM*   1,211.55

ANNUAL PREMIUM $ 1,211.55

*Premium is based on the following discounts: 5-year good driving record; anti theft device; designated professional group.

LESSON 3

Could you tell me the arrival time?

UNIFIED
INSURANCE
COMPANY

YUMIKO SAZAKI

THINGS TO DO

1 Warm Up

Work with your classmates to answer the questions below.

1. What do you think the people in each scene are saying?
2. Look at the map of Florida. What route would you take to get from Miami to Tampa? From Miami to Ft. Myers?

2 Put in Sequence 🎧

Number the pictures about Tom and his accident in order from 1 to 5. Then listen to 5 conversations and check your guesses.

3 Listen for Specific Information 🎧

Read the statements below. Then listen to the conversations again and check (✓) True or False. Next, correct the false statements.

	True	False
1. Tom asks the police officer for her name.	☐	☐
2. Tom doesn't have proof of insurance.	☐	☐
3. Tom is polite to the police officer.	☐	☐
4. Yumiko asks Tom about the weather conditions at the time of the accident.	☐	☐
5. Yumiko's phone number is 555-3465.	☐	☐
6. Tom's car has only a damaged windshield and bumper.	☐	☐
7. It will take a few hours to fix Tom's car.	☐	☐
8. The mechanic offers to take Tom to Tampa.	☐	☐
9. Tom buys a bus ticket for the 1:45 bus.	☐	☐
10. Tom buys a round-trip ticket.	☐	☐
11. Bill is Tom's boss.	☐	☐
12. Tom asks to borrow Bill's car to go to the beach.	☐	☐

4 Use the Communication Strategy 🎧

Role-play a telephone conversation between a customer and a ticket agent at a bus station. Use information from the bus schedule on page 27.

A: Blueway Bus Service. Can I help you?

B: Yes. Could you tell me if you have a bus to Tampa from downtown Miami leaving around 9:00 in the morning tomorrow?

A: Around 9:00? Let me see . We have a bus that departs at 9:45.

B: Can you give me the arrival time?

COMMUNICATION STRATEGY

Pausing Expressions

When you need a moment to respond to someone's question or comment, use the following expressions.

Let me see.

Just a minute.

Hold on a minute.

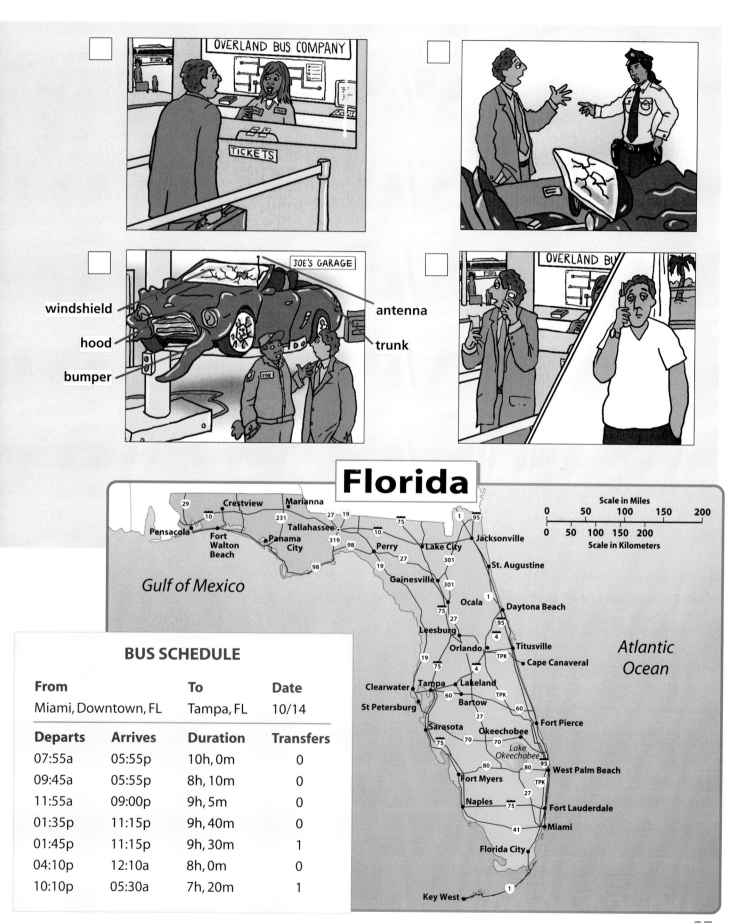

windshield

hood

bumper

antenna

trunk

Florida

BUS SCHEDULE

From	To	Date
Miami, Downtown, FL	Tampa, FL	10/14

Departs	Arrives	Duration	Transfers
07:55a	05:55p	10h, 0m	0
09:45a	05:55p	8h, 10m	0
11:55a	09:00p	9h, 5m	0
01:35p	11:15p	9h, 40m	0
01:45p	11:15p	9h, 30m	1
04:10p	12:10a	8h, 0m	0
10:10p	05:30a	7h, 20m	1

LESSON 4

Planning a Trip

Follow signs to the airport.

THINGS TO DO

1 Warm Up

Work with your classmates to answer the questions below.

1. What is your favorite way to travel short distances? Long distances?
2. What was the last trip you took? How did you get there?

2 Read and Compare

Read the email on page 29 and take notes in the chart below. Then add your own ideas under "Other Expenses."

Check the departure board for gate information.

Travel Options	Travel Time	Cost of Ticket (Round Trip)	Other Expenses
Plane		$300.00	• bus to airport • $100.00 to change ticket
Bus			
Train			
Car			

Compare charts with a classmate and answer the questions below.

1. What's the fastest way for Jackie to get to California? What's the slowest way?
2. What are the advantages of traveling by train? What are the disadvantages?
3. If Jackie decides to travel across the country by car, what expenses would she have in addition to gasoline?
4. If Jackie travels by train, what cities will she go through?
5. How does Jackie plan to get to California?

A bus tour is a good way to see the U.S.

3 Interview

Talk to different classmates. Find someone who has done each thing below. Then ask questions to get more details.

Find someone who	Person's name	Details
1. has rented a car		
2. has never been on a plane		
3. has booked a flight online		
4. wants to take a long trip		

Traveling by car offers the most flexibility.

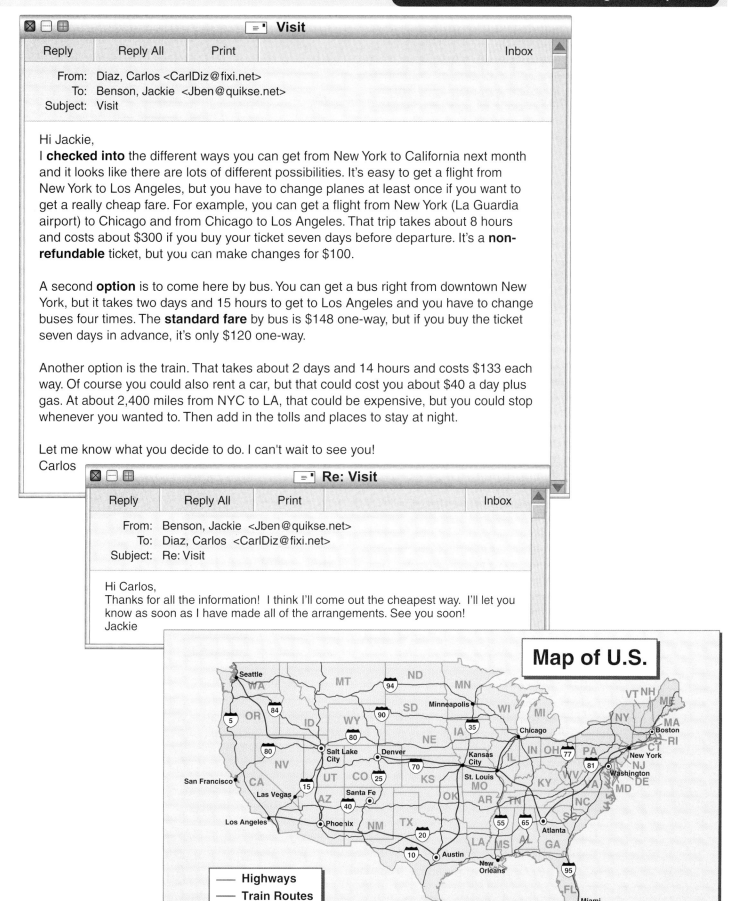

Visit

Reply   Reply All   Print   Inbox

From: Diaz, Carlos <CarlDiz@fixi.net>
To: Benson, Jackie <Jben@quikse.net>
Subject: Visit

Hi Jackie,

I **checked into** the different ways you can get from New York to California next month and it looks like there are lots of different possibilities. It's easy to get a flight from New York to Los Angeles, but you have to change planes at least once if you want to get a really cheap fare. For example, you can get a flight from New York (La Guardia airport) to Chicago and from Chicago to Los Angeles. That trip takes about 8 hours and costs about $300 if you buy your ticket seven days before departure. It's a **non-refundable** ticket, but you can make changes for $100.

A second **option** is to come here by bus. You can get a bus right from downtown New York, but it takes two days and 15 hours to get to Los Angeles and you have to change buses four times. The **standard fare** by bus is $148 one-way, but if you buy the ticket seven days in advance, it's only $120 one-way.

Another option is the train. That takes about 2 days and 14 hours and costs $133 each way. Of course you could also rent a car, but that could cost you about $40 a day plus gas. At about 2,400 miles from NYC to LA, that could be expensive, but you could stop whenever you wanted to. Then add in the tolls and places to stay at night.

Let me know what you decide to do. I can't wait to see you!
Carlos

Re: Visit

Reply   Reply All   Print   Inbox

From: Benson, Jackie <Jben@quikse.net>
To: Diaz, Carlos <CarlDiz@fixi.net>
Subject: Re: Visit

Hi Carlos,
Thanks for all the information! I think I'll come out the cheapest way. I'll let you know as soon as I have made all of the arrangements. See you soon!
Jackie

Map of U.S.

— Highways
— Train Routes

5 LESSON

I should have stayed home.

The Past Form of *Should*

You can use *should (not) have* + a past participle to give an opinion on or express regret about something in the past.

EXAMPLES:

Tom **should have slowed** down. (Slowing down was advisable, but Tom didn't do it.)

I **shouldn't have stopped** the car. (Stopping the car was <u>not</u> a good thing to do, but I did it.)

They **should have taken** the bus instead of driving. (Taking the bus was advisable, but they drove instead.)

I	
You	
He/She/It	**should have slowed** down.
We	**should have bought** some insurance.
They	**shouldn't have gotten** angry.

Note

For a list of irregular past participles, see page 148.

---

1 Complete the Sentences

Complete the sentences with *should* + *have* and the past participle of the verb in parentheses.

1. I _____should have taken_____ the bus to Tampa, but I drove instead. (take)

2. He _____ comprehensive insurance, but he only bought liability. (buy)

3. To get cheaper plane tickets, they _____ reservations seven days **in advance**. (make)

4. You _____ when the light turned yellow instead of speeding up. (slow down)

5. You _____ a discount on your car insurance because you haven't ever gotten a ticket. (get)

6. When she saw smoke coming from the engine, she _____ right away. (stop)

2 What's Your Advice?

For each situation below, write a sentence telling what you think the person should have done and shouldn't have done.

1. Nan forgot to put on the emergency brake when she parked her car and it rolled down the road and into another car. She was lucky because it could have caused a much worse accident.

   _____

   _____

2. Jamal had to pay a lot more for his plane ticket because he waited until the day before his vacation to buy it.

   _____

   _____

3. Keiko missed her train because she spent an hour looking for her wallet and got to the station late.

   _____

   _____

The Past Form of *Could*

You can use *could (not) have* + a past participle to identify something that was possible (or impossible) in the past. This structure is used to talk about an option not taken.

EXAMPLES:

I **could have left** on Monday, but I decided to wait until Tuesday.
Jude **could have bought** a new car, but he decided to buy a used car.
You **couldn't have booked** a ticket because your name is not on the flight list.

I / You / He/She/It / We / They	
	could have taken the train instead of the bus.
	could have gotten a cheaper fare by booking early.
	couldn't have seen the accident because it was too dark.

3 Write

Answer each question with a complete sentence.

1. Ann rented a car to travel from Miami, Florida to New York. How else could she have traveled to New York?

   She could have flown.

2. Mohamed used a credit card to buy his plane ticket. How else could he have bought his ticket?

   _____

3. Fatima only bought liability insurance for her car. What other kind of coverage could she have bought?

   _____

4. Andrea left her computer in the car and someone stole it. What could she have done to avoid losing her computer?

   _____

5. Ray was late to the meeting because he got caught in rush hour traffic. How could he have avoided being late?

   _____

6. Tranh tried to stop his car, but the streets were wet and he crashed into the car in front of him. What could Tranh have done (or not done) in this situation?

   _____

7. Marcos bought his plane ticket from a travel agent. Where else could he have bought his ticket?

   _____

UNIT 2: Getting Around

What To Do in a Car Accident

1 Warm Up

Work with your classmates to answer the questions below.

1. Have you ever seen or been in a car accident? What happened?
2. What should you do if you see a car accident? What shouldn't you do?

2 Read and Respond

Do you know what to do if you are in a car accident? Read the information below and answer the questions on page 33. Then fill in the missing information about Tom Rideout's accident. See page 25 for his insurance information.

Car Accident Checklist

- Stop immediately. Keep calm. Do not argue, accuse anyone, or make any admission of guilt for the accident.
- Do not leave the scene; however, if the vehicles are operable, move them to the **shoulder of the road** and out of the way of **oncoming** traffic.
- **Warn** oncoming traffic.
- Call medical assistance for anyone injured. Dial 911. Do what you can to provide first aid, but do not move them unless you know what you are doing.
- Call appropriate law enforcement authorities.
- Get the information requested in the form below.

Other Vehicle Information	Accident Facts
Owner: _Thomas Rideout_ Phone: _(305) 555-3465_	Date: _Nov. 6_ Time: _8:45 AM_
Address: _____	City, State/Street: _Miami, FL / Route 41_
Make/Model/Year: _____	Condition of Road/Weather: _dry / clear and sunny_
Vehicle ID: _____	Direction of your Car: _west_
License Plate #/State: _883WE / Florida_	Speed of your Car: _I was stopped._
Driver's Name: _____	Direction of other Car: _west_
Phone: _(305) 555-3465_	Speed of other Car: _About 25 mph. Ran into backend_
Address: _564 Philips St. Miami, FL 33136_	Did the police take a report? _Yes._
Driver's License #/State: _FLD000590 / Florida_	Responding Police Department: _Florida Highway Patrol_
Area of Damage: _bumper, windshield, headlights_	Case/Report Number: _FL2222XYZ_

Witnesses

Name: _Han Chen_ Phone: _(813) 555-1263_	Name: _N/A_ Phone: _____
Address: _1275 75 St. Tampa, FL 33619_	Address: _____

Source: AAA Insurance, http://www.ouraaa.com

QUESTIONS

1. According to the car accident checklist, what are 3 things you should do if you are in an accident? What are 3 things you shouldn't do?
2. In a serious accident, which would you do first—call 911 or move your car onto the shoulder of the road? Why?
3. How could you warn oncoming traffic that there has been an accident?
4. Why shouldn't you move an injured person?
5. Why is it important to get the names of any witnesses?

3 Apply

Work with one or more classmates. Read each situation below and answer the questions.

1. Oscar ran into a parked car leaving a big scratch along the side. He parked his car and left a note on the other car giving his name, address, and phone number. What else could he have done? What do you think he should have done?
2. Barbara was standing on the street corner when a truck ran a red light and hit another car. "I was probably the only witness to the accident," Barbara said, "but I was in a hurry to get home, so I just left quickly." What do you think Barbara should have done?

WINDOW ON PRONUNCIATION 🎧
Reduction of Past Modals

 Listen to the words. Then listen and repeat.

should have (sounds like *shuduv*)	shouldn't have (sounds like *shudnuv*)
could have (sounds like *cuduv*)	couldn't have (sounds like *cudnuv*)

 Listen to the sentences. Write the missing words. Use the correct spelling.

1. I _____ renewed my driver's license earlier this month.
2. He _____ taken an earlier flight.
3. They _____ chosen a worse time to travel.
4. She _____ slowed down at the intersection.
5. You _____ purchased insurance from that company.
6. We _____ bought our tickets online.

 Work with a partner. Ask the questions below. Write your partner's answers.

1. Think about the last trip you took. What are two things you should have done differently?

   _____

2. What could you have done to help someone last week?
   What did you do to help someone last week?

   _____

7 LESSON

What do you know?

1 Listening Review 🎧

Listen to each conversation and choose the best answer to the question you hear. Use the Answer Sheet.

1. A. by bus
   B. at 3:15
   C. to Miami

2. A. road assistance
   B. the police
   C. a flat tire

3. A. a higher deductible
   B. a discount for good driving
   C. collision coverage

4. A. He wants to have a good time.
   B. It's cheaper than flying.
   C. He wants to see the country.

5. A. The man was speeding.
   B. The man wasn't paying attention.
   C. The man was driving too close to the car ahead.

ANSWER SHEET

1	Ⓐ	Ⓑ	Ⓒ
2	Ⓐ	Ⓑ	Ⓒ
3	Ⓐ	Ⓑ	Ⓒ
4	Ⓐ	Ⓑ	Ⓒ
5	Ⓐ	Ⓑ	Ⓒ
6	Ⓐ	Ⓑ	Ⓒ
7	Ⓐ	Ⓑ	Ⓒ
8	Ⓐ	Ⓑ	Ⓒ
9	Ⓐ	Ⓑ	Ⓒ
10	Ⓐ	Ⓑ	Ⓒ

Listen and choose the sentence that is closest in meaning to the sentence you hear. Use the Answer Sheet.

6. A. My car is just like new.
   B. When I bought my car it was worth $5,000.
   C. My car is worth less now.

7. A. My insurance coverage starts on August 1.
   B. My insurance coverage ends on August 1.
   C. My insurance coverage is very expensive.

8. A. She bought a nonrefundable ticket.
   B. She bought her ticket a week before her trip.
   C. She bought a bus ticket seven days in advance.

9. A. She bought liability insurance.
   B. She has liability insurance.
   C. She didn't buy liability insurance.

10. A. I took the train.
    B. I took the bus.
    C. I could have taken the bus.

2 Vocabulary Review

Use the clues to complete the crossword puzzle.

ACROSS

2 The verb form of the word "collision" is _____.

3 You shouldn't drive on the _____ of a road, but you can stop there in an emergency.

6 An insurance contract is called a _____.

9 This word means "to repay."

10 The amount of money you pay each year for your insurance.

11 This is what you look through while you are driving a car.

12 Someone who sees a car accident is a _____ to the accident.

DOWN

1 This word means "to go down in value."

4 Traffic that is coming towards you is called _____ traffic.

5 "Watch out!" and "Be careful!" are examples of _____.

7 Another word for car or truck is _____.

8 Another word for "choice" is _____.

✔ **LEARNING LOG**

I know these words:

NOUNS
- ☐ actual cash value
- ☐ antenna
- ☐ bumper
- ☐ claim
- ☐ collision
- ☐ coverage
- ☐ deductible
- ☐ flat tire
- ☐ hood
- ☐ liability
- ☐ option
- ☐ policy
- ☐ policyholder
- ☐ premium
- ☐ reimbursement
- ☐ rush hour
- ☐ shoulder (of a road)
- ☐ standard fare
- ☐ trunk
- ☐ vehicle
- ☐ windshield
- ☐ witness

VERBS
- ☐ check into
- ☐ depreciate
- ☐ warn

ADJECTIVES
- ☐ comprehensive
- ☐ effective
- ☐ nonrefundable
- ☐ oncoming
- ☐ uninsured

OTHER
- ☐ in advance

I practiced these skills, strategies, and grammar points:
- ☐ setting goals for the unit
- ☐ making inferences
- ☐ analyzing transportation problems
- ☐ learning synonyms
- ☐ reading road maps
- ☐ reading a bus schedule
- ☐ understanding car insurance
- ☐ listening and sequencing events
- ☐ listening for specific information
- ☐ using pausing expressions
- ☐ comparing means of travel
- ☐ using the past forms of *should* and *could*
- ☐ dealing with a car accident
- ☐ practicing reduction of past modals

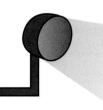

Spotlight: Reading Strategy

IDENTIFYING THE TOPIC AND MAIN IDEA
The topic of a paragraph tells what the paragraph is about. For example, the topic of a paragraph might be: *wearing seatbelts, buying a plane ticket,* or *my trip to Georgia*.   The main idea of a paragraph is the writer's attitude or opinion about the topic. For example, the main idea of a paragraph might be: *wearing a seatbelt is essential, it's important to buy your plane ticket early,* or *my trip to Georgia was a disaster.*

1 Think of a main idea for each topic below and write it in the chart. Then write your own topic and main idea. Compare your ideas with your classmates.

Topic	Main Idea
1. driving too fast	*Driving too fast can be fatal.*
2. traveling by car	
3. buying auto insurance	
4. making travel plans	
5. driving while drunk	
6. traveling by plane	
7. hitchhiking	
8.	

2 Read paragraphs 1 through 4 and identify the topic and the main idea.

Paragraph #1

Traveling is something that most people enjoy, though the way people travel differs greatly. Some people like to (or have to) travel **on a shoestring**, finding hotels, restaurants, and means of transportation that are inexpensive. Other people like (or can afford) the luxurious route in which they stay in the finest hotels, travel in first class, and eat delicious food along the way. Still others like to travel alone and explore things on their own, while others enjoy traveling with a tour group and sharing adventures with others. What kind of traveler are you?

Topic: _____

Main Idea: _____

Paragraph #2

To drive a car in the United States, you have to have a driver's license. However, a driver's license is necessary for more than driving a car. In the United States, a driver's license is also a major form of identification. If you want to cash a check or use a credit card, you may be asked to show your driver's license.

Topic: _____

Main Idea: _____

Paragraph #3

To get a driver's license in California, you have to take a four-part test. The first part of the test is a written examination with questions about the rules of the road. Another part of the exam tests your knowledge of road signs. To get a license, you also have to pass a vision test, but luckily you can wear glasses when you take this test. The last part of the test is the actual driving test. That's when you drive on the road and try not to make any mistakes.

Topic: _____

Main Idea: _____

Paragraph #4

Be sure to **do your homework** if you're buying a pre-owned car. Pre-owned cars are cheaper than new cars, but they might come with unknown problems. It's best to look online and elsewhere to read as much as you can to learn about the car and determine the value of the car. Also, you should have a mechanic test it before you buy it. If you buy a pre-owned car from a car dealer, you might want to get a warranty on it. But if you buy from a private owner, make sure that they have all of the paperwork showing regular maintenance throughout their ownership.

Topic: _____

Main Idea: _____

Spotlight: Writing Strategy

USING COMPOUND SUBJECTS, VERBS, AND OBJECTS

The word *compound* means having more than one part. A simple sentence might have two or more subjects (a compound subject), verbs (a compound verb), or objects (a compound object).

EXAMPLES:

Compound subject:	The **bus** and the **train** both leave at 9:45.
Compound verb:	They **picked up** the car and **drove** it away.
Compound object:	Uninsured motorist coverage pays for **treatment** and/or **property damage**.

---

1 Complete these sentences by adding another subject, verb, or object. Use your own ideas.

1. My sister and _____*her friend*_____ got lost on their way to California.

2. He is a good driver but a bad _____.

3. If you have a car accident, you should get the name of the driver of the other car and

   _____.

4. If you have a car accident you should stop immediately and _____.

5. Both the bus and _____ leave the city at noon.

6. I like to _____ in the morning and practice the piano in the evening.

7. To get a driver's license, you have to take a written test and _____.

8. You can get to the airport by taxi or _____.

9. The ambulance and _____ arrived at the scene of the accident within minutes.

10. Be careful when driving in rain or _____.

11. He needed to talk to his mechanic and _____ his insurance company.

12. I have insurance on my car and _____.

Be careful when you drive in rain or snow.

WRITING COMPOUND SENTENCES

A compound sentence consists of two or more simple sentences joined by a coordinating conjunction (*and, but, or*) or by a semicolon (;) if a coordinating conjunction is not used.

EXAMPLES:

Traveling by plane can be inexpensive, **but** you may need to spend a lot of time looking for a cheap fare.

Even numbered interstates run east-west; odd numbered interstates run north-south.

2 Join each pair of sentences below to make compound sentences.

1. Hitchhiking is not common in the United States.

   In many parts of the country, hitchhiking is illegal.

   _____

2. Taxis are more expensive than most other kinds of public transportation.

   Taxis take you exactly where you want to go.

   _____

3. In some states, you can make a right turn at a red light.

   Before you make a right turn at a red light, you must come to a complete stop.

   _____

4. Each state has different rules for getting a driver's license.

   All states require you to take a driving test.

   _____

5. Driving across the country takes a lot of time.
   Driving across the country allows you to see more than if you fly.

   _____

3 Choose a topic from Activity 1 on page 36 and write your ideas in a paragraph. Make sure your paragraph has a main idea and try to use several compound sentences.

UNIT 3: Your Health

Call 911!

LESSON 1

THINGS TO DO

1 Warm Up

Work with your classmates to answer the questions below.

1. What are 5 reasons that someone would call 911?
2. What is happening in pictures 1 to 9? Share ideas with classmates.

2 Put in Sequence

Match each picture to a sentence below. Write the number of the picture next to the sentence.

___ The ambulance took him to the emergency room.

___ While he was in the hospital, the nurses took his **vital signs** frequently.

_1_ Oscar and Rita were at home playing cards.

___ When Oscar and Rita saw the hospital bill, they suddenly felt a sharp pain in their chests.

___ Suddenly he felt a sharp pain in his chest.

___ In the emergency room, the doctors were able to **revive** him.

___ Oscar got out of the wheelchair and went home.

___ A month later, a bill from the hospital arrived in the mail.

___ Oscar **passed out** and fell to the floor. His wife ran to the phone and called 911.

3 Write

Match the synonyms below. Then rewrite the story in your own words. Use at least 5 words from the lists below and add at least 5 new details to the story.

1. _e_ frequently
2. ___ passed out
3. ___ took in a wheelchair
4. ___ vital signs
5. ___ revived
6. ___ ran
7. ___ arrived

a. lost consciousness
b. came
c. hurried
d. brought back to life
e. often
f. temperature and blood pressure
g. wheeled

2 LESSON

Who's your doctor?

THINGS TO DO

1 Warm Up

Work with your classmates to answer these questions.

1. Do you know anyone who works as a health care professional? What does this person do?
2. Circle one of the health professionals on page 42 or 43 that you or someone you know has visited. What happened?

2 Read and Take Notes

Read the information about the 12 health care professionals on pages 42–43 and make a chart like this with 12 rows. Complete the chart. Then answer the questions below.

Health care professional	Specialty
1. *Cardiologist*	*treats heart diseases*
2.	

1. Which of the health care professionals in the chart is a medical doctor?
2. What are the similarities and differences between a respiratory therapist and a physical therapist? A psychiatrist and a psychologist?

3 Apply

Read about the people below and answer the questions.

1. Jeb frequently feels **depressed** and last night he told a friend that he had thoughts about dying. What kind of doctor might be able to help Jeb?
2. Sharon just moved to a new area and she needs to find a doctor for her 5-year-old son. What kind of doctor should she look for?
3. Soon after hip surgery, Hamid's doctor wanted him to start walking again. Who could help Hamid walk?
4. Marta gets her teeth cleaned twice a year. Who does this for her?

---

1 Cardiologist

A cardiologist is a medical doctor who **specializes** in diseases of the heart.

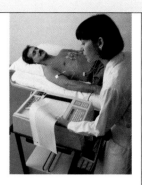

FYI: Cardiovascular diseases (diseases of the heart and **blood vessels**) are the number one cause of **death** in the U.S. Each day, more than 2,000 people in the U.S. die from heart disease.

5 General Practitioner (GP)

General practitioners are medical doctors, but they are not specialists. A GP treats common health problems and when necessary **refers** patients to the correct specialist.

 TRY THIS STRATEGY ◆ ◆ ◆ ◆ ◆ ◆ ◆ ◆ ◆ ◆ ◆ ◆ ◆ ◆ ◆ ◆ ◆ ◆ ◆
Learn Word Forms Expand your vocabulary by learning different forms of a word. Look in this lesson to find the missing word forms in the chart below.

NOUN	VERB
specialist	
treatment	
	die
performance	
	prepare
diagnosis	
prescription	

◆ ◆ ◆ ◆ ◆ ◆ ◆ ◆ ◆ ◆ ◆ ◆ ◆ ◆ ◆ ◆ ◆ ◆ ◆

HEALTH CARE PROFESSIONALS

2 Dental Hygienist

A dental hygienist **performs** a variety of dental **procedures** such as cleaning teeth and providing preventive care.

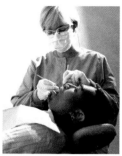

FYI: Most dental hygienists work in private dentists' offices.

3 Dermatologist

A dermatologist is a medical doctor who **treats** skin problems and diseases.

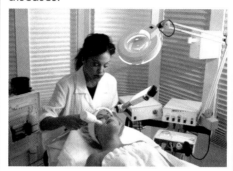

FYI: The average person has about 6 pounds of skin.

4 Dietician/Nutritionist

Dietitians and nutritionists plan meals and **nutrition** programs and supervise the **preparation** of meals.

FYI: Many dieticians work in hospitals and schools.

6 Obstetrician/Gynecologist

Obstetricians and gynecologists are medical doctors who specialize in women's health, pregnancy, and childbirth.

7 Physical Therapist (PTs)

Physical therapists help patients use a part of the body after an illness or accident.

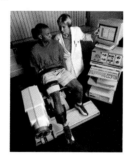

FYI: A physical therapist is not a medical doctor, but he or she must have special training and a license to practice.

8 Optometrist

An optometrist examines people's eyes to **diagnose** eye diseases and **vision** problems.

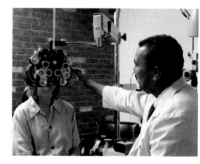

FYI: Optometrists are not medical doctors; rather, they are doctors of optometry.

9 Respiratory Therapist

A respiratory therapist treats patients with breathing or other **cardiopulmonary** problems.

FYI: The majority of respiratory therapists work in hospitals.

10 Pediatrician

A pediatrician is a medical doctor who takes care of children.

11 Psychiatrist/Psychologist

Both psychiatrists and psychologists help people with emotional rather than physical problems. Psychiatrists are medical doctors, so only they, not psychologists, can prescribe medicines to their patients.

That was the 22nd, not the 28th.

THINGS TO DO

1 Warm Up

Work with your classmates to answer the questions below.

1. Why would someone call a doctor's office? List 10 reasons.
2. Look at the photo and caption on page 44. What do you think the person is doing?
3. Look at the appointment book on page 45. At what times does Dr. McCoy have openings?

2 Listen and Take Notes 🎧

Listen to conversation #1 and take notes in the chart below. Then repeat with conversations #2 to #6.

	Name of caller	Purpose for calling
1	Jeff _Bartell_	_make an appointment—1:00_
2		
3	Maria	
4		
5		
6	Coralia Torres	

Compare notes with your classmates. Then add the information to the appointment book on page 45.

3 Use the Communication Strategy 🎧

Work with a partner. Role-play a telephone conversation between a patient and a receptionist. Replace the underlined words with your own ideas. Use the communication strategy.

A: Dr. Smith's office.
B: Hello. This is <u>Jan Li</u>. I need to cancel an appointment.
A: When is your appointment?
B: It's on the <u>15th</u> at <u>3:00</u>.
A: I don't see your name on the <u>5th</u>.
B: Excuse me, but it's <u>the 15th</u>.
A: OK. Here it is. I'll cancel it.
B: Thank you.

"The doctor can see you on the 15th at 3:00."

Dr. McCoy
555-4000

Patient: _____

Date: _____ Time: _____

Mon.   Tues.   Wed.
Thurs.   Fri.

Many medical offices give their patients appointment cards.

COMMUNICATION STRATEGY

Correcting Someone

If someone misunderstands something you say, use the phrases below to clarify.

Excuse me, but . . .

Excuse me, but I said . . .

That was . . . not . . .

Sorry, but I meant . . . not . . .

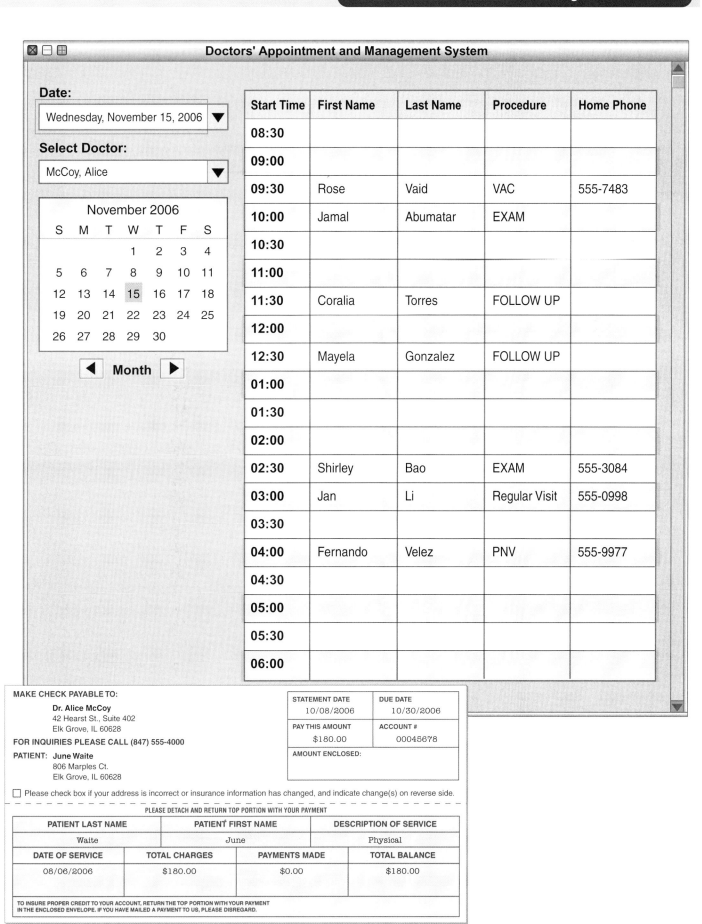

Doctors' Appointment and Management System

Date:
Wednesday, November 15, 2006 ▼

Select Doctor:
McCoy, Alice ▼

November 2006

S	M	T	W	T	F	S
			1	2	3	4
5	6	7	8	9	10	11
12	13	14	15	16	17	18
19	20	21	22	23	24	25
26	27	28	29	30		

◄ **Month** ►

Start Time	First Name	Last Name	Procedure	Home Phone
08:30				
09:00				
09:30	Rose	Vaid	VAC	555-7483
10:00	Jamal	Abumatar	EXAM	
10:30				
11:00				
11:30	Coralia	Torres	FOLLOW UP	
12:00				
12:30	Mayela	Gonzalez	FOLLOW UP	
01:00				
01:30				
02:00				
02:30	Shirley	Bao	EXAM	555-3084
03:00	Jan	Li	Regular Visit	555-0998
03:30				
04:00	Fernando	Velez	PNV	555-9977
04:30				
05:00				
05:30				
06:00				

MAKE CHECK PAYABLE TO:
Dr. Alice McCoy
42 Hearst St., Suite 402
Elk Grove, IL 60628
FOR INQUIRIES PLEASE CALL (847) 555-4000

PATIENT: June Waite
806 Marples Ct.
Elk Grove, IL 60628

STATEMENT DATE	DUE DATE
10/08/2006	10/30/2006
PAY THIS AMOUNT	ACCOUNT #
$180.00	00045678
AMOUNT ENCLOSED:	

☐ Please check box if your address is incorrect or insurance information has changed, and indicate change(s) on reverse side.

- -

PLEASE DETACH AND RETURN TOP PORTION WITH YOUR PAYMENT

PATIENT LAST NAME	PATIENT FIRST NAME	DESCRIPTION OF SERVICE
Waite	June	Physical

DATE OF SERVICE	TOTAL CHARGES	PAYMENTS MADE	TOTAL BALANCE
08/06/2006	$180.00	$0.00	$180.00

TO INSURE PROPER CREDIT TO YOUR ACCOUNT, RETURN THE TOP PORTION WITH YOUR PAYMENT
IN THE ENCLOSED ENVELOPE. IF YOU HAVE MAILED A PAYMENT TO US, PLEASE DISREGARD.

Food Labels

4 LESSON

THINGS TO DO

1 Warm Up

Work with your classmates to answer the questions below.

1. How often do you read the nutritional information on food labels?
2. Why do you think the U.S. government requires nutritional information on food labels?
3. Is your diet very healthy, somewhat healthy, or not very healthy? Why? Describe your diet.

2 Read and Compare

Study the food labels and read the sentences below. Then check (✓) *Peanuts* or *Spinach*.

	Label 1 Peanuts	Label 2 Spinach
1. Which food has more calories per serving?	☐	☐
2. Which has more calories from fat?	☐	☐
3. Which provides more calcium?	☐	☐
4. Which has more servings per **container**?	☐	☐
5. Which provides more Vitamin A?	☐	☐
6. Which has more sodium?	☐	☐
7. Which food has no cholesterol?	☐	☐
8. Which has more protein?	☐	☐

3 Apply

Work with a classmate to answer the questions below. Then compare answers with your classmates.

1. June ate two servings of peanuts. How many calories did she consume?
2. Climbing stairs for 10 minutes uses 100 calories. How many minutes do you have to climb stairs to burn a serving of peanuts?
3. Paul needs to **cut back on** the amount of fat in his diet. Do you think he should eat fewer vegetables? Why or why not?
4. Mei is worried that her children are not getting enough vitamins in their diet, so she gives them a handful of peanuts for their snack every day. Do you think this is a good idea? Why or why not?
5. Laura's cardiologist told her to eat foods with less fat. Based on that, should she eat less spinach or fewer peanuts?

The Serving Size

Food labels tell you the size of a serving of that food and the number of servings in the container. For this particular food, one serving equals 39 peanuts. If you ate the whole container, you would eat 16 × 39 peanuts. How many peanuts does this container hold? _____

Calories

Calories are a unit of measurement. They tell you how much **energy** you get from a serving of the food. How many calories are in 39 peanuts? _____
How many in a serving of spinach? _____

Peanuts are high in protein.

Label 2: Spinach

Nutrition Facts

Serving Size 1-1/2 cups (85g) (3 oz)

Servings per container 3+

Amount Per Serving

Calories 40   Calories from Fat 0

	% Daily Value*
Total Fat 0g	0%
Saturated Fat 0g	0%
Cholesterol 0mg	0%
Sodium 160mg	7%
Potassium 130 mg	4%
Total Carbohydrate 10g	3%
Dietary Fiber 5g	19%
Sugars 0g	
Protein 2g	

Vitamin A 70%	•	Vitamin C 25%
Calcium 6%	•	Iron 20%

* Percent Daily Values are based on a 2,000 calorie
diet. Your Daily Values may be higher or lower
depending on your calorie needs.

		Calories:	2,000	2,500
Total Fat	Less than		65g	80g
Sat. Fat	Less than		20g	25g
Cholesterol	Less than		300mg	300mg
Sodium	Less than		2,400mg	2,400mg
Potassium			3,500mg	3,500mg
Total Carbohydrate			300g	375g
Dietary Fiber			25g	30g
Protein			50g	65g

Calories per gram:
Fat 9   Carbohydrate 4   Protein 4

Label 1: Peanuts

Nutrition Facts

Serving Size 28g/About 39 pieces

Servings per container 16

Amount Per Serving

Calories 170   Calories from Fat 130

	% Daily Value*
Total Fat 14g	21%
Saturated Fat 2g	10%
Trans Fat 0g	
Polyunsaturated Fat 4g	
Monounsaturated Fat 7g	
Cholesterol 0mg	0%
Sodium 190mg	8%
Potassium 190 mg	5%
Total Carbohydrate 5g	2%
Dietary Fiber 2g	10%
Sugars 2g	
Protein 8g	

Vitamin A 0%	•	Vitamin C 0%
Calcium 0%	•	Iron 2%

*Percent Daily Values are based on a
2,000 calorie diet.

The Percent Daily Value (%DV)

The %DV shows you how much of the
recommended daily amount of a
nutrient (fat, sodium, fiber, etc.) is in a
serving of that food. For example, one
serving of peanuts has 21% of the
amount of fat you should have in a
day. What %DV of fat does a serving
of spinach have? _____

Spinach has 0 grams of sugar.

LESSON 5

It hurts when I breathe.

Adverb Clauses of Time

An adverb clause of time adds information about the timing of something that happened in the main clause.

EXAMPLES:

Main clause	Adverb clause of time
You should eat something	before you take that pill.
She felt sick	when she woke up in the morning.

Adverb clauses of time can begin with *before, after, when, whenever, while, since, until*, or *as soon as*.

Tip

as soon as = immediately after
since = from that time to now
until = before
whenever = any time that

EXAMPLES: **Before** I leave, I want to finish this report.
I always feel better **after** I get some exercise.
Nancy was shocked **when** she learned she was pregnant with twins.
Whenever I feel a headache coming on, I try to relax.
He felt a sharp pain in his chest **while** he was reading the newspaper.
Judy has had a headache **since** she got back home.
I can't reschedule my dentist appointment **until** I check my work schedule.

The adverb clause can come before or after the main clause. If the main clause comes after the adverb clause, put a comma (,) after the adverb clause.

EXAMPLE: **As soon as** I got his message, I called him back.

---

1 Find It

Read the sentences below and underline the adverb clauses. Add a comma (,) where necessary.

1. As soon as the ambulance arrived, the nurses rushed out through the main door.
2. When she saw the bill from the hospital she passed out.
3. Whenever you have a question about your diet you should talk to a nutritionist.
4. After his GP looked at the results of the tests she referred him to a cardiologist.
5. The cardiologist called as soon as he got the results of the test.
6. The doctor couldn't make a diagnosis until she saw the blood test.
7. Julia had to stay in bed for a month while she was pregnant.
8. After Jean saw her GP she had to go to a specialist.

2 Complete the Sentences

Complete these sentences with your own ideas.

1. Whenever I feel tired, _____.
2. I _____ while I'm studying.
3. I usually feel good whenever _____.
4. I _____ as soon as I get up in the morning.

Adverb Clauses of Reason and Contrast

An adverb clause of reason gives an explanation for something in the main clause. Adverb clauses of reason can begin with *because*, *since*, or *now that*.

EXAMPLES: Thomas went to the doctor **because** he had a bad headache.
Since she was sick, I went over to visit.
Now that she is a doctor, she can write prescriptions.

> **Tip**
>
> now that = because
> since = because

An adverb clause of contrast adds unexpected or surprising information to a sentence. Adverb clauses of contrast begin with *even though* or *although*.

EXAMPLES: Manuel refused to go to the doctor **even though** he had a temperature of 104°.
Although she exercises and eats well, she has high blood pressure.

3 Write

Combine each pair of sentences using *because*, *since*, *even though*, or *although*.

1. Larry felt a sharp pain in his chest. He went to the emergency room.

   Because Larry felt a sharp pain in his chest, he went to the emergency room.

2. He has health insurance. He got a big bill from the hospital.

3. She is a licensed physical therapist. She can't find a job.

4. Ali hopes to become a pediatrician. He really enjoys working with children.

5. Jim was rude to Laura. Laura is his boss.

6. Marta finished her degree as a dietician. She wants to find a full-time job.

7. Robert was in the hospital for 2 weeks and couldn't come to class. I took our assignments to him.

8. Masako finally got a promotion at work. She is going to get a raise and will probably buy a house.

FAMILY

6

LESSON

FAQs about Immunizations

1 Warm Up

Work with your classmates to answer the questions below.

1. When was the last time you got a shot? What was it for?
2. When you got your last shot, did it hurt?
3. Read the dictionary definition below. What is the noun form of the word **vaccinate**?

> **vaccinate** *v.* **-nated, -nating, -nates** to give someone a shot with medicine to prevent them from getting a disease: *The nurse vaccinated all of the children against the measles.* *-n.* **vaccination**

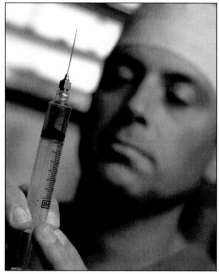

Preparing for a vaccination

2 Read and Respond

Read this information and answer the questions on page 51.

FAQs about Immunizations

FAQs = Frequently Asked Questions

1. Why should children be immunized?

Children need **immunizations** (shots) to protect them from dangerous childhood diseases such as **measles** and **mumps**. Most newborn babies are immune to many diseases because of antibodies they get from their mother. However, this immunity lasts for only about a year.

2. Why do adults sometimes need to be immunized?

- Some adults were never vaccinated as children.
- Newer vaccines were not available when some adults were children.
- Immunity can begin to fade over time. For example, it is **recommended** that adults get a tetanus and diphtheria shot every 10 years.
- As we age, we become more **susceptible** to serious disease caused by common infections (e.g., flu, pneumococcus).

3. What are the possible side effects of immunizations?

It is extremely unusual to have a **serious reaction** to a vaccine. Depending on the type of vaccine, however, a person might develop a slight fever, a soreness at the site of the shot, or a rash.

4. Is it possible to get free vaccinations?

Children without health insurance coverage can get free vaccines through a government program.

5. Does my child have to be immunized?

Not all states require immunization, but some states and local school districts do. Currently, some states allow refusal of immunization due to religious or personal reasons. Deciding to immunize or not is a serious decision.

Source: Centers for Disease Control and Prevention

QUESTIONS

1. Why don't newborn babies need immunizations?
2. What is one example of a dangerous disease that children can get?
3. How long will a vaccination protect you from disease?
4. How likely is it for someone to have a serious reaction to a vaccination?
5. What are some possible side effects of a vaccination?

3 Read a Graph

Study the graph below. What can you infer about the effectiveness of the measles vaccine from this graph? Share ideas with your classmates.

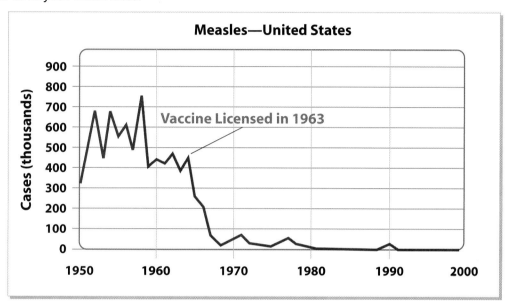

Measles—United States

Vaccine Licensed in 1963

Source: Centers for Disease Control

WINDOW ON MATH
Converting Numbers to Percentages

 Read the information.

To convert numerical information to a percentage, you should divide the part by the whole and multiply by 100.

1. 130 calories (from fat) ÷ 170 calories (total) × 100 = 76.5% total calories from fat

2. 5 calories (from protein) ÷ 14 calories (total) × 100 = 36% total calories from protein

 Calculate the percentages.

1. One package of peanut butter crackers contains 180 calories. Ninety calories come from fat. What percentage of the calories are from fat? _____

2. A serving of pasta has 42 grams of total carbohydrates. The recommended daily amount of carbohydrates is 300 grams. What percent of the recommended daily amount is the serving of pasta? _____

7 What do you know?

LESSON

1 Listening Review 🎧

Listen to each conversation and choose the best answer to the question you hear. Use the Answer Sheet.

1. A. a dental hygienist
   B. a dermatologist
   C. an optometrist

2. A. a dental exam
   B. an eye exam
   C. a skin exam

3. A. She's a cardiologist.
   B. She's a psychiatrist.
   C. She's a gynecologist.

4. A. to reschedule an appointment
   B. to cancel an appointment
   C. to inquire about a bill

5. A. the number of calories
   B. the serving size
   C. the amount of fat

ANSWER SHEET			
1	Ⓐ	Ⓑ	Ⓒ
2	Ⓐ	Ⓑ	Ⓒ
3	Ⓐ	Ⓑ	Ⓒ
4	Ⓐ	Ⓑ	Ⓒ
5	Ⓐ	Ⓑ	Ⓒ
6	Ⓐ	Ⓑ	Ⓒ
7	Ⓐ	Ⓑ	Ⓒ
8	Ⓐ	Ⓑ	Ⓒ
9	Ⓐ	Ⓑ	Ⓒ
10	Ⓐ	Ⓑ	Ⓒ

Listen and choose the statement that is closest in meaning to the statement you hear. Use the Answer Sheet.

6. A. A GP is not a specialist.
   B. A GP is a medical doctor.
   C. A GP sends patients to specialists.

7. A. You have an appointment on Monday the 5th at 4:00 in the afternoon.
   B. Your appointment is on Monday the 15th at 4:00 P.M.
   C. Your appointment is scheduled for Monday the 15th at 10:00 A.M.

8. A. She woke up feeling sick.
   B. She has felt sick all day.
   C. She didn't feel sick until this afternoon.

9. A. John has high blood pressure because he doesn't exercise.
   B. Although John exercises, he has high blood pressure.
   C. John doesn't exercise because he has high blood pressure.

10. A. Although Sandra had a high fever, she refused to go to the doctor.
    B. Sandra didn't have a high fever, but she went to the doctor anyway.
    C. Since she had a high temperature, Sandra went to the doctor.

2 Dictation 🎧

Listen and write the sentences you hear.

1. _____

_____

2. _____

_____

3 Vocabulary Review

Use the clues to complete the crossword puzzle.

ACROSS

7 This type of medical doctor helps people with emotional problems.

8 Some doctors are general practitioners while others are _____.

10 Dieticians and _____ prepare healthy meals for people to eat.

11 A doctor who specializes in diseases of the heart is called a _____.

12 The noun form of the verb "prepare" is _____.

DOWN

1 Doctors try to _____, or identify, diseases or illnesses.

2 Another word for "faint" is "_____ out."

3 If someone stops breathing, the doctors will try to _____ him.

4 A bag, box, and jar are different types of _____.

5 Your _____ signs include your body temperature and blood pressure.

6 A general practitioner may _____, or send, you to a specialist.

7 A doctor for children is called a _____.

9 If you have a _____ problem, you should go to an optometrist.

✔ LEARNING LOG

I know these words:

NOUNS
- ☐ blood vessel
- ☐ calorie
- ☐ cardiologist
- ☐ container
- ☐ death
- ☐ dental hygienist
- ☐ dermatologist
- ☐ dietician
- ☐ energy
- ☐ general practitioner
- ☐ gynecologist
- ☐ immunization
- ☐ measles
- ☐ mumps
- ☐ nutrition
- ☐ nutritionist
- ☐ obstetrician
- ☐ optometrist
- ☐ pediatrician
- ☐ physical therapist
- ☐ preparation
- ☐ procedure
- ☐ psychiatrist
- ☐ psychologist
- ☐ respiratory therapist
- ☐ serious reaction
- ☐ side effect
- ☐ specialty
- ☐ vision
- ☐ vital signs

VERBS
- ☐ cut back on
- ☐ diagnose
- ☐ immunize
- ☐ pass out
- ☐ perform
- ☐ recommend
- ☐ refer
- ☐ revive
- ☐ specialize

- ☐ treat
- ☐ vaccinate

ADJECTIVES
- ☐ cardiopulmonary
- ☐ cardiovascular
- ☐ depressed
- ☐ susceptible

OTHER
- ☐ FYI

I practiced these skills, strategies, and grammar points:

- ☐ sequencing events
- ☐ writing synonyms
- ☐ reading and taking notes
- ☐ applying health care information
- ☐ listening and taking notes
- ☐ listening for specific information
- ☐ correcting someone

- ☐ comparing food labels
- ☐ applying new knowledge about food labels
- ☐ using adverb clauses of time
- ☐ using adverb clauses of reason and contrast
- ☐ converting numbers to percentages

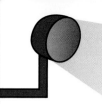

Spotlight: Reading Strategy

USING CONTEXT CLUES

When you come across an unfamiliar word, try to use context (the surrounding words and ideas) to figure out the meaning of the word. The context often gives you hints, or clues, about the general meaning of the unfamiliar word. Below are some types of context clues you can look for.

a synonym

Children need immunizations (<u>shots</u>) to protect them from dangerous childhood diseases.

a comparison or a contrast

She had a high fever yesterday, <u>but today her temperature is normal</u>.

a definition or description

It is unusual for a vaccine to have serious side effects. However, you might develop a <u>rash</u> or <u>a slight fever</u> after getting vaccinated.

words in a series

A first aid kit has items you can use for small injuries, such as <u>bandages</u>, **antiseptic wipes**, <u>pain medicine</u>, and <u>ice packs</u>.

cause and effect

Because he has a cardiopulmunary problem, <u>he has trouble breathing</u>.

---

1 Use context clues to guess the general meaning of each underlined word. Decide if the word tells about something that is good for your health or something that is bad for your health. Write *G* or *B*.

1. Her grandmother died from <u>melanoma</u>. _B_

2. Call 911 if your child is seriously <u>scalded</u>. _____

3. <u>Meditating</u> can help you relax. _____

4. <u>Stress busters</u> come in different forms, such as walking on the beach, listening to good music, and watching a funny movie. _____

5. Foods such as potato chips and candy have lots of <u>empty calories</u>. These foods are high in calories but they have little in them that is good for you. _____

6. He felt much better when he started doing <u>pilates</u>. _____

7. The <u>wound</u> on my leg wouldn't stop bleeding. _____

8. Jeff finally went to the doctor to find a reason for his <u>fatigue</u>. _____

9. I was <u>congested</u> yesterday, but today I feel much better. _____

10. Her diagnosis improved after she began exercising, eating better, getting more rest, and taking <u>prenatal supplements</u>. _____

2 Use context clues to guess the general meaning of the underlined words. Write your ideas on the lines. Then compare ideas with your classmates.

1. <u>Side effects</u> can occur with any medicine, including vaccines. Depending on the vaccine, these can include: slight fever, rash, or soreness at the site of the injection.

   unwanted effects from a medicine

2. If your child has a <u>severe</u> reaction to a vaccine, call your doctor right away.

   _____

3. The %DV shows you how much of the recommended daily amount of a <u>nutrient</u> (fat, sodium, fiber, etc.) is in a serving of that food.

   _____

4. Many things in your home can be poisonous if they are <u>swallowed</u>. These can include cleaning products, medicine, paint, alcohol, and cosmetics.

   _____

5. In the U.S., there are federal, state, and local law enforcement agencies that protect the public. In your community, law enforcement officers are the police or <u>sheriff</u>.

   _____

6. If you need a blood <u>transfusion</u> during surgery, you can use your own blood if you get it saved at least a week before surgery.

   _____

7. A <u>profusion</u> of recent research shows that aspirin may be good for more than headaches. The numerous new findings suggest that aspirin may also help prevent heart attacks and certain types of cancer.

   _____

8. In its regular form, aspirin is an <u>analgesic</u>—a painkilling drug—available without a prescription.

   _____

9. Many pills come in <u>buffered</u> form. The coating makes pills easier to swallow and easier on the stomach than tablets.

   _____

10. The American Lung Association reports a dramatic rise in the number of Americans with <u>asthma</u>. As many as 12 million Americans currently suffer from this lung condition, which blocks airflow and makes breathing difficult.

    _____

11. If both parents suffer from an allergy, their child has a 50 to 75 percent chance of <u>inheriting</u> it.

    _____

Spotlight: Writing Strategy

IDENTIFYING PUNCTUATION MARKS

Punctuation marks are like road signs. They help your reader follow your ideas. Here are the names of some important punctuation marks.

In Written Materials

apostrophe	'		comma	,		hyphen	-
quotation marks	" "		period	.		bullet point	•
question mark	?		parentheses	( )		colon	:
exclamation point	!		slash	/		semicolon	;

On a Computer (when talking about a website or an email address)

back slash	\		dash	–		"at" mark	@
forward slash	/		underscore	_		dot	.

On a Phone (on an automated telephone message)

pound	#		star	*

---

1 Count and identify the punctuation marks in each sentence below.

1. A first aid kit has items you can use for small injuries or for pain, such as bandages, antiseptic wipes, instant ice packs, and gloves. _4 commas and 1 period_

2. If you need help during the night, call Dr. Fanning-White at (800) 555-2255.

   _____

3. You can get more information at http://www.redcross.org. This is called a "url."

   _____

4. The recording said, "Using the number keys on your phone, enter your credit card number followed by the # key." _____

5. Do <u>not</u> call 911 to do the following:
   • Ask for directions.
   • Ask for information about public services. _____

2 Write the correct punctuation marks in the sentences below.

1. The doctor■s patient didn■t arrive on time■

2. Can you email me at drfranklin■help■net■

3. My next appointment is on 03■21■07. That■s the first day of spring■

4. You can find information about immunizations at http■■■www■cde■gov■

5. When she saw the child run into the street, she yelled, "Stop■"

USING COMMAS

Use commas to separate the day of the month from the year. Do not use a comma if only the month and year are given.

> January 10, 2005
> I have lived here since January 1990.

Use a comma before the conjunction in a compound sentence.

> Psychologists help people with emotional problems, but they are not medical doctors.

Use a comma to separate items in a series.

> This food contains a lot of fat, sodium, and potassium.

Use a comma after an introductory word or phrase in a sentence.

> By 1980, there were few cases of measles in the U.S.
> There are many kinds of medical specialists. For example, a dermatologist specializes in skin diseases.

Use commas before and after words that interrupt the flow of words in a sentence.

> Today I went to work. Yesterday, however, I stayed at home.

3 Add commas where appropriate in each paragraph below.

Stop Smoking

In 1960 the Surgeon General of the U.S. announced that smoking was bad for your health. Since then many Americans have stopped using tobacco products. Recently however there has been an increase in the number of young people who smoke. Some people think that movies are influencing young people to start smoking.

Get Moving

According to the U.S. Surgeon General people aren't getting enough exercise and this is causing serious health problems. There are some easy ways to get more exercise. For example you can walk up the stairs instead of taking the elevator. You can also take an exercise class join a gym or take up a sport.

1 LESSON

They marched on Washington.

THINGS TO DO

1 Warm Up

Work with your classmates to answer the questions below.

1. What city is in the picture? How do you know?
2. What do you see people in the picture doing?

2 Check *True* or *False*

Look at the picture and read the article. Then read the statements below and check (✓) *True* or *False*. Write 2 more true sentences.

	True	False
1. Some people in the picture are protesting unpaid overtime work.	☐	☐
2. All of the protesters in the picture are protesting peacefully.	☐	☐
3. There is more than one protest march taking place in the picture.	☐	☐
4. The U.S. flag has 13 stripes.	☐	☐
5. Only young people are involved in protest marches.	☐	☐
6. Protest marches are unusual in the U.S.	☐	☐
7. _____	☐	☐
8. _____	☐	☐

3 Give Opinions

Work with a partner to answer the questions below. Then report your answers to the class.

1. Why do you think people **participate** in protest marches?
2. Do you think protest marches are useful? Why or why not?
3. What social issues are the people in the picture concerned about?
4. What social issues are people concerned about in your community or another place you know?
5. What should and shouldn't people do during a protest march?

Compare answers with your classmates.

SUPPORT WORKERS

Capitol Building

Washington Monument

A Tradition of Marches

Marches on Washington are an American tradition. In 1894, several hundred unemployed workers **marched** from Ohio to Washington to bring the government's attention to the problem of unemployment. In 1913, thousands of women marched on Washington to demand the right for women to vote. Since then, people have marched on Washington for a variety of reasons, such as to **protest** wars, to influence government policy, and to demand their rights.

2 LESSON

It's your right.

THINGS TO DO

1 Identify

What are the rights and responsibilities of a U.S. citizen? Study the information on pages 60–61 and complete the chart below. Then add your own ideas.

Rights	Responsibilities
• to be treated equally	• to report unfair treatment

2 Use the Vocabulary

Add the missing words to the chart below. Then write 5 *wh*- questions using any of the words. Ask a partner your questions.

> EXAMPLE: What are the requirements to vote in another country you know?

NOUN	VERB	ADJECTIVE
1. discrimination	*discriminate*	discriminatory
2.	**elect**	elected
3. registration		registered
4. tolerance	tolerate	
5. requirement		required
6.	authorize	authorized

3 Interview

Talk to different classmates. Find someone who answers *yes* to your questions. Then ask questions to get the details.

Find someone who:	Person's name	Details
has voted in an election		
understands basic ideas about the U.S. Constitution		
has a child in school		
stays informed about current events		

Equal Rights

The Constitution of the U.S. says that all citizens must be treated equally. That means it is illegal to **discriminate** against someone because of his or her race, color, religion, age, sex, or national origin. If you are treated unfairly, it is your responsibility to report it to the proper **authorities**.

4 Taxes

It is the responsibility of citizens to pay their taxes **honestly** and on time.

TRY THIS STRATEGY **Understanding Homonyms** Some pairs of words sound the same but have a different spelling and a different meaning. *See* and *sea* is an example. Find a homonym in this lesson for each word below.

write: _____   two: _____

there: _____   due: _____

RIGHTS AND RESPONSIBILITIES

The Constitution of the United States and the laws passed by the U.S. Congress spell out the rights and responsibilities of citizens. Below are a few examples.

2 Voting

Citizens of the U.S. who are at least 18 years old have the right to vote in **elections**. In order to vote, however, it is the responsibility of citizens to **register** to vote. It is also the responsibility of citizens to keep informed about important issues and to vote on election day.

3 Education

People in the U.S. have the right to a free education through high school. In most states, school is **compulsory** for students up to age 16. It is the responsibility of parents to make sure their children go to school and do their homework.

5 Free Speech/Freedom of Assembly

In the United States, people have the right to speak freely and to **get together** in public to protest a government policy. However, public gatherings and demonstrations must remain **peaceful**. In addition, it is everyone's responsibility to **respect** people with different opinions. Martin Luther King, Jr. is speaking in the picture below. He was a Civil Rights leader in the 1960s.

6 Freedom of Religion

People in the United States have the right to follow any **religious** belief. You cannot discriminate based on someone's religion. It is the responsibility of all citizens to be **tolerant** of the religious beliefs of others. How many different religions can you name?

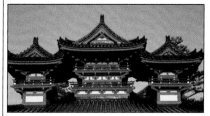

3 LESSON

Should high school be compulsory?

THINGS TO DO

1 Warm Up

Work with your classmates to answer the questions below.

1. What do you see people in the pictures doing?
2. Read the information in each box and answer the questions.
3. Study the bar graph on page 63. What is the relationship between level of education and income in the U.S.?

2 Listen and Take Notes 🎧

Listen to 6 people's opinions about education. Summarize each opinion.

Speaker's opinion	Agree	Disagree
1. *Parents should be involved in their child's school and education.*		
2.		
3.		
4.		
5.		
6.		

Check (✓) if you agree or disagree with each opinion.

3 Listen and Circle Your Answer 🎧

Listen to 5 conversations. Check (✓) if the people agree or disagree.

	#1	#2	#3	#4	#5
They agree.					
They disagree.					

4 Use the Communication Strategy 🎧

Talk to different classmates. Ask for opinions about 3 things that interest you. Use the communication strategy.

A: Do you think <u>students should speak only English in school?</u>
B: <u>No, I don't.</u>
A: <u>I don't either</u>.
B: Do you think <u>high school should be compulsory?</u>
A. Yes, I do.
B: <u>I do too.</u> I think high school is very important.

PUBLIC SCHOOLS IN THE U.S.

1

In the U.S., parents are encouraged to take an active role in their children's education. Why is this important?

2

Many students participate in **extracurricular activities** such as sports, drama, or publishing a school newspaper. What extracurricular activities did you participate in?

3

In most states, children begin public school at age 5. The first year of school is called kindergarten. When do children begin school in other countries that you know?

4

Physical punishment, such as hitting or **spanking**, is illegal in most, but not all U.S. schools. Was physical punishment legal in your school?

5

Classes in most public school are **coeducational**; girls and boys study together. Did you go to a coeducational school?

6

Students take **required** classes, such as math and history. In high school, students can also take **elective** classes such as photography, music, or cooking. Did you take any elective classes in school?

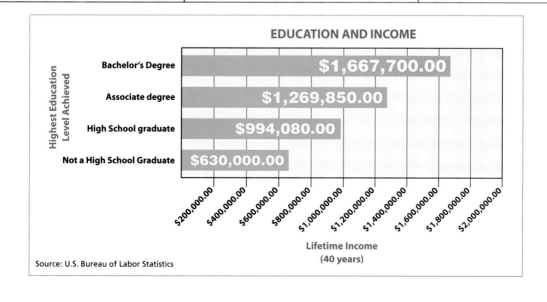

EDUCATION AND INCOME

Highest Education Level Achieved	Lifetime Income (40 years)
Bachelor's Degree	$1,667,700.00
Associate degree	$1,269,850.00
High School graduate	$994,080.00
Not a High School Graduate	$630,000.00

Source: U.S. Bureau of Labor Statistics

4 LESSON

Government Agencies

THINGS TO DO

1 Scan

Scan the information on pages 64–65 to answer these questions. Share your answers with a partner.

1. How many of these agencies have you heard of?
2. What do the **initials** FTC mean?
3. What is the purpose of the CPSC?

2 Read and Respond

Read the information on pages 64–65 and answer the questions below.

1. What do all of these agencies have in common?
2. Which agencies focus on issues of safety?
3. Which agencies help people at work?
4. Which agency looks the most useful to you? Why?

3 Predict

Which agency would you **contact** to get the information below? Write the initials of the agency.

1. Information about discrimination at work

   _____

2. What to do in an emergency _____
3. How to find out about an oil spill_____
4. The names of products that have been
   recalled for safety reasons _____
5. How to apply for assistance after a hurricane _____
6. How to report dangerous conditions at work

   _____

7. How to report a missing person _____
8. How to report an unfair business practice _____

Federal Emergency Management Agency (FEMA)

Helps local communities recover from **disasters** such as hurricanes, earthquakes, and floods.

Equal Employment Opportunity Commission (EEOC)

Makes sure that people are not discriminated against when they apply for a job and when they are at work.

TRY THIS STRATEGY

Understanding Acronyms An acronym is a word formed from the first letters of other words. Unlike initials, an acronym is said as a word rather than as individual letters. For example, the acronym FEMA is said as one word (fee-ma) while the intials FBI are said as separate letters (F-B-I). Find one more acronym in this lesson.

GOVERNMENT AGENCIES

There are many different kinds of government agencies. Some agencies make rules and regulations while others enforce laws. Below are some of the important government agencies in the United States.

Consumer Product Safety Commission (CPSC)

Tests products for sale to **consumers** to make sure that they are safe. Warns consumers about unsafe products.

In 2004, the U.S. Consumer Product Safety Commission told consumers to stop wearing a certain type of tennis shoe for safety reasons. The Commission also told consumers how to get a refund for the shoes.

Environmental Protection Agency (EPA)

Enforces laws on clean air and water and is responsible for cleaning up hazardous waste sites.

Federal Bureau of Investigation (FBI)

Investigates federal crimes such as manufacturing or stealing large amounts of money. They also collect statistics on crime in the United States.

Federal Trade Commission (FTC)

Makes sure that businesses operate fairly and that they **obey** the law.

Media Advisory:

May 28

FTC Announces Latest Campaign Targeting Bogus Weight Loss Claims

The Federal Trade Commission will host a press conference on **Tuesday June 7**, to announce a series of new law enforcement acts. <u>More.</u> . .

Occupational Safety and Health Administration (OSHA)

Makes sure that places where people work are safe and will not be **harmful** to their health.

LESSON 5

He was elected in 1789.

Active and Passive Verb Forms

A verb can be active or passive. In a sentence with an active verb, the subject does the action of the verb. In a sentence with a passive verb, the subject receives the action of the verb.

| Subject | Active verb |

The citizens **elect** the president.

| Subject | Passive verb |

The president **is elected** by the citizens.

It is common to use a passive verb when you don't know who did something.

EXAMPLES: The school **is locked up** at night.
All citizens **are encouraged** to vote.

You can use a passive verb to emphasize the action instead of the person who did the action. In these cases the passive verb is followed with *by* + a noun.

EXAMPLES: New laws are passed **by Congress**.
Children are required **by law** to attend school.

---

1 Identify

Read the sentences and write *A* (Active) or *P* (Passive).

1. __A__ The Bill of Rights spells out many of the rights of U.S. citizens.
2. _____ In the United States, citizens are not required to vote.
3. _____ Discrimination because of someone's race or age is illegal.
4. _____ U.S. citizens are allowed to follow any or no religion.
5. _____ Most public schools in the U.S. are coeducational, meaning that girls and boys study together.
6. _____ Employers are not allowed to pay their employees less than the minimum wage.
7. _____ In most states, parents are allowed to teach their children at home. This is called *home schooling*.
8. _____ What children learn at school is decided by the state.
9. _____ Education is paid for by income taxes and property taxes.
10. _____ The EPA enforces environmental laws.
11. _____ The FBI collects statistics on crime.

2 Choose the Correct Verb

Read the sentences and choose the active or passive verb form in parentheses. Write the verb in the blank.

1. Children _____ extracurricular activities after school. (do / is done)
2. Employees _____ a certain number of breaks during the work day. (give / are given)
3. In most states, children ages 5 to 16 _____ to go to school. (require / are required)
4. If your employer _____ you unfairly, you must report it. (treats / is treated)
5. After a disaster, communities _____ help from FEMA. (receive / is received)

Forming the Passive

To form the simple present passive, use *is* (*isn't*) or *are* (*aren't*) + a past participle.

EXAMPLES:

English **is spoken** in Australia.   Free daycare **isn't provided** here.
Many languages **are spoken** in the U.S.   Students **aren't allowed** to skip school.

To form the simple past passive, use *was* (*wasn't*) or *were* (*weren't*) + a past participle.

EXAMPLES:

He **was treated** unfairly by his boss.   The protestor **wasn't arrested**.
The children **were sent** outside.   Their differences **weren't resolved**.

3 | Complete the Sentences

Complete the sentences below with the correct passive form of the verb in parentheses.

1. The U.S. president *is elected* _____ every four years. (elect)

2. The first U.S. president _____ in 1789. (elect)

3. Before the U.S. became an independent country, it _____ by Great Britain. (rule)

4. Segregation in public schools _____ in 1954. (outlaw)

5. When you register to vote, your name _____ to a list of voters. (add)

6. The U.S. Declaration of Independence _____ on July 4, 1776. (sign)

7. The U.S. Constitution _____ in 1789. (write)

8. The Bill of Rights _____ to the Constitution in 1791. (add)

9. Major elections _____ on the Tuesday after the first Monday in November. (hold)

10. Your tax money _____ to the Internal Revenue Service (IRS). (send)

11. A sales tax _____ on a percentage of the cost of something. (base)

4 | Interview

Work with a partner. Take turns asking and answering the questions below. Use a complete sentence in your answer.

1. Where were you born?

_____

2. What language was spoken in your first school?

_____

3. What language was spoken in your home when you were a child?

_____

4. When was the current U.S. president elected?

_____

The Purpose of a Union

1 Warm Up

Look over the information in Activity 2 and answer the questions below.

1. Where is the information from—a newspaper, a book, a website, or a magazine? How do you know?
2. What kind of organization do you think the AFL-CIO is?

2 Read and Respond

Read the information below and answer the questions on page 69.

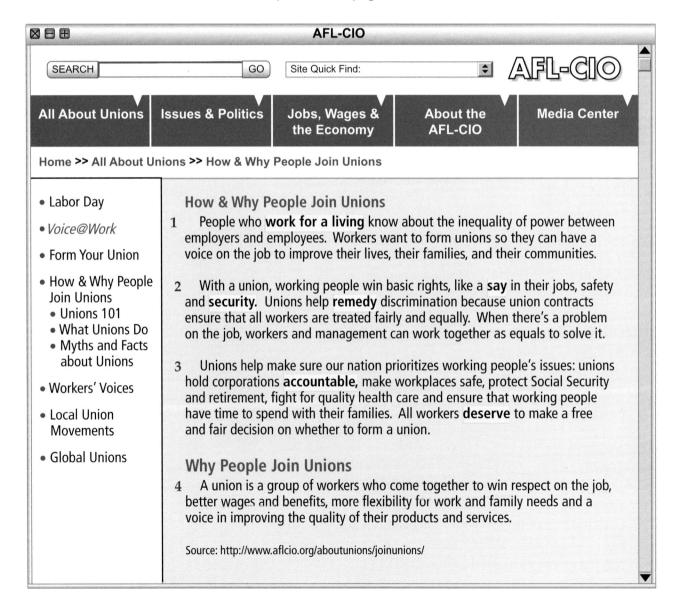

AFL-CIO

SEARCH [   ] GO   Site Quick Find: [   ]   AFL-CIO

| All About Unions | Issues & Politics | Jobs, Wages & the Economy | About the AFL-CIO | Media Center |

Home >> All About Unions >> How & Why People Join Unions

- Labor Day
- *Voice@Work*
- Form Your Union
- How & Why People Join Unions
  - Unions 101
  - What Unions Do
  - Myths and Facts about Unions
- Workers' Voices
- Local Union Movements
- Global Unions

How & Why People Join Unions

1   People who **work for a living** know about the inequality of power between employers and employees. Workers want to form unions so they can have a voice on the job to improve their lives, their families, and their communities.

2   With a union, working people win basic rights, like a **say** in their jobs, safety and **security**. Unions help **remedy** discrimination because union contracts ensure that all workers are treated fairly and equally. When there's a problem on the job, workers and management can work together as equals to solve it.

3   Unions help make sure our nation prioritizes working people's issues: unions hold corporations **accountable**, make workplaces safe, protect Social Security and retirement, fight for quality health care and ensure that working people have time to spend with their families. All workers **deserve** to make a free and fair decision on whether to form a union.

Why People Join Unions

4   A union is a group of workers who come together to win respect on the job, better wages and benefits, more flexibility for work and family needs and a voice in improving the quality of their products and services.

Source: http://www.aflcio.org/aboutunions/joinunions/

QUESTIONS

1. What is a union?

_____

2. What is the purpose of a union?

_____

3. What basic rights can a union help workers win?

_____

4. In paragraph 4, which issue is the most important to you?

_____

3 Apply

Work with a classmate to answer the questions below.

1. Pat heard that union members earn more money than non-union workers. Where on this website could she check this information out?

2. Ira wants to find out about unions in his city. Where on this website could he find this information?

3. Shirin would like to read some stories about the experiences of other workers. Where might she find this information on the website?

WINDOW ON MATH
Understanding Graphs

 A Read the information below.

> **Bar graphs:** Bar graphs contain a vertical axis (y-axis) and a horizontal axis (x-axis). Each axis presents different information. Numbers along an axis are called the scale. (See page 63 for an example.)
> **Line graphs:** Line graphs are a way to show how two pieces of information are related. They often show changes over time. (See page 51 for an example.)

 B Look at the bar graph on page 63. Answer the questions below.

1. What's the highest educational level included in the bar graph?_____

2. How many types of educational backgrounds are being compared in the bar graph?

_____

3. How much money do people with an associate degree (a 2-year college degree) usually earn during their lifetime? _____

C Look at the line graph on page 51. Answer the questions below.

1. What years does this line graph cover? _____

2. What 2 pieces of information are being shown? _____

3. In what decade did the number of cases of the measles drop most dramatically?

_____

7 LESSON

What do you know?

1 Listening Review 🎧

Listen and choose the statement that is closest in meaning to the statement you hear. Use the Answer Sheet.

1. A. Most children start school at age 5.
   B. School is compulsory.
   C. Schools are required to treat students fairly.

2. A. Many people in the U.S. are religious.
   B. People in the U.S. are required to follow a religion.
   C. People in the U.S. have religious freedom.

3. A. Public schools in the U.S. are coeducational.
   B. Both boys and girls are required to go to school in the U.S.
   C. Boys and girls take required classes in U.S. schools.

4. A. You can't vote until you register.
   B. You are not required to register in order to vote.
   C. It's easy to register to vote.

5. A. People disagree about things.
   B. People need to express their opinions about things.
   C. It's important to respect people with different opinions.

ANSWER SHEET			
1	A	B	C
2	A	B	C
3	A	B	C
4	A	B	C
5	A	B	C
6	A	B	C
7	A	B	C
8	A	B	C
9	A	B	C
10	A	B	C

Listen to each conversation and choose the best answer to the question you hear. Use the Answer Sheet.

6. A. voted in the election
   B. been elected
   C. registered to vote

7. A. take an elective class
   B. go to a school meeting
   C. meet her friend

8. A. a crime
   B. a federal agency
   C. an acronym

9. A. today's social problems
   B. why there are social problems
   C. the usefulness of protest marches

10. A. It's compulsory.
    B. It's useful.
    C. It's tolerant.

2 Vocabulary Review

Write the missing noun, verb, or adjective form.

	NOUN	VERB	ADJECTIVE
1.	investigation/investigator	*investigate*	——
2.	coeducation	——	
3.		——	constitutional
4.		consume	
5.		——	disastrous
6.	discrimination		discriminatory
7.		elect	elective
8.	harm	harm	
9.	participation/participant		participatory
10.	peace	——	

Choose 6 words from the chart above and write 6 questions. Then ask your classmates the questions.

EXAMPLE: Did you go to a coeducational elementary school?

✔ LEARNING LOG

I know these words:

NOUNS
- ☐ acronym
- ☐ authorities
- ☐ constitution
- ☐ consumer
- ☐ crime
- ☐ disaster
- ☐ election
- ☐ extracurricular activity
- ☐ initial
- ☐ physical punishment

- ☐ say
- ☐ security

VERBS
- ☐ contact
- ☐ deserve
- ☐ discriminate
- ☐ enforce
- ☐ get together
- ☐ investigate
- ☐ march
- ☐ obey

- ☐ participate
- ☐ protest
- ☐ recall
- ☐ register
- ☐ remedy
- ☐ respect
- ☐ spank
- ☐ work for a living

ADJECTIVES
- ☐ accountable
- ☐ coeducational

- ☐ compulsory
- ☐ elective
- ☐ federal
- ☐ harmful
- ☐ peaceful
- ☐ religious
- ☐ required
- ☐ tolerant

ADVERBS
- ☐ honestly

I practiced these skills, strategies, and grammar points:
- ☐ giving personal opinions
- ☐ learning about U.S. citizens' rights and responsibilities
- ☐ interviewing classmates
- ☐ identifying personal rights and responsibilities
- ☐ understanding homonyms
- ☐ listening and taking notes
- ☐ listening for agreement and disagreement
- ☐ understanding the U.S. educational system
- ☐ understanding U.S. government agencies
- ☐ reading and responding
- ☐ predicting
- ☐ using active and passive verb forms
- ☐ understanding unions
- ☐ understanding graphs

Spotlight: Reading Strategy

ADJUSTING YOUR READING SPEED

Good readers are flexible. They change the way they read to match their reading goals.

Ways to Read

Skim. When you skim a text, you move your eyes quickly across the words. Skimming helps you to learn the topic of the text.

Scan. When you scan a text, you move your eyes quickly across the text to look for specific words or information. For example, you might scan the text for the names of countries or dates.

Read quickly. When you read quickly, you try to read groups of words together. You don't read each word separately.

Read slowly. When you come to a part of a text that you want to remember, you can read the information slowly and try to restate it in your own words.

5 Common Reading Goals
• to get the gist or general meaning
• to decide if you want to read something
• to find specific information
• to read for fun
• to learn and remember what you read

---

1 How would you read the following items? Check (✓) your answer. Answers will vary, depending on your reading goals.

	Skim	Scan	Read quickly	Read slowly
1. a chart with tonight's TV programs	☑	☐	☐	☐
2. a letter from your boss	☐	☐	☐	☐
3. a paycheck	☐	☐	☐	☐
4. instructions for taking a test	☐	☐	☐	☐
5. a funny story	☐	☐	☐	☐
6 a movie review	☐	☐	☐	☐
7. a very big bill	☐	☐	☐	☐
8. a newspaper article about you	☐	☐	☐	☐

Work with your classmates. Compare ideas and give reasons for your answers.

2 Follow the steps below to read the article on page 73.

Step 1. How interesting does the article look to you? Skim it and circle your answer.

   Very interesting   Somewhat interesting   Not very interesting

Step 2. What is the topic of the article? Skim it again and write your answer below.

   Topic: _____

Step 3: What numbers appear in the article? Scan the reading to find them.

Step 4: What is the writer's main idea? Read the article quickly and write your idea below.

   Main Idea: _____

Step 5: Which paragraph in the article was the most interesting to you? _____ Read this part again slowly and then summarize it in your own words.

Rights at Work for Immigrant Workers

1   Immigrant workers are **particularly** likely to say more protection is needed for rights at work. Seventy-eight percent of Latino immigrants and 73 percent of Asian immigrants—compared with 68 percent of workers overall—say "much more" or "somewhat more" protection is necessary.

2   Employers **take advantage of** recent immigrants, according to 65 percent of black workers, 66 percent of Asians and 74 percent of Latinos. And 85 percent of black workers, 83 percent of Asians and 86 percent of Latinos say immigrants are more likely than others to be treated unfairly by employers.

3   Immigrants also are more likely than workers overall to say they have experienced discrimination at work. Thirty-one percent of Latino immigrants and 25 percent of Asian immigrants say they have experienced discrimination based on race or ethnicity.

4   The survey shows significant differences between immigrants and workers overall in employer-provided workplace benefits. Only 31 percent of Latino immigrants and 42 percent of Asian immigrants say they have pensions to which their employers contribute, compared with 51 percent of all workers. Forty-four percent of Latino immigrants and 51 percent of Asian immigrants say they are covered by their employer's health plans, compared with 60 percent of workers overall.

Source: AFL-CIO Workers' Rights in America survey.

3 Use information from the article above to complete the bar graph.

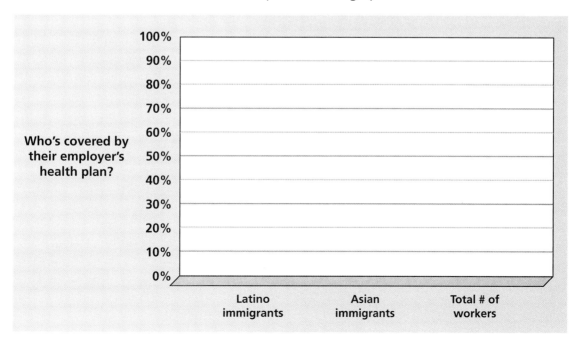

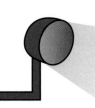

Spotlight: Writing Strategy

IDENTIFYING YOUR PURPOSE FOR WRITING

There are many different reasons for writing. For example, you might want to:

- give your opinion about something
- ask for information
- ask for help
- inform someone about something
- identify a community problem
- persuade someone
- invite someone to something
- entertain someone
- thank someone

In a business letter, it is especially important to make your purpose for writing clear.

1 Read letters 1 to 3 that follow. Identify the writer's purpose for writing each letter.

1

244 SW 15th Street, Apt 23
Miami, Florida 33129
July 23, 2006

Senator Mell Martinez
United States Senate
317 Hart Senate Office Building
Washington D.C. 20510

Writer's purpose:
_____
_____

Dear Senator Martinez:

I am writing to you to voice my opinion of the government's plan to take away overtime pay from millions of workers in the U.S. It is my strong belief that every worker has the right to get overtime pay. For many of us, overtime pay is a necessity. The extra money helps to pay for housing, food, and transportation. I hope you will consider this when you next vote on this issue.

Sincerely,

Gerald Santiago
Gerald Santiago

2

4536 Santini Street
Jersey City, NJ 07306
April 12, 2006

Representative Robert Menendez
United States House of Representatives
2238 Rayburn House Office Building
Washington, D.C. 20515

Dear Representative Menendez:

I am writing to ask for help in getting my social security checks. I have written to the proper authorities several times, but I have not yet received a response. Please find enclosed copies of this correspondence.

I thank you in advance for your help.

Sincerely,

Sonya Bluvosky
Sonya Bluvosky

Writer's purpose:
_____
_____

3

642 South Beverly Dr.
Palm Springs, CA 92264
August 21, 2006

Congresswoman Mary Bono
404 Canon House Office Building
Washington D.C. 20515

Dear Congresswoman Bono:

I am writing to invite you to speak at a meeting of the Durham Voter's Network. The Voter's Network is a nonpartisan group that is interested in many of the environmental issues that you have supported in the past. Our members would especially be interested in hearing about the environmental issues you are currently working on in the House. If you are available on any of the dates on the attached sheet, we would be honored to have you speak to our group.

I look forward to hearing from you.

Sincerely,

Dora Lasky
Dora Lasky

Writer's purpose:
_____
_____

2 Identify an issue or problem in your community. For example: Do people drive too fast on streets with children? Is there too much graffiti or litter in public places? Do people play loud music late at night? Write a letter to the mayor of your town or city. Explain the problem and suggest a solution. Write your purpose in the box.

_____

_____

_____

_____

_____

_____

_____

Writer's purpose:
_____
_____

Everything must go.

THINGS TO DO

1 Warm Up

Work with your classmates to answer these questions.

1. What do you like and dislike about shopping?
2. Have you ever **purchased** something you didn't really need? What was it? Why did you buy it?
3. What's being advertised in the picture?

2 Analyze

Work with one or more classmates to discuss the questions below. Then report your answers to the class.

1. Why do you think there are so many people going into May's?
2. Which advertisements in the picture are especially effective? Why do you think so?
3. What do you think "false advertising" is? Can you find an example of false advertising in the picture?
4. The average person sees and hears hundreds of advertisements a day. What effect do you think this has on people?

3 Interview

Work with a partner. Take turns asking the questions below. Write your partner's answers.

What was the last thing you bought . . .

with cash? _____

with a credit card? _____

with a personal check? _____

on layaway? _____

Report one of your partner's answers to the class.

EXAMPLE: The last thing my partner bought
<u>with a credit card</u> was <u>a pair of pants.</u>

Setting Goals Below are some things you will do in this unit. Number them in order from most useful to you (1) to least useful (6).

____ read shopping tips ____ ask tag questions

____ listen to salespeople ____ read and write ads

____ compare prices ____ learn shopping terms

2 LESSON

Are you an impulse buyer?

THINGS TO DO

1 Use Context Clues

Read the *Tips for Consumers* and use context clues to guess the meaning of the highlighted words. Make a chart like the one below and write your answers there. Then compare ideas with your classmates.

Word or phrase	Your definition
purchases	
impulse buyer	
end up	

2 Read and Respond

Read the Tips for Consumers again and answer the question in each box. Check (✓) *Yes* or *No*. Then compare answers with a classmate and complete these statements.

1. Both of us _____.
2. Neither of us _____.

3 Use the Vocabulary

Talk to different classmates. Find someone who answers *Yes* to each question below. Then ask another question to get more information.

Find someone who . . .	Classmate's name	More information
is an impulse buyer		
has returned something to a store		
has been to a yard sale or consignment shop		
has an extended warranty on something		
likes to buy things in bulk		

4 Write

Write a shopping tip for your classmates to read.

---

1 Plan your **purchases** before you go shopping. Don't be an **impulse buyer**. Impulse buyers usually buy things they don't need and **end up** spending more money than they need to.

Are you an impulse buyer?
❑ Yes   ❑ No

4 An **extended warranty** is really a **service contract**. It covers repairs after the initial warranty has expired. Extended warranties can be **profitable** for stores because most products don't need repair during the first few years. Also, **keep in mind** that salespeople usually get a **commission** for selling you an extended warranty.

Have you ever purchased an extended warranty?
❑ Yes   ❑ No

7 Be **suspicious** when something is offered for free. For example, when there is an offer to "Buy one, get one free," the seller may **increase** the price of the first item to **cover** the cost of the free item. The free item might also be of a much lower **quality**.

BUY 1 GET 1 FREE!

Have you ever gotten something for free?
❑ Yes   ❑ No

TIPS FOR CONSUMERS

2 What can you do when something is advertised for sale on TV but is **out of stock**, or sold out, when you get to the store? If the store didn't advertise "a limited quantity in stock," it must give you a **rain check**. This allows you to buy the product at the special price when more arrive at the store.

Have you ever asked for a rain check?
❑ Yes   ❑ No

3 Some products come with a written warranty; it's included in the purchase price. The warranty says that the company will fix or repair the product for a certain period of time. Before you buy something, it's a good idea to compare the warranties on different **brands** of the same item.

XZ400 COMPACT DISC PLAYER
LIMITED 1 YEAR WARRANTY

A. XYZ standard Products are warranted against defects in workmanship and material for a period of one (1) year from the date of purchase.

B. XYZ's sole responsibility under this warranty shall be to either repair or replace, at its option, any component which fails during the applicable warranty period because of a defect in workmanship and material, provided PURCHASER has promptly contacted XYZ in writing or by telephone.

C. XYZ will honor the warranty at XYZ's repair facility in Rochester, New York, U.S.A. It is the PURCHASER's responsibility to return, at their expense, the allegedly defective Product to XYZ. PURCHASER must obtain a Service Request Order (SRO) number and shipping instructions from XYZ prior to returning any Product under warranty.

D. All above warranties are contingent upon proper use of the Product. These warranties will not apply (i) if adjustment, repair or parts replacement is required because of accident, unusual electrical or electromagnetic stress, neglect, misuse, failure of electric power, environmental controls, transportation, not maintained in accordance with XYZ specifications, or abuses other than ordinary use, (ii) if Product has been modified by PURCHASER or has been repaired or altered outside XYZ's repair facility, unless XYZ specifically authorizes such repairs or alterations; (iii) where XYZ serial numbers, warranty data or quality assurance decals have been removed or altered

This Product is registered to: _Mark L. Burke_

Serial Number: XZ400FHA3009493   *XYZ ELECTRONICS*

Do you usually look at the warranty before you buy something expensive?
❑ Yes   ❑ No

5 You can buy used clothes and other things at **thrift stores** and **yard sales**. You can also buy and sell used clothes at **consignment shops**. Used clothes may be more expensive at a consignment shop, but the **selection** is usually better.

Have you ever bought something at a thrift store, consignment shop, or yard sale?
❑ Yes   ❑ No

6 Don't let a salesperson pressure you into buying **merchandise** you don't want. If you don't want help from a salesperson, you can say, "I'm just looking, thank you."

Would you like to be a salesperson?
❑ Yes   ❑ No

8 When you buy something, be sure to keep your receipt and make sure you understand the store's refund **policy**. Find out if the store gives a cash refund or **store credit** if you return the item. You should also ask if there is a **time limit** for returning a purchase.

Have you ever gotten a cash refund for something you bought?
❑ Yes   ❑ No

9 You can save money by buying food or household goods **in bulk**. Many stores sell loose grains, pasta, cereal, and other foods, and the customer can select as much as they want. Stores also sell large amounts of certain products in one package.

Did you buy anything in bulk last month?
❑ Yes   ❑ No

3
LESSON

Do you have your receipt?

THINGS TO DO

1 Warm Up

Work with your classmates to answer the questions below.

1. What are 4 common questions that customers ask salespeople?
2. What do you think the people in each picture are saying?

2 Listen and Match

Listen to 5 conversations. Match each conversation to a picture. Write the number of the conversation in the circle next to the picture.

3 Listen for Specific Information

Listen to the conversations again. What does each customer want? Take notes in the chart below.

	What does the customer want?
1.	
2.	
3.	
4.	
5.	

Compare answers with your classmates.

TRY THIS STRATEGY

Summarizing
Summarizing helps you remember what you read and hear. To summarize, retell only the most important ideas and information. Write a summary of one of the *Tips for Consumers* on pages 78–79.

EXAMPLE: Tip #9: Many stores sell food and household goods in bulk. Buying in bulk can save you money.

4 Use the Communication Strategy

Work with a partner. Role-play a conversation between a customer and a salesperson. Try to use the communication strategy in your conversation.

A: Could you tell me if this comes with a warranty?
B: I think it does, but I'm not positive.
A: Could you check for me?
B: Yes, of course. Just give me a minute. I'll be right back.
A: Thanks.

COMMUNICATION STRATEGY

Expressing Doubt

If you aren't certain your answer to a question is 100% correct, it's important to say so. Use these sentences:

- I think ____, but I'm not positive.
- It's possible that ____, but I'm not sure.
- It seems to me that ____, but I'm not sure.
- I'm pretty sure that ____, but I'm not absolutely certain.

Best Buys

LESSON 4

THINGS TO DO

1 Warm Up

Work with your classmates to answer these questions.

1. What's your favorite place to buy groceries? Why?
2. Which of these things do you use when you shop for groceries—coupons, store fliers, a grocery list?
3. Why is it a good idea to be a **comparison shopper**?

2 Read and Respond

Read the food shopping tips and answer these questions.

1. In picture 1, which cereal is the better buy? Why?
2. In picture 2, which type of rice is the better deal?
3. Why do you think grocery stores put more expensive items at eye level?
4. What can you do if you find a mistake on a receipt?
5. What are 3 other grocery shopping tips?

3 Compare

Use the store flyers to choose the store with the best price for each food below. Check (✓) your answers. Then compare ideas with your classmates.

Where is _____ cheaper?	Henry's	Foodbasket
pasta	☐	☐
grapes	☐	☐
toilet paper	☐	☐
_____	☐	☐

4 Write

Plan a meal for 20 people. Choose 4 items you need from the store flyers. Make a chart like this and answer the questions below.

Item	Quantity/Size	Henry's Price	Foodbasket Price
pasta	(12) 16 oz packages	$10.68	$8.00

1. How much would you spend if you bought all 4 items at Henry's?
2. How much would you spend if you bought all 4 items at the Foodbasket?
3. Which item on your list is the best bargain?

---

1 When you buy packaged food, be sure to check the **net weight**. A large box might have less in it than a small box.

Henry's **FOODMART**

2 FOR $4
Southern Bath Tissue, 300 sq. ft. 4-roll

89¢
Vito's Whole Tomatoes, 28 oz.

1 29
Fresh Bunch Broccoli, High in Vitamin C

1 09 per pound
California Red Seedless Grapes, High in vitamin C

1 19
Plaza 10" Flour Tortillas, 12 tortillas

1 99
Sunrise Orange Juice, 48 oz.

49¢ per lb.
Southwest Sweet Onions

89¢
Aunt Tillie's Pasta, 16 oz.

2 99 per gal.
Henry's Milk

3 10 per pound
Boneless Chicken Breast

79¢ ea.
Tyler's Yogurt, 8 oz.

FOOD SHOPPING TIPS

2 Read the **unit price** when you are comparing different brands. The unit price, for example, the price per ounce, is usually listed on the store shelf. The store brands or the generic brands are often the cheapest.

3 More expensive items are often placed on the store shelf at eye level. Lower priced items of the same food are up higher or down lower.

SOUP .95 ea.

SOUP 1.59 ea.

SOUP 1.39 ea.

4 Watch as the cashier **rings up** your purchase. The **scanners** at the checkout line don't always register the correct amount. Check your receipt and say something if you think there is a mistake.

THE FOODBASKET

Prices That Can't Be Beat!

3/$2
Bari's pasta, 16 oz.
All Varieties

2/$5
Tropics Pure Orange Juice
96 oz., All Varieties

$2.80 BUY 1 GET 1 FREE!
Texas Sweet Onions
2 lb. bag

$2.99 lb.
Boneless Chicken Breast,
Grade A Fresh, Family Pack,
Approximately 3 lbs

$2.69
Good Milk, gallon
All Varieties

3/$4 32 oz.
10/$5 8 oz.
Mambo Yogurt

$1.79 lb.
Fresh Broccoli

$1.59 OR **2/$3**
Rosa's 8" Flour Tortillas
12 tortillas

69¢
Renata's Tomatoes
28 oz., Selected Varieties

2/$9
Anna's Soft Bath Tissue
600 sq. ft.
4-roll package

$1.29 lb.
Seedless Grapes

SOME ITEMS MAY NOT BE AVAILABLE IN ALL STORES

That's really expensive, isn't it?

Asking Tag Questions

A tag question is a statement with a short question at the end. A positive statement is followed by a negative tag. A negative statement is followed by a positive tag.

EXAMPLES: **Positive Statement** **Negative Tag**   **Negative Statement** **Positive Tag**

She's a smart shopper, <u>isn't she</u>?   She isn't very happy today, <u>is she</u>?
That's very expensive, <u>isn't it</u>?   That isn't cheap, <u>is it</u>?

The subject in the statement is the same in the tag question, but the tag question always uses a pronoun. The verb tense is also the same in both parts.

EXAMPLES: **Margaret is** very intelligent, <u>is</u>n't <u>she</u>?   **He was** very helpful, <u>was</u>n't <u>he</u>?

These **shoes are** really nice, <u>are</u>n't **they**?   **They were**n't very helpful, <u>were they</u>?

When the verb is *be* or a modal like *can, could,* or *should,* we use the same verb or modal in the tag question. For other verbs, we use *do, does,* or *did* in the tag.

EXAMPLES: You **can** come to the party, **can**'t you?   She **runs** extremely fast, **does**n't she?
You **live** in Los Angeles, **do**n't you?   The children **had** fun, **did**n't they?

People often use a tag question when they give an opinion that other people will probably agree with. When used this way, they are not really asking questions; rather, they are sharing an opinion. In this type of tag question, the speaker's intonation drops at the end.

Tag questions can also be used when the speaker is asking a true *yes/no* question and needs information. In that type of tag question, the intonation rises at the end of the tag.

Note

See page 87 for pronunciation tips on tag questions.

---

1 Complete the Sentences

Add a tag question to these statements. Write *was she, aren't they, wasn't it,* or *are they.*

1. These books are cheap, _____?
2. These shoes are nice, but they aren't very cheap, _____?
3. That was a terrible movie, _____?
4. She wasn't very polite, _____?

Add a tag question to these statements. Write *did they, does she, didn't they,* or *doesn't he.*

5. She doesn't live here, _____?
6. He cooks very well, _____?
7. They didn't close at 5:00, _____?
8. They bought a new house, _____?

Answering Tag Questions

Usually when people use a tag question to give an opinion, they expect the listener to agree.

When someone asks:	**The expected answer is:**
This is a nice store, isn't it?	→ Yes, it is.
These are really cheap, aren't they?	→ Yes, they are.
This isn't very good, is it?	→ No, it isn't.
These aren't very well made, are they?	→ No, they aren't.
These grapes look delicious, don't they?	→ Yes, they do.

If you disagree with the person asking a tag question, it's rude to say so directly. It's more polite to say "Actually" and give a reason why you disagree.

EXAMPLE: A: This is really pretty, isn't it?
B: Actually, I don't really like the color that much. I prefer bright colors.

2 Write

Complete the questions below with your opinion. Then practice with a partner.

1. This dress is _really_ _____ _cute, isn't it?_

2. This dessert looks _____ _____?

3. These shoes are _____ _____?

4. This tie is _____ _____?

5. This red pepper isn't _____ _____?

6. This car isn't _____ _____?

3 Compare

Complete the sentence below with your opinion. Then rewrite the sentence as a tag question. Talk to different classmates and ask them your question.

Learning a foreign language is _____. / Learning a foreign language is _____, _____?

Classified Ads

1 Warm Up

Work with your classmates to answer the questions below.

1. In addition to the newspaper, where can you find information about houses for rent?
2. What do you think is the best way to find a house or an apartment for rent?
3. What advice would you give to someone looking for a house for rent?

2 Read and Respond

Read this information and answer the questions on page 87.

Houses for Rent   453

North End, 2 BR, 2 baths on dead-end street. $1000/mo. + sec. dep. Call Karen 555-3590

2BR, newly remodeled, W/D hkup, 1.5 BA, no pets/smoking, $1200/mo. Patty or Sam 555-8998

2BR Ranch, Stv, frig, dshwshr, W/D include'd. Lg bkyard. $1200/mo. + utils. 555-5827

Exc. cond. 3 BR house, lrg deck & private setting $900/mo. Immed. occupancy. 555-3325

3 BR, 2.5 bath, 2 car gar, avail. 12/15, short term, no lease $1200/mo. Cell 555-0949

Contemporary 3 BR, 2 baths, cent. air, garage, pet ok. $1100/mo. Call Peter 555-3356

Nice 2 BR home w/porch & 2 stall garage, on lg. lot, $1100. No pets. Call Dick 555-2113

Condominium Rentals   457

2 BR, open concept, ample prkg. Inc. heat/hw/gas, central a/c. $900/mo. Call Jennifer 555-7867

Brand NEW condo. 6 rms, 2BR, central air. $1200/mo. Call Kathleen after 8 PM 555-3354

WEST SIDE Large 1 BR, new paint/carpet, pets ok, parking, a/c, ht & hw included $850/mo. 555-0878

Furnished Apartments   459

So. Beech. 1st flr, 1 BR/LR, kitchen, bath, prkg, deposit, $200/wk, incls all utils. 555-6584

2 1/2 rms, 1 bath, compl furn'd, no pets/smkrs, parkg & all utils provided. $750/mo. 555-4463

Unfurnished Apartments   461

WEST SIDE Lg 1 BR, include. Ht/HW, gar, porch. Nice yard, small dog ok. $800/mo. 555-9984

EAST SIDE. 2 BR completely renovated, off-st prkg, no utils., $900/mo. 555-6657

DOWNTOWN Lrg 2 BR, new windows, lndry., $675/mo. 555-9068

So. Beech. Safe nghbh'd, 1 BR, new windows/paint/flr. No smkg/pets. Landlord/credit refs checked. Avail. 2/1. $900/mo. 555-3256

EAST SIDE 2BR, nice area, nice bldg., storage room, owner occup'd bldg, no dogs, $800/mo. 555-3657

DOWNTOWN, super clean lg 2 BR, new kitchen, near hospital. 555-5884

Housing to Share   467

QUESTIONS

1. You are looking for a condo to rent. Which section of the want ads should you look at?
2. You want to rent an apartment that you will furnish. Which section would you look at?
3. You are looking for a house with 3 bedrooms to rent. Which number would you call?
4. You are looking for an apartment that allows pets. Which number would you call?
5. Choose 2 of the 1-bedroom apartments for rent. How are they similar and different?
6. Which ad looks the most interesting to you? Why?

3 Apply

Write a classified ad for your own house or apartment.

WINDOW ON PRONUNCIATION 🎧
Intonation in Tag Questions

 Read the information.

When tag questions are used to give an opinion or confirm something, they have rising and then falling intonation. When tag questions are used like a *yes/no* question, they have rising intonation.

 Listen to the questions. Then listen and repeat.

Question	Confirmation	Yes/No
1. That's a really good price, isn't it?	❏	❏
2. You didn't bring your credit card, did you?	❏	❏
3. We paid that bill last month, didn't we?	❏	❏
4. They can't cancel our subscription without notice, can they?	❏	❏
5. These cookies aren't very fresh, are they?	❏	❏

 Listen to the questions again and check the appropriate box.

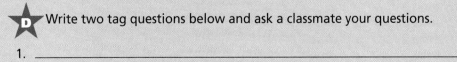 Write two tag questions below and ask a classmate your questions.

1. _____

2. _____

7 LESSON

What do you know?

1 Listening Review 🎧

Listen to each conversation and choose the best answer to the question you hear. Use the Answer Sheet.

1. A. to see the return policy

B. to pay for something

C. to return something

2. A. an extended warranty

B. a computer

C. both of the above

3. A. He paid too much for milk.

B. The sales clerk refused to correct the mistake on his receipt.

C. He didn't want to buy milk.

4. A. rice

B. 5 pounds

C. several bags

5. A. The coat is nice.

B. The coat is expensive.

C. The coat is a good price.

ANSWER SHEET			
1	A	B	C
2	A	B	C
3	A	B	C
4	A	B	C
5	A	B	C
6	A	B	C
7	A	B	C
8	A	B	C
9	A	B	C
10	A	B	C

Listen and choose the sentence that is closest in meaning to the sentence you hear. Use the Answer Sheet.

6. A. You have to pay extra for the warranty.

B. You don't have to pay extra for the warranty.

C. The warranty on this product has expired.

7. A. If I return this, will I get my money back?

B. Can I return this for a store credit?

C. How many days do I have to return this?

8. A. I'm certain you can return this.

B. I'm not positive, but I think you can return this.

C. You can return this for a store credit.

9. A. I don't think this is very good.

B. This is terrible, isn't it?

C. This tastes good, doesn't it?

10. A. Grapes aren't expensive.

B. Grapes are expensive.

C. Grapes are cheap.

2 Dictation 🎧

Listen and write the questions you hear.

1. _____

_____

2. _____

_____

3. _____

_____

3 Vocabulary Review

Use the clues to complete the crossword puzzle.

ACROSS

2 A _____ store sells used clothing.

5 A grocery store that has many different kinds of fruit has a good _____ of fruit.

9 Another word for "buy" is _____.

10 A business that makes more money than it spends is _____.

11 A _____ person doesn't believe everything advertisements say.

12 You should ask for a "rain _____" when a store doesn't have something that was advertised for sale.

13 Another word for the things a store sells is _____.

DOWN

1 Most stores offer a cash refund or store _____ if you return a purchase.

3 If you have an _____ warranty, you can get something repaired after the initial warranty has expired.

4 Some salespeople get extra money, or a _____, each time they sell something.

6 If you have a _____ contract, you can get free repairs.

7 Grocery stores sell many different _____, or kinds, of cereal.

8 When you buy rice "in _____," you can choose any amount you want.

✔ LEARNING LOG

I know these words:

NOUNS
- ☐ brand
- ☐ commission
- ☐ comparison shopper
- ☐ consignment shop
- ☐ extended warranty
- ☐ impulse buyer
- ☐ merchandise
- ☐ net weight
- ☐ policy
- ☐ purchase

- ☐ quality
- ☐ rain check
- ☐ scanner
- ☐ selection
- ☐ service contract
- ☐ store credit
- ☐ thrift store
- ☐ time limit
- ☐ unit price
- ☐ yard sale

VERBS
- ☐ cover
- ☐ end up
- ☐ increase
- ☐ keep in mind
- ☐ purchase
- ☐ ring up

ADJECTIVES
- ☐ profitable
- ☐ suspicious

OTHER
- ☐ in bulk
- ☐ out of stock

I practiced these skills, strategies, and grammar points:

- ☐ analyzing advertisements
- ☐ interviewing classmates
- ☐ prioritizing goals for the unit
- ☐ understanding words in context
- ☐ understanding shopping tips
- ☐ listening for general information

- ☐ listening for specific information
- ☐ expressing doubt
- ☐ comparing prices
- ☐ asking and answering tag questions
- ☐ reading and responding to classified ads
- ☐ practicing intonation in tag questions

Spotlight: Reading Strategy

USING A DICTIONARY

There is a lot of interesting and useful information in an English language learner's dictionary. In addition to finding the definition of a word, you can:

- ✓ learn how to pronounce a word.
- ✓ learn the part of speech of a word.
- ✓ learn the number of syllables in a word.
- ✓ learn irregular forms of nouns and verbs.
- ✓ find a synonym for a word.
- ✓ read sample sentences with the word.
- ✓ learn phrasal verbs such as "look into" and "find out."
- ✓ learn cultural information about the word.

Words in English often have more than one meaning. When you look up a word in a dictionary, make sure you choose the correct definition. The first definition is usually the most common, but it might not be the one you are looking for.

---

1 Read the dictionary definitions below and answer the questions.

> **bulk**/ bûlk/ *n.* **1** large size: *Big animals, such as elephants and whales, have huge bulk.* **2** the most of s.t., (syn.) the majority: *The bulk of the students passed the exam.* **3 in bulk**: large amount: *You can save money by buying things in bulk.*
>
> —*adj.* a bulk shipment: a large quantity: *The bulk shipment was 500 boxes of shoes.*
>
> **bulk•y**/ bûlki / *adj.* -ier, -iest large and difficult to handle, (syn.) unwieldy: *A mattress is bulky for one person to carry.*

1. What is the most common meaning of the word *bulk*?

   _____

2. What is the superlative form of the word *bulky*?

   _____

3. What does *s.t.* mean? (Hint: *s.o.* means *someone*)

   _____

4. What is a synonym for one definition of *bulk*?

   _____

5. What is a synonym for the adjective *bulky*?

   _____

2 Read the dictionary definitions and the usage note and answer the questions below.

> **garage sale** *n.* a sale of used household items (old lamps, tables, etc.) inside or near a person's garage: *When my parents moved to a smaller house, they held a garage sale one weekend.*
>
> ---
>
> USAGE NOTE: Also known as yard sales, rummage sales, tag sales, or sidewalk sales, *garage sales* are popular in both cities and suburbs. Homeowners may post signs around their neighborhood to advertise a sale. People who live in apartments usually just put things out on the sidewalk and wait for passersby: *I need some bookshelves. Let's drive around the university area and look for a garage sale.*
>
> ---
>
> **yard sale** *n.* the sale of unwanted household items, such as old lamps, and tables, in a person's yard: *We bought a beautiful old table at a yard sale for $10!* *See:* garage sale, USAGE NOTE.

1. What is the difference between a yard sale and a garage sale?

2. This dictionary provides sample sentences in italics. Do the sample sentences help you to understand the meanings of the words?

3. What is the purpose of a usage note?

4. How helpful is this usage note to you?

3 Read the sentences and choose the correct definition for the word *yard* in each context. Circle 1 or 2.

> **yard** /yard/ *n.* **1** a length of three feet or 36 inches (0.91 meter): a yard of cloth **2** an area usually behind or in front of a house: *The children went outside to play in the yard.*

1. I spent an hour yesterday cleaning the yard.   1   2

2. I need 3 yards to make a new dress.   1   2

3. I found a yard of rope downstairs.   1   2

4. My new tie is a yard long.   1   2

5. My yard is about 20 yards wide.   1   2

Source for definitions: *Newbury House Dictionary,* Fourth Edition.

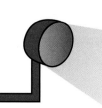
Spotlight: Writing Strategy

WRITING A LETTER OF COMPLAINT

Writing a letter of complaint is often the best way for a consumer to correct a problem. Be concise and direct in a letter of complaint and include the following information:

- the date and place of the purchase
- a description of the purchase
- a copy of the receipt

- an explanation of the problem
- the length of time you are willing to wait
- what you want

---

1 Read the written complaints and check (✓) the information each one provides.

	Email	Letter
1. the date the complaint was written	☐	✓
2. the date of the purchase	☐	☐
3. the recipient's name and address	☐	☐
4. the recipient's title	☐	☐
5. a description of the purchase	☐	☐
6. an explanation of the problem	☐	☐
7. what the writer wants	☐	☐
8. how long the writer will wait	☐	☐
9. the writer's name and address	☐	☐
10. a copy of the receipt	☐	☐

Email

> Dear Sir/Madam:
>
> In February, I went to the Lucky Sam's toy store in Oyster, New Jersey to buy a Sander's Wood Gym (Product #2678). This product was advertised in the store's flyer, but when I got to the store, they did not have any in stock. I asked for a rain check and they gave me one, but now I have waited more than 10 weeks, and I still don't have a Sander's Gym.
>
> I feel strongly that the company needs to do something soon to resolve this problem. I look forward to your reply.
>
> Sincerely,
> Frank Muller
>
> 5677 Torrence Avenue
> Millville, New Jersey 08332
> FMuller@freeemail.net

Letter

4567 Melody Avenue, Apt 4A
San Carlos, CA 94070

May 6, 2006

Bridget Jones
Consumer Service Manager
Dyno Electronics
432 Southwest Avenue
Modesto, CA 95350

Dear Ms. Jones:

On April 15, I bought a Dyno stereo (serial number 45605048844) at your store in San Carlos. Unfortunately, the CD changer on this stereo has not worked properly since the day I bought it. I called the store the day after I purchased the equipment to report the problem, but the store manager refuses to repair or exchange the stereo. Enclosed you will find a copy of my receipt.

To resolve the problem, I feel strongly that I should be able to exchange this stereo for one that works properly.

I look forward to your reply and a resolution to my problem. I will wait until June 1 before seeking help from a consumer protection agency or the Better Business Bureau. Please contact me at the address above or by phone at (914) 555-4993.

Sincerely,

Jon Phillips

Jon Phillips

2 Think of something you have bought but weren't satisfied with. Write a letter of complaint explaining the situation. Then read a classmate's letter and identify the information in Activity 1 that the letter provides.

LESSON 1

She has jury duty.

THINGS TO DO

1 Warm Up

Work with your classmates to answer the questions below.

1. Have you ever seen a courtroom in real life or in a movie? Describe what happened.
2. What are the people in this courtroom doing?

2 Identify

Who in this courtroom does each thing below? Write your guesses. Then compare ideas with a classmate. Find the words in the glossary on **page 171** to check your answers.

_____ decides if the defendant is guilty or not guilty

_____ records what people say

_____ is in charge of the courtroom

_____ keeps peace in the courtroom

_____ tries to prove the **defendant** is not guilty

_____ tries to show the defendant is guilty

_____ describes what he or she saw

3 Put in Sequence

Read the journal entries on **page 94** and put the events below in order from first (1) to last (8).

_____ The **jury** went into a special room.

_____ She went to court for the first time.

_____ She became a member of the jury.

_____ A **judge** and two lawyers interviewed her.

_____ She received a summons for jury duty in her mailbox.

_____ She received a check from the court.

_____ The jury made a decision.

_____ She listened to the **testimony** of many **witnesses**.

Compare ideas with a classmate. Then take turns telling the story in your own words.

My Journal

May 21: There was an unexpected piece of mail in my mailbox today—a **summons** for jury duty. The summons says I should appear in court at 9 A.M. on June 22.

June 22: I signed in at court at 9 A.M. A lot of other people were there too, and we waited for several hours until finally someone told us to go into the courtroom. Each person was interviewed by a judge and two **lawyers**. Some people were **dismissed** and some were asked to stay. When it was my turn, I answered all their questions. I guess they liked my answers because they told me to come back tomorrow to be a member of the jury.

June 23: My first day on a jury. I'm not allowed to talk about the case, but I can write about it in my journal. It's a **criminal** case! The defendant is accused of **battery**, disturbing the peace, and using language intended to **incite** violence! We listened to the **testimony** of witnesses all day. It seems pretty clear to me that he is **guilty**.

July 9: I've been listening to testimonies for over 2 weeks, and today the trial ended. I wasn't so sure the man was guilty. In the afternoon all of us—the jury members—went into a special room to make a decision. We worked for 4 hours to come to a decision. He was found guilty on the first count, **innocent** on the two others—disturbing the peace and using language to incite violence.

Aug. 2: There was a check from the court in my mailbox today. They paid me $5.00 a day to serve on the jury.

94

2 LESSON

It's a felony.

"You're under arrest."

THINGS TO DO

1 Read a Bar Graph

Work with your classmates to answer the questions below.

1. According to the bar graph on page 97, which type of crime was the most common in the U.S. in 1980? In 2000?
2. According to the bar graph, which types of crime have decreased since 1980?
3. What information in the graph is surprising to you? Why?

2 Use the Vocabulary

Use the chart on page 96–97 to answer the questions below.

1. Which is the most serious—an **infraction**, a **misdemeanor**, or a **felony**?
2. What is an example of an infraction, a misdemeanor, and a felony?
3. What type of crime is **punishable** by a year or less in prison?
4. For what crimes can a person go to **prison** for more than a year?
5. What type of offense is **jaywalking**? What's the consequence?
6. Which is more serious—shoplifting or burglary?

Work with a partner. Take turns asking and answering the questions.

3 Expand Your Vocabulary

Write the missing noun or verb form. Then complete the questions with the correct form of the word.

NOUN	VERB	NOUN	VERB
1. *violation*	violate	4. payment	
2. punishment		5.	imprison
3.	vandalize	6.	burglarize

1. Is jaywalking a _____ of the law?
2. What is the _____ for arson?
3. Is _____ a felony?
4. For what kinds of crimes do you have to _____ a fine?
5. Can trespassing be punishable by _____?
6. Is _____ punishable by more than a year in prison?

Work with a partner. Take turns asking and answering the questions.

Types of Illegal Action

Infraction

Misdemeanor

Felony

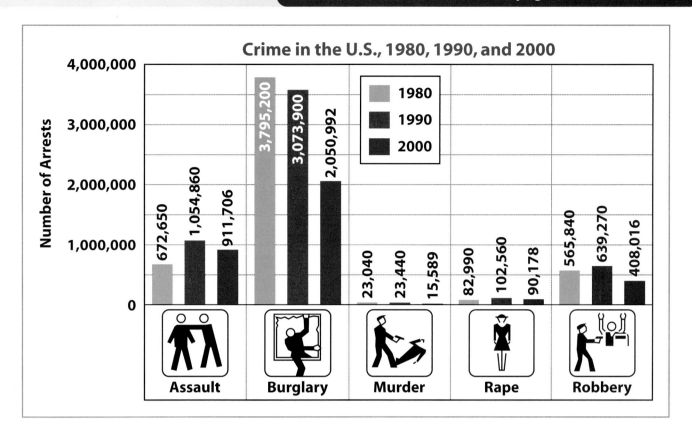

Crime in the U.S., 1980, 1990, and 2000

Definitions	Examples	Consequences
An infraction is a minor **offense**. It is the least serious type of offense.	• littering • jaywalking • minor traffic **violations**	People who **commit** an infraction usually have to **pay a fine**. Jaywalking fines vary from city to city, ranging from under $50 to $700.
A misdemeanor is more serious than an infraction but less serious than a felony. In general, misdemeanors are crimes punishable by less than one year in prison.	• petty theft (in many states, this includes shoplifting) • trespassing • vandalism	People who commit a misdemeanor may be punished with a fine, **probation**, community service, or **imprisonment** for one year or less.
A felony is a very serious crime. In many states, a felony is any crime punishable by more than one year in prison.	• arson • burglary • murder • rape • aggravated assault	Felony crimes are punishable by imprisonment for more than a year. The most serious felonies can be punishable by death.

To hear this message again, press 9.

THINGS TO DO

Couples must get a marriage license before getting married.

1 Warm Up

Work with your classmates to answer the questions below.

1. What do you need a permit or license for in your community? Check (✓) your answers.

   □ to get married   □ to ride a bicycle

   □ to vote   □ to ride a motorcycle

   □ to build a house   □ other: _____

2. What do you have to do to get a marriage license and a driver's license? Read questions 1 and 2 on page 99 and check (✓) your guesses in the *Before Listening* column.

2 Listen and Compare 🎧

Listen to a recorded message about getting a marriage license. Check (✓) the things you have to do in the *After Listening* column on page 99. Repeat with the recorded message about getting a driver's license.

3 Listen for Specific Information 🎧

Read the questions in the *Note-Taking Chart* on page 99. Then listen again for the answers to the questions and take notes. Then get together with a classmate and take turns asking and answering the questions.

A vision test is required to get a driver's license.

4 Use the Communication Strategy 🎧

Work with a partner. Take turns asking and answering the questions below. Try to use the communication strategy in your answers.

> EXAMPLE:
> A: Do I need to have a blood test to get a marriage license?
> B: No, it's not necessary.
> A: So, a blood test is not required?
> B: Yes, that's right.

Questions

1. Is it expensive to get a marriage license?
2. How long is a marriage license valid?
3. Where do I go to get a marriage license?
4. Where do I go to get a driver's license?
5. How long is a temporary driver's license valid?
6. How many times can I take the written test?

COMMUNICATION STRATEGY

Paraphrasing to Check Understanding

When you paraphrase, you put information into your own words. Paraphrasing is a good way to check your understanding of something.

A: It usually takes about 30 minutes to issue a marriage license.

B: So, I can get a license in just half an hour?

A: Yes, that's right.

You have reached the County Clerk's automated information system.

1. What do you have to do to get a marriage license?

Before Listening			After Listening
☐	a. You have to get a blood test.		☐
☐	b. You have to complete an application.		☐
☐	c. You have to make an appointment.		☐
☐	d. You have to go to the county clerk's office.		☐
☐	e. You have to show a picture ID.		☐
☐	f. You have to show your social security card.		☐
☐	g. You have to take a test.		☐
☐	h. You have to have your picture taken.		☐
☐	i. You have to pay a fee.		☐
☐	j. You have to be fingerprinted.		☐

Thank you for calling the Department of Motor Vehicles.

2. What do you have to do to get a driver's license?

Before Listening			After Listening
☐	a. You have to get a blood test.		☐
☐	b. You have to complete an application.		☐
☐	c. You have to make an appointment.		☐
☐	d. You have to go to the county clerk's office.		☐
☐	e. You have to show a picture ID.		☐
☐	f. You have to show your social security card.		☐
☐	g. You have to take a test.		☐
☐	h. You have to have your picture taken.		☐
☐	i. You have to pay a fee.		☐
☐	j. You have to be fingerprinted.		☐

Note-Taking Chart

Marriage License Questions	Notes
1. What forms of identification can you use to get a marriage license? 2. How much does a marriage license cost in this county? 3. How long do you have to wait in the office to get a marriage license in this county?	

Driver's License Questions	Notes
4. In this state, what forms of identification can you use to get a driver's license? 5. How much does it cost to get a driver's license in this state? 6. How many questions are there on the test?	

LESSON 4

Traffic Infractions and Misdemeanors

THINGS TO DO

1 Warm Up

Work with your classmates to answer the questions below.

1. Have you ever gotten a parking or a driving ticket? If so, what happened?
2. Look at the ticket on this page. What did the person get a ticket for?
3. What are some other reasons for getting a parking or driving ticket?
4. What does each of the traffic signs on page 101 say you should or shouldn't do?

2 Read and Take Notes

Read the information on page 101 and take notes in a chart like the chart below. Then compare notes with a partner.

Topic	Important details
Parking tickets	• you don't have to go to court • cost of ticket is on the ticket
Infraction tickets	

3 Summarize

Use your notes from Activity 2 to write a summary of the text on page 101. Your summary should be about 1/3 the length of the original text.

TRY THIS STRATEGY

Asking Questions Ask yourself questions before you read, while you are reading, and after you read. This can help you understand and remember information. Below are some useful questions to ask after reading something. Ask yourself these questions about the article on page 101.

- What is the main idea?
- What was interesting to me?
- What are 2 things that I learned?
- How do any of these ideas connect to other things I've read?

Impound Tag Number   *0—432Y*
            Case Number

NON-MOVING TRAFFIC TICKET

Jose D. Bayron
Name
12 Mountain Rd.
Address
El Paso   *TX*   *79924*
City   State   Zip
ELT456   *JH4DC445XIT006950*
Lic #   VIN #
black   *Acura*   *Integra*
Color   Make   Model

The Undersigned States That On or About

04 / *23* / *06* At *4:15* __ AM ☒PM
Mo.   Day   Year

At or Near: *Main St.*

The defendant violated the following section of the Municipal Code.

☐ OVERTIME PARKING   ☒ ILLEGAL PARKING   ☐ ILLEGAL PARKING DESIGNATED HANDICAPPED

SECTION 27-644   SECTION *27-608* SECTION 27-616
FINE **$15.00**   FINE **$25.00**   FINE **$100.00**

"Your license and registration, please."

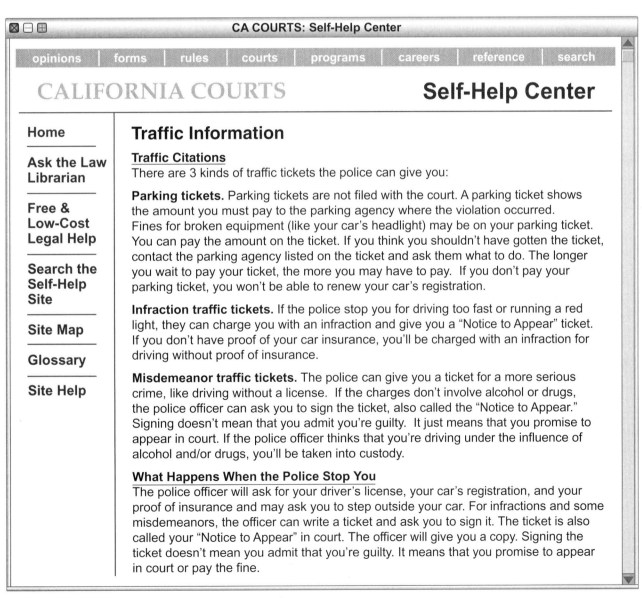

It shows the amount that you must pay.

LESSON 5

Adjective Clauses, Part 1

A clause is a group of words with a subject and a verb. A clause can be independent or dependent. An independent, or main clause, is a complete sentence. A dependent clause is not a complete sentence. It is always connected to a main clause.

An adjective clause is a dependent clause. It gives more information about a person or thing in the main clause. Most adjective clauses begin with the pronoun *that, which,* or *who*.

	Main Clause	Adjective Clause
EXAMPLES:	A crime is any behavior	**that** is punishable by imprisonment, a fine, or both.
	I paid the parking ticket	**which** I received last week.

1st part of Main Clause	Adjective Clause	2nd part of Main Clause
A person	**who** is charged with an infraction	is not entitled to a trial by jury.

Tip
- Use *who* for people.
- Use *which* for things.
- Use *that* for people and things.

---

1 Match

Match each main clause with an adjective clause.

Main clause

1. She was on the jury of a case ___c___
2. I was polite to the police officer _____
3. A criminal is someone _____
4. A felony is a crime _____
5. The police caught the person _____
6. I just got a temporary license _____
7. She didn't see the sign _____
8. The police couldn't find the person _____

Adjective clause

a. which is good for 60 days.
b. that said no parking.
c. that lasted for several months.
d. that is punishable by imprisonment.
e. who vandalized the building.
f. who **witnessed** the crime.
g. who commits a crime.
h. who stopped me for speeding.

2 Write

Complete these adjective clauses with your own ideas.

1. I have a friend who is _____
2. I would like to own a car that is _____
3. I live in a house that is _____
4. Do you know the name of the actor who was _____
5. Do you know the name of a city that is _____

Adjective Clauses, Part 2

The pronoun at the beginning of an adjective clause is either the subject or the object of the adjective clause.

EXAMPLES:

The police interviewed the woman **who witnessed the crime**. (*who* = the subject of the adjective clause)

The police interviewed the woman about the crime **that she witnessed**. (*that* = the object of the adjective clause)

The case **that ended last week** was a criminal case. (*that* = the subject of the adjective clause)

The case **that we heard** was a criminal case. (*that* = the object of the adjective clause)

When the pronoun is the object of the adjective clause, it can be omitted. When the pronoun is the subject of the adjective clause, it cannot be omitted.

EXAMPLE:

He was charged with a crime **that he didn't commit**. = He was charged with a crime **he didn't commit**.

3 Identify and Rewrite

Identify the boldfaced pronoun at the beginning of each adjective clause as a *subject* or *object*. Write your answer on the line.

1. I visited the prisoner **who** is in jail for 3 months. _subject_
2. He got a parking ticket **that** he didn't deserve. _____
3. She did something **that** is a minor offense. _____
4. The officer **that** I was telling you about is on the phone. _____
5. He paid the ticket **that** he got for speeding. _____
6. The stop sign **that** I drove through was taken down. _____
7. The police stopped a man **who** was driving dangerously. _____
8. My husband opened the summons **that** I received yesterday in the mail. _____

Now rewrite the 5 sentences from above that have an object pronoun in the adjective clause. Omit the pronoun from your sentence.

1. _He got a parking ticket he didn't deserve._
2. _____
3. _____
4. _____
5. _____

4 Write

Complete these adjective clauses with your own ideas.

1. I live in a city that I _____
2. I saw a movie that you _____
3. I have a friend who I _____
4. I saw a movie that I _____
5. My friend is getting married to someone that I _____

103

Neighborhood Watch

NEIGHBORHOOD CRIME WATCH

We immediately report all **SUSPICIOUS PERSONS** and activities to our Police Dept.

1 Warm Up

Work with your classmates to answer the questions below.

1. What are the biggest problems in your neighborhood?
2. How safe is your neighborhood?
3. What can individuals do to make their neighborhoods safer?

2 Read and Respond

Read the information below and answer the questions on page 105.

Making Changes

Neighborhood Watch is an organization of citizens in a neighborhood. The members of a Neighborhood Watch program work with the police to protect their community. Neighborhood Watch members watch for unusual activity in their neighborhood and report it to the police.

It's a story of hard work and pride. In 1975, Trong Nguyen arrived in Chicago from Vietnam. He and his family were fleeing the last days of war.

But the "Uptown" area the refugees moved into seemed like another war zone. The streets were filled with muggers, drug addicts, and other dangerous people. It was not a good place for families with children.

But people like Trong Nguyen were determined to save the neighborhood. They worked with police and other community leaders. Groups were formed to watch for trouble. Before long, much of the crime stopped.

Meanwhile, Trong opened a small restaurant. Other people from Laos, Cambodia, and Vietnam started businesses in stores that had been empty. Soon, the addicts and gangs disappeared.

Today, Chicago's "Uptown" is no longer a dangerous, run down area, thanks to Trong and others. People from all over the city come to visit its stores and restaurants. It's a special place.

Source: *U.S. Express*, Scholastic, Inc.

QUESTIONS

1. Why wasn't Trong's neighborhood in Chicago a good place to live?
2. What did Trong do to change his neighborhood?
3. What is Trong's neighborhood like now?
4. Do you think the Neighborhood Watch program is a good idea? Why or why not?

3 Apply

Below are some things you can do to help keep your neighborhood safe. Choose one to pursue. Report to your class any information that you learn.

1. Get to know your neighbors. Talk with them about what to do in an emergency in your area.
2. Call the local police to find out if there is a Neighborhood Watch in your area.
3. Get more information about Neighborhood Watch by looking on the internet. Visit http://www.usaonwatch.com.

WINDOW ON PRONUNCIATION 🎧
Changing Stress with *That*

 Read the information.

The word *that* is often stressed when it is a pronoun or a demonstrative.

> He needs **that** book, not this one.
> We don't want **that**.

It is not usually stressed, however, when it is at the beginning of an adjective clause.

> I can't find the book that I left on the desk.

 Listen to the statements and questions. Listen again and repeat.

1. That's the man that was on TV.
2. Remember the movie that I told you about? It's at that theater over there.
3. Did you meet the girl that Matt likes? That's her.
4. Not that book. I want the one that I gave you last week.
5. The neighbor that had an accident last week lives in that house.

 Listen to the statements and questions again. Circle *that* each time it is stressed.

 Work with a partner. Answer the questions using an adjective clause with *that*.

1. How would you describe a good law?
2. What are the characteristics of a responsible citizen?

★7 LESSON

What do you know?

1 Listening Review 🎧

Listen and choose the sentence that is closest in meaning to the sentence you hear. Use the Answer Sheet.

1. A. An infraction is less serious than a misdemeanor.
   B. An infraction is not as serious as a felony.
   C. A misdemeanor is less serious than a felony.

2. A. Jaywalking is an example of an infraction.
   B. An infraction is the least serious type of offense.
   C. An infraction is punishable by a fine.

3. A. You have to get a blood test before you can get married.
   B. You might need a blood test to get married.
   C. You don't need a blood test to get married.

4. A. You can take the test 3 times.
   B. You can pass the test 3 times.
   C. You can fail the written test 3 times.

5. A. The defendant was accused of an infraction.
   B. The defendant was accused of a felony.
   C. The defendant was accused of a misdemeanor.

	ANSWER SHEET		
1	Ⓐ	Ⓑ	Ⓒ
2	Ⓐ	Ⓑ	Ⓒ
3	Ⓐ	Ⓑ	Ⓒ
4	Ⓐ	Ⓑ	Ⓒ
5	Ⓐ	Ⓑ	Ⓒ
6	Ⓐ	Ⓑ	Ⓒ
7	Ⓐ	Ⓑ	Ⓒ
8	Ⓐ	Ⓑ	Ⓒ
9	Ⓐ	Ⓑ	Ⓒ
10	Ⓐ	Ⓑ	Ⓒ

Listen to each conversation and choose the best answer to the question you hear. Use the Answer Sheet.

6. A. She committed a crime.
   B. She saw someone commit a crime.
   C. She talked to a witness to the crime.

7. A. a photo ID
   B. a work ID
   C. a picture

8. A. a blood test
   B. a marriage license
   C. an application form

9. A. a parking ticket
   B. an infraction traffic ticket
   C. a misdemeanor traffic ticket

10. A. the book that was on the chair
    B. the book that was on the table
    C. the table that was in the dining room

2 Vocabulary Review

Write the missing noun, verb, or adjective form.

	NOUN	VERB	ADJECTIVE
1.	aggravation	*aggravate*	aggravated
2.	commitment	commit	
3.		defend	——
4.	fatality	——	
5.	guilt	——	
6.	innocence	——	
7.	jaywalker		——
8.	judgment / judge		——
9.		punish	
10.	violation		

Choose 6 words from the chart above and write 6 questions. Then ask your classmates your questions.

EXAMPLE: Why do people commit crimes?

✔ LEARNING LOG

I know these words:

NOUNS
- ☐ aggravated assault
- ☐ assault
- ☐ bailiff
- ☐ battery
- ☐ burglary
- ☐ court reporter
- ☐ defendant
- ☐ defense attorney
- ☐ felony
- ☐ imprisonment
- ☐ infraction
- ☐ jaywalking
- ☐ judge
- ☐ jury
- ☐ lawyer
- ☐ misdemeanor
- ☐ murder
- ☐ offense
- ☐ prison
- ☐ probation
- ☐ prosecutor
- ☐ rape
- ☐ summons
- ☐ testimony
- ☐ violation
- ☐ witness

VERBS
- ☐ commit
- ☐ dismiss
- ☐ incite
- ☐ pay a fine
- ☐ witness

ADJECTIVES
- ☐ criminal
- ☐ guilty
- ☐ innocent
- ☐ punishable

I practiced these skills, strategies, and grammar points:

- ☐ identifying roles in a courtroom
- ☐ putting a story in sequence
- ☐ summarizing
- ☐ reading a bar graph
- ☐ understanding types of crime
- ☐ comparing recorded phone messages
- ☐ listening for specific information
- ☐ paraphrasing to check information
- ☐ reading about traffic citations
- ☐ understanding traffic signs
- ☐ asking questions before reading
- ☐ using adjective clauses
- ☐ reading and responding to local issues
- ☐ changing stress with *that*

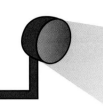

Spotlight: Reading Strategy

RECOGNIZING CAUSE AND EFFECT

A **cause** is an event or action that makes something else happen. An **effect** is what happens because of a certain event or action.

	Cause	Effect

EXAMPLES: If you don't pay your parking ticket, you won't be able to register your car.

	Effect	Cause

She took time off from work because she had jury duty.

When you are reading, it's important to recognize any cause and effect relationships. You may see the words below when you are reading about a cause and effect relationship.

if	because	since
as a result	for this reason	consequently

It's also important to recognize false cause and effect relationships. Just because one event follows another does not mean there is a cause and effect relationship. The following have no cause and effect relationship.

EXAMPLES: Jane had jury duty and I went to work.

We were talking on the phone when she fainted.

---

1 Read the paragraph and take notes in the chart below. What are the possible effects of running a red light?

> If you think running a red light is a minor thing, think again. If you get just one traffic ticket for breaking this law, the cost of your car insurance can go up. And this price increase can last for five years or more. That makes running a red light a very expensive offense. Running a red light could also cause a horrific accident. I once witnessed a **fatal** car crash that was caused by a car that didn't stop for a red light.

Cause *Running a red light*	→	Effects

2 Read the paragraph below and complete the chart. What is the cause and effect relationship in the paragraph?

> Is it wise to drive under the influence of alcohol? Not at all. Drunk driving is a serious offense. More than 50% of all fatal car accidents in the U.S. every year are alcohol related. If you drink and drive, you could hurt yourself, or worse, you could injure or even kill another person. You will also lose your driver's license if you are caught drinking and driving. Face it. Drinking and driving is not a smart thing to do.

Cause	→	Effects

3 Read the article and take notes in the chart below. Then use your notes to summarize the article.

Violence on TV

Do you think it is **no big deal** if somebody gets killed on TV? Is it funny to you if people on TV hit each other? If so, maybe you are watching too much violence on TV.

Shows with violence should tell the truth, but often they do not. In real life, violence hurts. Flattened animals and people don't become round again and walk away. Bad guys are not always ugly so that you can tell right away who they are. Bad guys are not always caught. Bad guys do not always break down when police question them.

If you watch too many violent shows, you may start thinking that violence is more common and less serious than it is. It may seem to you that bad guys are on every corner and that you will have to use violence to defend yourself.

Violence *is* a part of life, but it is not a part of life to take lightly. Violence usually creates problems instead of solving them, and the problems it creates are very tough to solve. That is why, in real life, most people try hard to avoid ever using violence.

What TV puts in your brain is likely to stay there. Keep that in mind when you watch it.

Source: *The Macmillan Book of Fascinating Facts,* by Ann Elwood and Carol Madigan

Cause *watching too many violent shows on TV*	→	Effects

Summary:

_____

_____

_____

_____

_____

_____

Spotlight: Writing Strategy

USING GRAPHIC ORGANIZERS FOR WRITING

It is a good idea to organize your ideas before your start writing. Organizing your ideas is really a way to "think on paper." Taking notes in a graphic organizer is one good way to collect and organize your ideas.

- If you want to compare or contrast two things, use a Venn Diagram. In the overlapping area of the two circles, identify how the two things are similar. In the outer part of each circle, write how each thing is different.

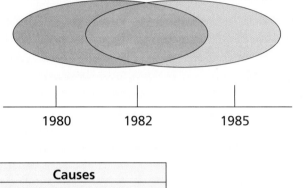

- If you want to identify a sequence of events, use a time line.

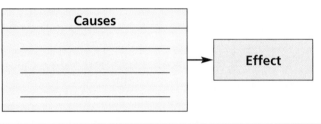

| | 1980 | 1982 | 1985 |

- If you want to identify a cause and effect relationship, use a cause/effect diagram.

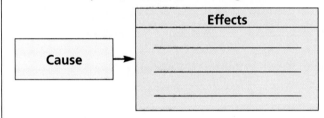

| Cause | → | **Effects** _____ _____ _____ |

| **Causes** _____ _____ _____ | → | Effect |

---

1 Use a graphic organizer to organize your answers to the questions below. Then write a paragraph to answer each question.

a. What do you think are 3 causes of crime in the U.S.? Write them in the *Causes* box below.

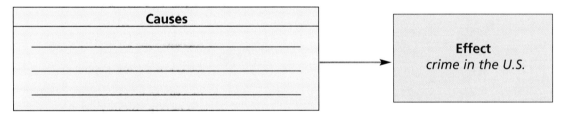

| **Causes** _____ _____ _____ | → | **Effect** *crime in the U.S.* |

Your paragraph:

_____

_____

_____

_____

_____

_____

_____

b. How are infractions and misdemeanors similar? How are they different? See pages 96–97 for help.

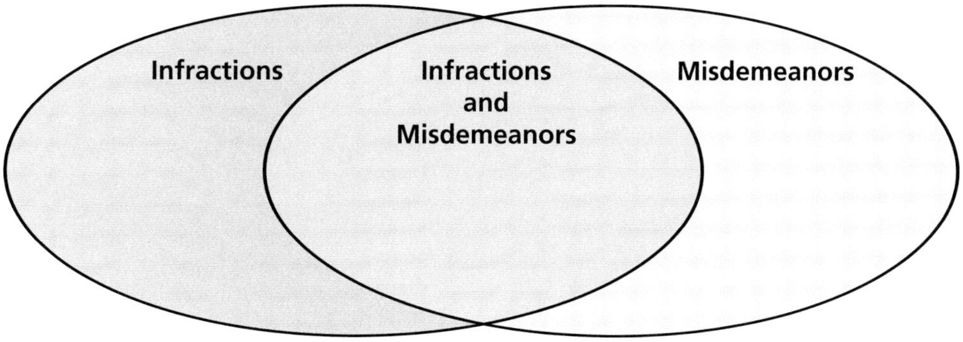

Infractions   Infractions
                      and
                     Misdemeanors   Misdemeanors

Your paragraph:

_____
_____
_____
_____
_____
_____
_____
_____

c. What are the steps a person takes to get married?

Your paragraph:

_____
_____
_____
_____
_____
_____
_____

1 LESSON

Who's in charge?

THINGS TO DO

1 Warm Up

Work with your classmates to answer these questions.

1. What are the characteristics of a good job?
2. Would you like to work in the store in the picture? Why or why not?
3. What do you see employees in the picture doing?

2 Analyze

Study the picture and read the work rules. Then answer the questions below.

1. Which work rule is the most serious to break?
2. What are 5 other types of inappropriate work place behavior?
3. Find 5 people in the picture who are breaking a work rule. What are they doing?
4. Who in the picture do you think is in charge? Why?

3 Solve Problems

Work with a partner to discuss the situations below. Then share ideas with your classmates.

1. Simon is a new employee at the company and Joe, a coworker, is training him. Joe spends a lot of time on the job loafing. Simon doesn't like to loaf on the job, but Joe is training him. What should Simon do?
2. Nancy frequently makes lengthy personal calls during work hours. Jane, her coworker, can hear Nancy talking and laughing on the phone and it makes it hard for Jane to work. What should Jane do?

TRY THIS STRATEGY

Understanding prefixes Many prefixes change the meaning of an adjective from positive to negative.

il-	illegal (not legal)
im-	impolite (not polite)
dis-	disconnected (not connected)
un-	uncommon (not common)

Write 3 more examples of words with these prefixes.

WORK RULES

The company considers the following behavior **unacceptable**. Any employee who engages in these behaviors will be subject to **disciplinary** actions including **reprimand**, warning, or **dismissal**.

1. Fighting or engaging in horseplay or **disorderly** behavior.
2. Unexcused or **excessive absenteeism**.
3. **Ignoring** work duties or **loafing** during working hours.
4. Failing to wear appropriate clothing.
5. Willfully **violating** safety or health regulations.
6. Taking improper care of company equipment and tools.
7. Failing to observe time limits for lunch and other breaks.

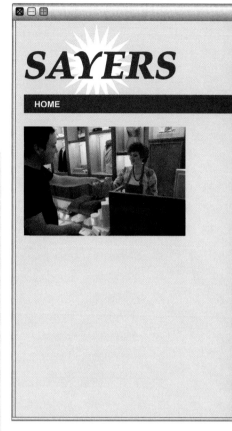

2 LESSON

Experience is preferred.

THINGS TO DO

1 Scan

Scan the job posting information on page 115 to find the answers.

1. What job is described in each of the job postings on page 115?
2. Which job requires more direct contact with customers?
3. Of these two jobs, which would you prefer? Why?

2 Use the Vocabulary

Write the missing verbs in the job tasks below. Then tell who is responsible for each task. Check (✓) SS (Shift Supervisor) and/or SM (Store Manager).

		SS	SM
1. _provides_	excellent customer service	☐	☐
2. _____	customer refunds	☐	☐
3. _____	customer complaints	☐	☐
4. _____	the daily activities of the store	☐	☐
5. _____	merchandise	☐	☐
6. counts and _____	money	☐	☐
7. _____	P&L reports	☐	☐
8. _____	daily banking activities	☐	☐
9. _____	the cash register	☐	☐
10. _____	recruitment	☐	☐
11. _____	customers receive good service	☐	☐
12. _____	deposits	☐	☐

3 Expand Your Vocabulary

Add the missing words to the chart. Write a sentence using each word.

NOUN	VERB	ADJECTIVE
supervisor	_supervise_	
	recruit	—
preparation		preparatory
	apply	applicable
preference		preferable

4 Write

Imagine you want to hire someone to help you with something at home or work. Write a job description for that position.

Welcome to Our Company

SEARCH OUR SITE [ ] GO

WHAT'S IN OUR STORE   OUR COMPANY   ABOUT US   CAREERS   COMMUNITY

Career Opportunities

Posting #
5443

Job Title
Shift Supervisor

Job Description
The Shift Supervisor has the following responsibilities, in addition to other duties as assigned:
- provides excellent customer service (uses the cash register to complete customer transactions, **handles** customer refunds and exchanges, **assists** customers with their shopping needs, and resolves customer complaints)
- counts and balances money, and **prepares** deposits
- **ensures** that **shipments** are correctly **processed**
- ensures that the store appearance is pleasing to the customer

Skills
Six (6) months of **retail** experience desired. **Previous** experience providing excellent customer service in a retail setting. Supervisory experience is **preferred**.

Education
High school diploma or general education degree (GED).

Welcome to Our Company

SEARCH OUR SITE [ ] GO

WHAT'S IN OUR STORE   OUR COMPANY   ABOUT US   CAREERS   COMMUNITY

Career Opportunities

Posting #
6544

Job Title
Store Manager

Job Description
The Store Manager has the following responsibilities, in addition to other duties assigned:
- ensures prompt and **courteous** service is given to all customers
- **oversees** the daily activities of a retail store to ensure its smooth operation
- orders merchandise
- oversees daily banking activities
- reviews profit and loss (P&L) reports
- provides leadership and development opportunities for store level associates
- does **recruitment** and training for store level associates

Skills
The successful candidate should have 2+ years supervisory experience in a retail setting. Must **possess** hands-on leadership skills. A proven record in building and working as part of a team is necessary. Applicants must have an ability to work varied shifts (including evenings/weekends).

Education
High school diploma or general education degree (GED) or higher. Candidates with a college degree are desired.

3 LESSON

He spoke very clearly.

Roberta submits her résumé.

THINGS TO DO

1 Warm Up

Work with your classmates to answer the questions below.

1. When was the last time you interviewed for a job? How did it go?
2. What should and shouldn't you do at a job interview?
3. What are 5 things you know about Roberta from her job application on page 117?

2 Listen for Specific Information 🎧

Listen to Roberta's interview and add the missing information to her job application on page 117.

3 Listen and Evaluate 🎧

Read the questions below. Then look at the pictures and listen to the interview again. Check (✓) your answers.

Do you think Roberta _____?	Yes, very.	Yes.	No.
1. was dressed appropriately	☐	☐	☐
2. was prepared for the interview	☐	☐	☐
3. spoke clearly	☐	☐	☐
4. was businesslike	☐	☐	☐
5. was polite	☐	☐	☐
6. had a friendly tone of voice	☐	☐	☐
7. had a positive attitude	☐	☐	☐

Now listen to Richard's interview. On another piece of paper, answer questions 1–7 about him. Then compare each interview.

4 Use the Communication Strategy

Work with a partner. Take turns asking the questions below. Write 2 of your own questions. Use the communication strategy when you answer the questions.

1. Do you like your school?
2. Do you have a job now?
3. Have you lived here for a long time?
4. _____?
5. _____?

Richard completes his application.

COMMUNICATION STRATEGY

Expanding Your Answers

It can seem rude or unfriendly if you give very short answers to questions. Expanding your answers helps to show that you want to have a conversation.

A: Do you like your school?

B: Yes, I do. The people are very friendly.

A: Did you go to school here last year?

B: No, I didn't. I wasn't here last year. I was in Haiti.

A: Where in Haiti did you live?

B: In Port-au-Prince. That's where I was born.

SAYERS

Welcome to Our Company

SEARCH OUR SITE [_____] [GO]

| HOME | WHAT'S IN OUR STORE | OUR COMPANY | ABOUT US | CAREERS | COMMUNITY |

Online Job Application

Please enter the following information to apply online or just enter your personal information and attach your resume on the next page:

Name
| Madera | Roberta | S |
| *Last* | *First* | *MI* |

Address
| 245 Longwood Blvd. | Hayworth | |
| *Street* | *City* | |

| Florida | 22222 | 123-45-6789 |
| *State* | *Zip Code* | *Social Security* |

Telephone
| 555-4959 | 555-5467 | fmd@metrocast.net |
| *Primary* | *Secondary* | *Email* |

Do you have the legal right to work in the United States? ● Yes ○ No

Are you under the age of 18? ○ Yes ● No

Position Applied For:

| Assistant Manager | Hayworth Store | |
| *Position* | *Location* | *Start Date* |

Have you ever had or do you currently have any restrictions to your license? ○ Yes ● No

Education:

Northeast Community College			
Name of School	*Years Completed*	*Diploma/Degree*	*Major*
Sanchez High School	4	H. S. Degree	N/A
Name of School	*Years Completed*	*Diploma/Degree*	*Major*
Name of School	*Years Completed*	*Diploma/Degree*	*Major*

General Information:

Have you ever been convicted of a felony or misdemeanor? ○ Yes ● No
(A Yes answer is not an automatic bar to employment.)

Have you ever been dismissed or forced to resign from any employment? ○ Yes ● No

1. Employer and Complete Address:

06/04	Floormart		
From Mo/Yr	*Name of Employer*	*Your Title*	*Reason for Leaving*
04/05	13600 Industrial Rd.	Miguel Sandor	
To Mo/Yr	*Address*	*Your Supervisor*	

2. Employer and Complete Address:

05/02	Reiko's		
From Mo/Yr	*Name of Employer*	*Your Title*	*Reason for Leaving*
05/04	1220 Bayside Dr.	Jean Phillips	
To Mo/Yr	*Address*	*Your Supervisor*	

117

LESSON 4

Performance Evaluations

THINGS TO DO

1 Warm Up

Work with your classmates to answer the questions below.

1. What are 5 characteristics of the ideal employee and the ideal employer? List your ideas in a chart like the one below. Then share ideas with your classmates.

The ideal employee	The ideal employer
is always on time	is fair

2. If you want to get a job promotion, what should you do? What shouldn't you do?

2 Read and Respond

Read the employee performance evaluation on page 119 and answer the questions below.

1. What do you know about Sarah Wang from her performance evaluation?
2. What are Sarah's greatest strengths on the job?
3. What is Sarah's greatest weakness on the job?
4. What are 3 things Sarah could do to improve her job performance?

3 Make Inferences

Match each comment below to one or more possible inferences.

Comments	Inferences
1. Petra completes her work on time. She _c, e, h_	a. is polite
2. Max prepares deposits accurately. He _____.	b. is creative
3. Tim often comes in early to work. He _____.	c. is dependable
4. Paul helped to train 3 new employees. He _____.	d. is punctual
5. Mei is very friendly with everyone. She _____.	e. is productive
6. Yoshiko does what needs to be done. She _____.	f. is cooperative
7. Hiro always has wonderful new ideas. He _____.	g. shows initiative
8. Patricia **delivers** her work on time. She _____.	h. has good job skills
9. Tony shows respect to everyone. He _____.	i. works independently
	j. other: _____

Sarah Wang relies on public transportation to get to work. Here, she waits for a bus.

Sarah Wang's manager discusses her performance evaluation with her.

Employee Performance Evaluation

EMPLOYEE	TITLE
Sarah Wang	Store Associate
DEPARTMENT	**EMPLOYEE NO.**
Housewares	214

TYPE OF EVALUATION

☒ ANNUAL ☐ PROMOTION ☐ MERIT ☐ OTHER

DIRECTIONS: Evaluate the employee's work performance as it relates to the requirements of the job. Write the number that best describes the employee's performance since the last evaluation.

1 = Excellent **2** = Very Good **3** = Satisfactory **4** = Decreased Performance **5** = Unsatisfactory

Job Responsibilities	Rating	Comments
DEPENDABILITY The employee is on time and follows the rules for breaks and **attendance**.	4	Ms. Wang was late to work more than ten times in the past three months due to transportation problems.
BEHAVIOR The employee is polite on the job.	3	There have been no customer complaints about Ms. Wang's behavior.
CREATIVITY The employee suggests ideas and better ways of accomplishing goals.	1	Ms. Wang suggested a new way to handle customer refunds that will save the company time and money. The customers also benefited.
RELIABILITY The employee can be relied on to efficiently complete a job.	4	Because Ms. Wang is often late to work, she cannot always be relied on to do her share of the work.
INDEPENDENCE The employee accomplishes work with little or no supervision.	2	Ms. Wang rarely requires assistance from her supervisor or coworkers. She knows what she has to do and she usually does it without being asked.
INITIATIVE The employee looks for new tasks and expands abilities professionally.	1	Ms. Wang is taking a design course because she would like to be more involved in improving the appearance of the store. She voluntarily set up an attractive display for the holiday season.
INTERPERSONAL SKILLS The employee is willing and able to communicate, cooperate, and work with coworkers, supervisors, and customers.	3	Ms. Wang works well with her coworkers. She's cooperative, and she listens well. She had a conflict with a coworker and because she was able to communicate well, they resolved the problem.
JOB SKILLS The employee has the appropriate skills to do the job well.	3	Ms. Wang has carefully and correctly completed the tasks assigned to her.

5
LESSON

If I had known, . . .

Past Perfect
Use the past perfect to show that one action happened before another in the past. In each example below, the underlined action happened first.

EXAMPLES: My sister got fired even though she **had worked** at the hospital for a long time.
She lost her job even though she **had** just **received** a great performance evaluation.
By the time she was 20, she **had** already **gotten** her diploma.

The adverbs *already, finally, just,* and *recently* often appear with past perfect verbs. The adverb comes immediately after the auxiliary "had."

EXAMPLE: I had **finally** gotten to sleep when the doorbell rang.

To form the past perfect, use *had* + the past participle of the verb.

I You She, He, It We They	**had**	already **left** work already **started** work already **taken** a break already **cleaned** the office just **finished** their meeting	when the boss arrived.

1 Complete the Sentences

Complete the sentences with the past perfect form of the verb in parentheses.

1. I _____*had*_____ already _____*gone*_____ to bed when the phone rang. (go)

2. He _____ just _____ a promotion when the company went out of business. (get)

3. Jan's supervisor _____ her several times by the time he fired her. (warn)

4. My friend was late to the interview because he _____ to set his alarm clock. (forget)

5. She _____ just _____ from college when she found the job she has now. (graduate)

6. I _____ just _____ one customer when another one asked me for help. (help)

7. Joan was reprimanded because she _____ jeans to work. (wear)

8. My boss was angry when he saw that no one _____ the tools away. (put)

2 Write

Complete each sentence. Use a verb in the past perfect tense.

1. When I got to work, _____.

2. When the electricity went out, _____.

3. By the time I got to class, _____.

4. When I got home last night, _____.

Past Unreal Conditional Statements

Use past unreal conditional statements to talk about imaginary or unreal situations in the past. To form these statements, use the past perfect in the *if* clause and *would have* + the past participle of the verb in the main clause.

If clause	Main clause

If Sam **had gotten** the job, he **would have stayed** in California.
(Sam didn't get the job and he didn't stay in California.)

EXAMPLES:
  If Rita and Marie **had applied** on time, they **would have gotten** the jobs.
  (They didn't apply on time, and they didn't get the jobs.)

  If Jim **hadn't lied** on his application, he **would have gotten** the job.
  (Jim did lie, and he didn't get the job.)

  Taka **wouldn't have lost** her job if she **had been** more cooperative.
  (She wasn't cooperative, and she lost her job.)

---

3 Complete the Sentences

Complete each sentence with the correct form of the verbs in parentheses.

1. If Donna ___*had had*___ more supervisory experience, she would have gotten the job. (have)

2. If Jon had resolved the customer's complaint, she _____ to see his supervisor. (not ask)

3. If Sam had taken care of the company's tools, he _____ his job. (not lose)

4. If she _____ more courteous to customers, she would have gotten the promotion. (be)

5. If I _____ how to use a cash register, I would have gotten the job right away. (know)

6. If someone _____ me, I wouldn't have left the store without buying anything. (assist)

7. If she had ordered the supplies on time, they _____ by now. (arrive)

8. If the supervisor had given clear instructions, we _____ them. (follow)

4 Write

Complete each sentence with your own ideas.

1. If _____, I wouldn't have gotten angry.

2. If _____, they wouldn't have fired him.

3. If _____, I would have gone to Hawaii.

4. If _____, I would have bought a new house.

5. I wouldn't have taken the job if _____.

6. I would have gotten the job if _____.

7. She wouldn't have lost her job if _____.

Family-Friendly Companies

1 Warm Up

Work with your classmates to answer the questions below.

1. Some companies and businesses are called *family-friendly* companies. What do you think that means?
2. What are 3 ways that work can **interfere with** your family life?
3. What do you think it means to balance work and family?

2 Read and Respond

Read the information below and answer the questions on page 123.

Employees participate at company picnics and parties.

> Name of Company: Wendall Corporation   Location: Lancaster, Ohio
> Type of Business: Table manufacturer   Number of Employees: 46
>
> Wendall Corporation has a reputation that many companies would love to have. Among its employees, Wendall is known as a great place to work. Employees rarely leave the company and Wendall's employment office is usually **flooded** with job applications. Among its customers, Wendall is known for providing quality workmanship and excellent customer service.
>
> In its hometown of Lancaster, Wendall is known for its commitment to both its customers and its employees. According to office manager Sheila Philips, Wendall is able to provide good customer service and great products because its employees want the company to succeed. "Wendall Corporation decided to become a family-friendly company about 10 years ago," Philips says. "We decided that anything we could do to keep our employees happy would only make the company better."
>
> What exactly does Wendall Corporation do for its employees? In addition to a good health care program, Wendall employees get **substantial discounts** on the company's wood products. They also receive generous **quarterly** bonuses and participate in company picnics and parties.
>
> Even more important for many employees is the fact that Wendall Corporation offers employees a flexible work schedule. This family-friendly company allows employees to work any hours between 7:00 A.M. and 7:00 P.M. as long as they put in the required 40 hours of work a week. Some employees, for example, work four 10-hour days while others choose to work the more common five 8-hour days. Wendall's flexible scheduling also makes it possible for parents to take time off during the day to attend meetings and participate in their children's activities at school.

Some companies allow employees to work offsite.

QUESTIONS

1. Employees at Wendall Corporation rarely leave the company. What can you infer from this fact?
2. What benefits does Wendall Corporation offer its employees?
3. Which of Wendall's benefits would be the most useful to you?
4. What are some other things that companies could do to help employees balance work and family?

3 Apply

Below is a list of family-friendly job benefits that some companies offer. Number them in importance to you from most important (1) to least important (10).

a. _____ Paid vacation of two weeks or more

b. _____ Health and dental insurance for all family members

c. _____ Tuition assistance

d. _____ Merchandise discount: the ability to buy the company's products at a discount.

e. _____ Flexible schedules: the ability to adjust work schedules to fit school or child-care schedules

f. _____ Telecommuting: the ability to work from home, when appropriate

g. _____ On-site day care

h. _____ Company help in finding child care

i. _____ Sixteen weeks of unpaid leave to take care of a sick family member, give birth, or adopt a child

j. _____ Job sharing: two half-time employees work to meet the demands of one full-time position

WINDOW ON MATH
Computing Averages

 Read the information.

You can find the average of a set of numbers by adding all the numbers and dividing by the number in the sample.

Daily classroom attendance for the week of January 8th:

Mon.		Tues.		Wed.		Thurs.		Fri.
17	+	15	+	13	+	14	+	16

Average daily attendance
    17 + 15 + 13 + 14 + 16 = 75 ÷ 5 (# of days) = 15

 Compute the average.

1. Six people work at Speedy Copy. Their hourly wages are as follows: Jim ($10), Cindy ($12), Ken ($11), Ivan ($15), Lucy ($13) and Chang ($14). What is the average hourly pay at Speedy Copy? _____

2. In one department at SouthWood, there are 8 full-time employees. Look at the number of sick days taken in one year by each employee. What is the average number of sick days taken by employees in that department?

Ming	7	Mahmoud	2
Park	3	Thomas	6
Sanders	2	Grant	1
Oliveira	5	Lopez	8

UNIT 7: Career Paths

LESSON 7

What do you know?

1 Listening Review 🎧

Listen to each conversation and choose the best answer to the question you hear. Use the Answer Sheet.

1. A. He ignored his work duties.
   B. He fought with a coworker.
   C. He violated a safety regulation.

2. A. She's courteous.
   B. She isn't very polite.
   C. She has good job skills.

3. A. He's creative.
   B. He is always on time.
   C. He's dependable.

4. A. She wanted to earn more money.
   B. She wasn't very dependable.
   C. She wanted a job with more responsibility.

5. A. He's creative.
   B. He's dependable.
   C. He's cooperative.

	ANSWER SHEET		
1	A	B	C
2	A	B	C
3	A	B	C
4	A	B	C
5	A	B	C
6	A	B	C
7	A	B	C
8	A	B	C
9	A	B	C
10	A	B	C

Listen and choose the statement that is closest in meaning to the sentence you hear. Use the Answer Sheet.

6. A. Joshua doesn't have to order merchandise.
   B. Ordering merchandise is part of Joshua's job.
   C. Joshua doesn't like to order merchandise.

7. A. Jill has worked for only two years.
   B. Jill has worked for two years with her supervisor.
   C. Jill has worked as a supervisor for two years.

8. A. Bob knows how to do refunds and exchanges for customers.
   B. The customer asked Bob for a refund or an exchange.
   C. Bob can't do refunds and exchanges for customers.

9. A. Tito left the job for a good reason.
   B. Tito didn't get the job for a good reason.
   C. Tito didn't have a reason for leaving the job.

10. A. Noah is creative.
    B. Noah works independently.
    C. Noah has good interpersonal skills.

2 Vocabulary Review

Write the missing noun, verb, or adjective form.

	NOUN	VERB	ADJECTIVE
1.	*absenteeism*	——	absent
2.	acceptance		
3.			assistant
4.	courtesy	——	
5.		deliver	
6.	discipline	discipline	
7.	excess	——	
8.	possession		possessive
9.	preference		
10.	resolution		——

Choose 6 words from the chart above and write 6 questions. Then ask your classmates your questions.

EXAMPLE: How did your parents discipline you?

✔ LEARNING LOG

I know these words:

NOUNS
- ☐ absenteeism
- ☐ attendance
- ☐ creativity
- ☐ discount
- ☐ dismissal
- ☐ independence
- ☐ initiative
- ☐ performance
- ☐ recruitment
- ☐ reprimand
- ☐ shipment

VERBS
- ☐ assist
- ☐ deliver
- ☐ ensure
- ☐ handle
- ☐ ignore
- ☐ interfere with
- ☐ loaf
- ☐ oversee
- ☐ possess
- ☐ prefer
- ☐ prepare
- ☐ process

ADJECTIVES
- ☐ courteous
- ☐ disciplinary
- ☐ disorderly
- ☐ excessive
- ☐ flooded
- ☐ previous
- ☐ quarterly
- ☐ retail
- ☐ substantial
- ☐ unacceptable

I practiced these skills, strategies, and grammar points:

- ☐ analyzing workplace behavior
- ☐ solving problems at work
- ☐ understanding prefixes
- ☐ reading job postings
- ☐ listening for specific information
- ☐ evaluating job interviews
- ☐ expanding your answers

- ☐ completing a job application
- ☐ understanding performance evaluations
- ☐ making inferences
- ☐ using the past perfect
- ☐ using the past unreal conditional
- ☐ understanding and ranking job benefits
- ☐ computing averages

Spotlight: Reading Strategy

IDENTIFYING A SEQUENCE OF EVENTS

When you are reading about a sequence of events, it's important to keep track of what happened and in what order. Below are some words that can help you follow a sequence of events.

after	before	later	previously
after that	first	meanwhile	today
afterwards	in + (year) then	now	

---

1 Read the paragraph below. Circle the words that help you follow the sequence of events.

    Working part-time can be a good way to get your foot in the door, says Nancy Lin. Her (first) job was as a part-time sales associate with Mill's Hardware at their store in Springvale. Meanwhile, she continued studying full time to get her degree. Immediately after graduating, she began working full time at the store. Soon after that she became an assistant store manager, and today she is a successful general manager of the Mill's store in San Bernardo. Who knows what's next, but before she started college, Nancy wasn't quite sure what kind of job she would have. She's happy with the outcome.

2 Read about Franklin Chang-Diaz on page 127. List some of the important events in his life in the boxes below. Sequence them from the beginning.

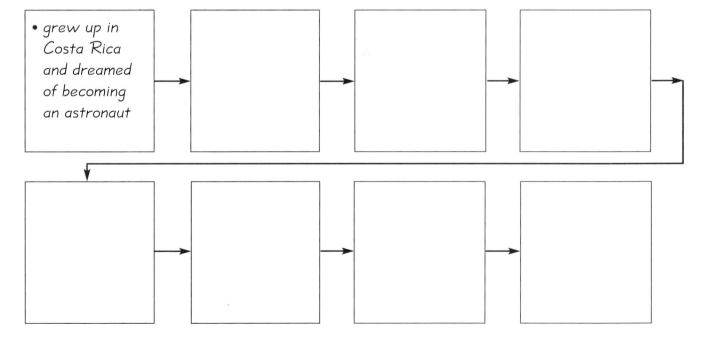

- grew up in Costa Rica and dreamed of becoming an astronaut

3 Use your notes to write a summary of the reading on page 127.

FRANKLIN CHANG-DIAZ NEEDS SPACE

Some people know what they want to do with their lives from the time they are very young. Franklin Chang-Diaz is one of those people. From the time he was a child in school, Chang-Diaz dreamt about exploring outer space. Unlike many people, however, Chang-Diaz held on to his dream and worked to make it come true.

Franklin Chang-Diaz grew up in Costa Rica. It was there that he became interested in space exploration, and he set his heart on becoming an astronaut. To make this possible, however, he knew he would have to move to the U.S. And to do that, he needed money. That's why as soon as he finished high school, he got a job as a bank teller at the National Bank of Costa Rica. In eight months he saved up enough money to move to Hartford, Connecticut where he could live with relatives.

Chang-Diaz's next step towards becoming an astronaut was to learn English and to get a university degree. Soon after he arrived in Hartford, he enrolled in high school so that he could improve his English. "The language was the number one problem for me," Chang-Diaz said. "After I learned English, things were 100% easier. His performance in high school was so outstanding that his teachers helped him get a scholarship to attend the University of Connecticut. After graduating from the University of Connecticut, Chang-Diaz received a scholarship for a PhD program at the Massachusetts Institute of Technology.

When Chang-Diaz finished his PhD studies, he decided it was time to apply for an astronaut position with NASA. The first time he applied, however, he was rejected. When he received his American citizenship in 1980, Chang-Diaz decided to apply again for a position at NASA. Four thousand people applied for just 19 jobs and Chang-Diaz got one of them. In 1981 he began his training as an astronaut.

On January 12, 1986, Chang-Diaz went up in space for the first time. Since then he has traveled into space numerous times. And what has he learned from traveling in space? "From space, we can really see how people are hurting the earth's environment," Chang-Diaz says. "So NASA is working hard to warn people that we must take care of our planet."

Most people have dreams, but it takes a truly exceptional person to make a dream come true. Chang-Diaz reminds us that with hard work and persistence it is possible to do the seemingly impossible.

Spotlight: Writing Strategy

UNDERSTANDING THE WRITING PROCESS

When you write something—a letter, a poem, a story, or an article—you probably aren't able to just sit down and quickly write the perfect piece. For most people, writing is a process made up of a number of steps. Below is one example of how you might write something.

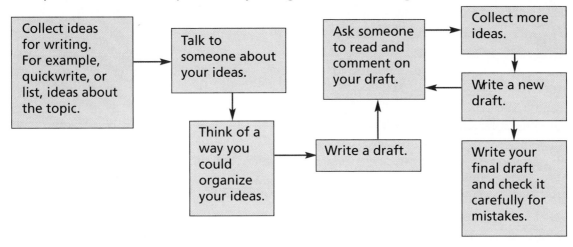

---

1 Follow the steps below to explore the writing process. You will write a paragraph about a person that you know well and admire.

Step 1: Choose a person you know well and admire. Collect ideas by quickwriting about the person. When you quickwrite, you simply write any ideas that come to mind. Don't worry about grammar mistakes, just write. If you can't think of something to write, just write, "I can't think of anything to write." After quickwriting for several minutes, look over your ideas and underline the ideas that you might want to use in your writing.

EXAMPLE: *One person I really admire is my friend Ann. I think I admire her because she is willing to try anything. She never says she doesn't want to do something. You can always depend on her to join you. I can't think of anything to write. I can't think of anything to write. Ann never worries about what people think about her. I mean, she just does what she thinks is right and if other people don't agree, well, too bad.*

Step 2: Talk to a partner. Describe the person you chose and tell why you admire him or her. Answer any questions your partner has.

I'm going to write about my friend Ann. She . . .

I admire her because . . .

Step 3: Try mapping to organize your ideas about this person. Add information about the person to the categories below and add your own categories.

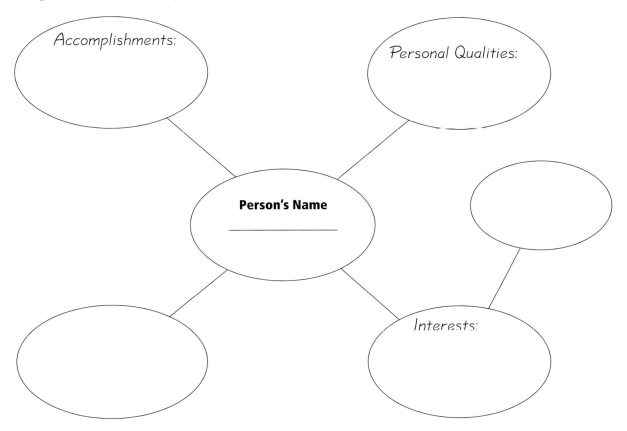

Step 4: Write a first draft. This is a first draft, so don't worry about making things perfect. Just try to get your ideas on paper.

Step 5: Ask a partner to read and comment on your draft. For example, your partner can tell you what is clear and unclear and what he or she likes about the draft and wants to know more about.

Step 6: Revise your writing as many times as you need to before you give it to your classmates to read.

It's not in the budget.

LESSON 1

THINGS TO DO

1 Warm Up

Work with your classmates to answer these questions.

1. Do you have a monthly **budget**, or spending plan? How closely do you follow it?

2. What is your biggest expense each month?

3. Look at the pictures on pages 130–131. What do the Lees spend money on each month? How much do they spend?

2 Evaluate

Study the monthly budget goals and actual spending of the Lee family and answer the questions below.

1. What percentage of their monthly budget did they actually spend in each category?

   See page 51 for math help.

2. What can you include in the miscellaneous category?

3. Which of their budget goals did the Lees meet?

4. What could the Lees do to meet their budget goals?

3 Plan

Write the percentage of your income that you would like to spend on each category below. What can you do to meet your goals?

My Budget Goals (% of income after taxes)			
Housing	___ %	Clothing	___ %
Savings	___ %	Miscellaneous	___ %
Entertainment	___ %	Food	___ %
Utilities	___ %	Transportation	___ %
Debts	___ %		

TRY THIS STRATEGY

Classifying Classifying or grouping words is a good way to remember them. Add 5 items to each group below in a similar chart.

CLOTHING	ENTERTAINMENT	TRANSPORTATION
pants	going to the movies	*car payment*

1 Housing
Actual Spending: $900

9 Transportation
Actual Spending: $450

8 Food
Actual Spending: $450

The Lee's Monthly Budget: March

2 Savings & Investments
Actual Spending: $100

3 Entertainment
Actual Spending: $150

Monthly Budget Goals
(Lee Family)
Income after taxes = $3,000.00

	Goals	Actual Spending
1. Housing	30%	_30%_
2. Savings/Investments	10%	_15%_
3. Entertainment	5%	___
4. Utilities	5%	___
5. Debts	0%	___
6. Clothing	5%	___
7. Miscellaneous	20%	___
8. Food	15%	___
9. Transportation	10%	___

4 Utilities
Actual Spending: $150

5 Debts
Actual Spending: $150

6 Clothing
Actual Spending: $150

7 Miscellaneous
Actual Spending: $300

2 LESSON

Do you have an IRA?

THINGS TO DO

1 Warm Up

Work with your classmates to answer these questions.

1. Read questions 1 to 9. Which question is the most interesting to you? Which is the least interesting?
2. What do you see in each picture?

2 Summarize

Read the questions and answers on pages 132 and 133. Then take turns asking and answering the questions with a partner. Use your own words to answer.

> EXAMPLE: Q: Are all credit cards the same?
> A: No they aren't. Credit cards have different perks, annual fees, and interest rates.

3 Use the Vocabulary

Talk to different classmates. Find someone who answers *Yes* to each question below. Write the person's name.

Find someone who _____.	Name
1. has more than one credit card	
2. has never maxed out a credit card	
3. has a budget deficit	
4. knows what the acronym IRA means	
5. has paid a credit card bill late	

4 Evaluate

Work with a partner. Read about each person below and answer the questions. Then share ideas with your classmates.

1. Carla always pays off her credit card bill in full. She never carries a balance. In choosing a credit card, should she get a no-fee card with 18% interest or a card with an annual fee of $50.00 and a 15% interest rate? Why?
2. You are saving money to buy a house. Should you put your money in an IRA account, a savings account, or in a CD? Why?

---

1 Q: Are all credit cards the same?

A: Absolutely not. Some credit cards charge an annual **fee** while others do not. Some credit cards offer **perks**, such as frequent flier miles, while others do not. In addition, the interest rate **varies** from one card to another.

4 Q: What happens if you pay your credit card bill late?

A: If you pay your credit card bill late, you will be charged a **penalty fee**. This could be $35 or more. Even if your credit card bill is only $25, you may have to pay a penalty fee of $35! In addition, your credit card rate can go up even when you are late in paying other bills such as your utility bill.

7 Q: Who owns McDonald's?

A: Thousands of people do. In 1980 you could buy one piece, or **share**, of **stock** in McDonald's for about $1.20. In 2000 one share cost about $30.00.

ALL ABOUT MONEY

2 Q: If you make the **minimum monthly payment** on a $5,000 credit card bill at 18% interest, how long will it take to pay off?

A: If you make the minimum $100 monthly payment, it will take more than 46 years to pay off your $5,000 credit card bill! You will also pay $13,931 in interest. However, if you pay $200 a month, you can pay off your bill in less than 3 years and you will pay $1,314 in interest.

Paying off a $5,000 Credit Card Bill
Option 1: Pay $100/month = 46 years = $13,931 in interest
Option 2: Pay $200/month = 3 years = $1,314 in interest

3 Q: What types of credit card problems do people have?

A: Credit card problems occur when you **max out** your credit card, make a late payment, or don't have enough money to pay your bill for a few months. If you frequently don't pay your bill when it's due, your case may be sent to a collection agency.

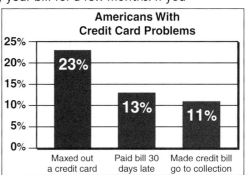

Americans With Credit Card Problems

	23%	13%	11%
	Maxed out a credit card	Paid bill 30 days late	Made credit bill go to collection

5 Q: Is it better to put your money in a savings account or to buy a **CD**?

A: A CD or **certificate of deposit** is a special kind of savings account. It earns a **fixed** interest rate over a **specific** period of time. The interest rate is higher than a savings account, but you cannot use the money for a certain amount of time.

6 Q: What are the advantages of **investing** in an **individual retirement account** (**IRA**)?

A: Federal tax law allows many employees to put money in an IRA. The money you invest doesn't count as part of your income so you don't have to pay taxes on it until you withdraw it. The purpose is to save it so you can use it after you retire.

8 Q: What is **inflation**?

A: Inflation is a continuous increase in the price of goods and services. As prices increase, the value of money goes down. For example, a coat that cost $10 in 1914 would **set you back** $189 in 2005.

$10
1914

$189
2005

9 Q: What is a **budget deficit** and why do governments sometimes have one?

A: If you spend more than you earn, you have a budget deficit. Governments have a budget deficit when they spend more money than they collect in taxes.

3
LESSON

Does this account earn interest?

THINGS TO DO

1 Warm Up

Work with your classmates to answer the questions below.

1. What banking services do you see in the pictures?
2. What other banking services can you think of?

2 Listen and Check 🎧

Read questions 1 to 9 on page 135. Then listen to a conversation between a bank officer and a customer. Check (✓) 4 questions the customer asks.

3 Listen and Take Notes 🎧

Listen again and add the missing information to the chart on page 135.

4 Write

Complete the sentences with information from the chart on page 135.

1. Neither the Green Account nor the Basic Account

_____.

2. Both the Circle and Basic Accounts _____

_____.

3. Unlike the Circle Account, the Green Account _____

_____.

4. Both the Green and Basic Accounts _____

_____.

5. All three accounts _____.

5 Use the Communication Strategy 🎧

Role-play a conversation between a bank officer and a customer. Take turns asking and answering questions about banking services. Try to use the communication strategy in your conversation.

A: How much money do I need to open a savings account?
B: Was that a savings account?
A: Yes, that's right.
B: A hundred dollars.
A: Did you say one hundred?
B: Yes, that's correct.

COMMUNICATION STRATEGY

Repeating to Confirm

Misunderstandings can cause a lot of problems. To avoid this, it's important to confirm what you hear.

- Did you say twenty-five dollars?

- You said twenty-five dollars?

- That was twenty-five dollars?

- Was that twenty-five dollars?

"I'd like to open a checking account."

Seattle Banking	Circle Checking Account	Green Checking Account	Basic Checking Account
1. ☐ How much money do I need to open a checking account?	$50		
2. ☐ Does this account earn interest?		No	
3. ☐ Will I be charged to use the ATM at other banks?			
4. ☐ Does this account provide free checks?		N/A*	
5. ☐ How much is the monthly maintenance fee?			
6. ☐ How much do I have to keep in my account to avoid a monthly maintenance fee?		N/A	N/A
7. ☐ Does a free ATM or debit card come with this account?	Yes		
8. ☐ Does this account provide free online banking?			
9. ☐ Can I pay my bills online free of charge?			

*N/A means *not applicable,* or *the question doesn't apply to this account.*

4
LESSON

Credit Card Fraud

THINGS TO DO

1 Warm Up

Make a chart like the one below. Work with your classmates to answer the questions in the chart.

1. What do you already know about credit card fraud?	2. What would you like to find out about credit card fraud?
You should report a stolen card right away.	How do you report a stolen card?

2 Read and Respond

Read the article on page 137 and answer the questions below.

1. Who really pays for credit card fraud? How?
2. What is a bogus credit card?
3. What would you do if a telemarketer called and asked for your credit card number?
4. In what ways do people become victims of credit card fraud?
5. What are 3 things you can do to prevent credit card fraud?

3 Give Advice

Read the stories below. Tell what each person should and shouldn't have done. Then tell what each person should do next.

1. Paul left his credit card on his desk overnight. Weeks later, Paul found a charge for a $1,300 computer he hadn't ordered on his credit card bill. He called his bank and discovered that someone had ordered the computer and had it sent to an unfamiliar address.

2. Pam went to lunch at a restaurant. When it was time to pay, her purse was gone. She rushed to a phone to call her credit card issuer and found that the card had already been used by the thief.

Make sure you use a safe website if you use your credit card online.

Individuals and businesses often shred receipts before throwing them away.

Don't Be a Victim of Credit Card Fraud

Problem

You open your credit card bill and notice several charges for things you didn't buy. Someone else is using your name and your credit card number to buy things. You are a victim of credit card fraud.

Credit card fraud is a major problem. It costs cardholders and businesses hundreds of millions of dollars each year. You can become a victim of credit card fraud if someone steals your wallet and gets your credit card. You can also become a victim of credit card fraud if someone finds a sales slip with your account number and the expiration date. That is all someone needs in order to use your credit card.

Solution

Fortunately, there are some simple things you can do to protect yourself from credit card fraud. Here are a few suggestions:

Do:

✓ Sign your credit card as soon as you get it. Many credit card companies also require you to call from your home phone to **activate** your credit card.

✓ Use only a **secure** website when you use your credit card online.

✓ Pay attention when you give your credit card to store employees. **Crooks** have been known to pay store employees to record a customer's credit card number. They then make a **bogus** credit card to sell on the **black market**. Unfortunately, that bogus credit card has your number on it.

✓ Immediately report any charges on your bill that you didn't make. Do this both by phone and in writing.

✓ Immediately report a stolen credit card.

✓ **Guard** both your credit card number and your credit card.

✓ Keep your credit card and statements in a safe place.

Don't:

✗ Don't give out your credit card number over the phone unless you made the telephone call to a business you can trust. Never give your credit card number to **telemarketers** who call with an offer of a prize or cheap merchandise.

✗ Don't throw away any credit card receipts unless you **tear** them **up** into very small pieces.

5
LESSON

She said it was a good deal.

Quoted Speech
When you write a person's exact words, you should use quotation marks around the words.

Quoted Speech

Sandra asked, "Where are you going?"
Mark answered, "To the bank."
"We need to cut taxes," the president said.

1 Write the Quotation Marks

Add quotation marks around each person's exact words. The first one is done as an example.

1. "Stay out of debt," his father said.

2. Laura said happily, I cut up all my credit cards last night.

3. I always pay my credit card bills in full, Jane said.

4. Jane asked, Did you have to pay a late fee?

5. Rob said, I decided to put money in an IRA.

6. The interest rate is 18%, Joel answered.

7. How did you max out your credit card, Fernando asked.

8. His accountant asked, Do you own any stocks?

9. How much money can I put in my IRA, Lisa asked her accountant.

10. You need to pay off your credit card bill first, Janet said.

2 Interview and Write

Ask a partner the questions below. Then write your classmate's exact words using quotation marks.

1. What did you do last night?
   "I went to work," Juanita said.

2. What did you do in the evening yesterday?

   _____

3. What did you have for breakfast today?

   _____

4. Where do you live?

   _____

5. What are you going to do tomorrow?

   _____

Reported Speech

When you report someone's words and ideas, you don't have to use the speaker's exact words or quotation marks. You can paraphrase what the person said. When the information is paraphrased and reported soon after it is said or in informal situations, the verb form doesn't change.

Quoted Speech		Reported Speech
Maria said, "I **paid** that bill."	→	Maria said she **paid** the bill.
Otto said, "I'**m** not in debt."	→	Otto said he **is**n't in debt.

In formal English or when the information is reported much later, the verb form changes.

Quoted Speech		Reported Speech
"It'**s** a good deal," the bank officer said.	→	The bank officer said it **was** a good deal.
"I **have** a headache," Rob said.	→	Rob said he **had** a headache.
"I'**m eating**," Jacob said.	→	Jacob said he **was eating**.
"I just **got** a new credit card," Don said.	→	Don said he **had** just **gotten** a new credit card.
"I **can**'t **pay** for it," Celia said.	→	Celia said she **could**n't pay for it.
"I'**ll finish** it later," Ada said.	→	Ada said she **would finish** it later.

3 Complete the Sentences

Complete the conversations below. Then practice the coversations with classmates.

1. Ben: Do you want to go out tonight?
   Celia: No, I just want to stay home.
            (a little later)
   Sam: What does Celia want to do tonight?
   Ben: She said she just _____ to stay home.

2. Celia: What are you going to do tomorrow?
   Sam: Oh, I have class all day.
            (a little later)
   Ben: Is Sam coming over tomorrow?
   Celia: No, he can't. He said he _____ class all day.

3. Sam: Where's the key to the back door?
   Celia: It's in the kitchen drawer next to the fridge.
            (a week later)
   Celia: Where's the key to the back door? I can't find it.
   Sam: You said it _____ in the kitchen drawer.

Deductions from a Paycheck

1 Warm Up

Work with your classmates to answer the questions below.

1. What kinds of information appears on a pay stub?
2. What kinds of things are often deducted from a paycheck?

2 Read and Respond

Read the information on the pay stub below and answer the questions that follow.

ATWOOD INDUSTRIES

Employee: Osualdo Vargas   Check Number: 947930
Social Security Number: 123-45-6789
Pay Period Date: 3/1/05 to 3/15/05
Check Date: 3/20/05

EARNINGS	Rate	Hours	This Period	Year to Date
	20.00	80	1,600.00	8,000.00
GROSS PAY			1,600.00	8,000.00

DEDUCTIONS		
Federal Income Tax	208.00	1,040.00
Social Security	176.00	880.00
Medicare	41.60	208.00
CA Income Tax	48.22	241.10
CA State Disability Ins.	22.40	112.00
Total Deductions	496.22	2,481.10
NET PAY	1,103.78	

QUESTIONS

1. How much is Osualdo's take home pay this pay period?
2. How much money was deducted from his paycheck this pay period?
3. How often does he get a paycheck?
4. How much did he earn from January 1 to March 1?
5. How much federal income tax has he paid this year?

3 Apply

When you get a paycheck, it's important to check it over carefully. Look at Osualdo's pay stub on the right and fill in the missing numbers. You can look at the pay stub on page 140 to help you. Then compare ideas with your classmates.

ATWOOD INDUSTRIES

Employee: Osualdo Vargas   Check Number: 947941
Social Security Number: 123-45-6789
Pay Period Date: 3/16/05 to 3/31/05
Check Date: 4/5/05

EARNINGS	Rate	Hours	This Period	Year to Date
	20.00	40		
GROSS PAY				

DEDUCTIONS	This Period	Year to Date
Federal Income Tax	104.00	1,144.00
Social Security	88.00	
Medicare	20.80	228.80
CA Income Tax	24.11	
CA State Disability Ins.	11.20	123.20
Total Deductions		2729.21
NET PAY		

WINDOW ON MATH
Understanding Rates

A Read the information.

A *rate* is a comparison of 2 measurements that is expressed as a fraction, where the 2 measurements have different units, such as: $30/5 hours.

A *unit rate* is the rate in which the bottom number (or *denominator*) is 1: $6/1 hour. You can convert a rate to a unit rate if you divide the top number (or *numerator*) by the denominator: $30 divided by 5 hours = $6 for 1 hour.

EXAMPLE: Tina was charged $40 in bank fees on her checking account for the first four months of 2005. The rate was $40/4 months. The unit rate was $10 per month.

B Change the following rates to unit rates.

1. $5 for two hours: _____ per hour
2. 12 sick days per year: _____ per month
3. $30 for 6 months: _____ per month
4. $9 for 3 pounds: _____ per pound

C Solve the following.

1. Henry is thinking of changing jobs. At his current job, he works 40 hours and earns $500 a week. At his new job, Henry would earn $15 an hour. At which job, would Henry make more money? _____
2. Paula drives to work every day. She notices that she can go about 500 miles on a tank of gas. Her tank holds 20 gallons. What is the unit rate? _____

7 LESSON

What do you know?

1 Listening Review 🎧

Listen and choose the sentence that is closest in meaning to the sentence you hear. Use the Answer Sheet.

1. A. Their biggest expense is housing.
   B. Thirty percent of their income goes for housing.
   C. They budgeted $900.00 for housing.

2. A. She has a no-fee credit card.
   B. She refuses to pay a fee for her credit card.
   C. Her credit card has an annual fee.

3. A. John owns a company that makes medicines.
   B. John owns shares of stock in a company.
   C. John works for a company that makes medicines.

4. A. Sue has invested in an individual retirement account.
   B. Every year Sue pays taxes on her income.
   C. Sue frequently puts money in her savings account.

5. A. Carlos didn't pay his credit card bill because he forgot.
   B. When Carlos forgot to pay his credit card bill, he had to pay a fee.
   C. Carlos paid a penalty fee when he received his credit card.

ANSWER SHEET			
1	A	B	C
2	A	B	C
3	A	B	C
4	A	B	C
5	A	B	C
6	A	B	C
7	A	B	C
8	A	B	C
9	A	B	C
10	A	B	C

Listen to each conversation and choose the best answer to the question you hear. Use the Answer Sheet.

6. A. Put it in a savings account.
   B. Buy a certificate of deposit.
   C. Buy some stock.

7. A. a free ATM card
   B. a free check
   C. an account with free checks

8. A. fifty dollars
   B. fifteen dollars
   C. five dollars

9. A. Buy a new TV set over the phone.
   B. Get a credit card.
   C. Give out his credit card number.

10. A. the interest rate on a CD
    B. the interest rate on a savings account
    C. the interest rate on a student loan

2 Vocabulary Review

Use the clues to complete the crossword puzzle.

ACROSS

2 The opposite of "general" is _____.

5 A synonym for "luckily" is _____.

9 A _____ interest rate doesn't change. It is always the same.

10 These people try to sell you things over the telephone.

11 The acronym IRA stands for individual _____ account.

DOWN

1 Another word for a spending plan is a _____.

3 A bank CD is a _____ of deposit.

4 If you spend more than you earn, you have a budget _____.

5 You have to pay a _____ to get a driver's license.

6 Another word for a "thief" is a _____.

7 Some credit cards offer _____, such as frequent flier miles.

8 During a period of _____, prices rise and the value of money goes down.

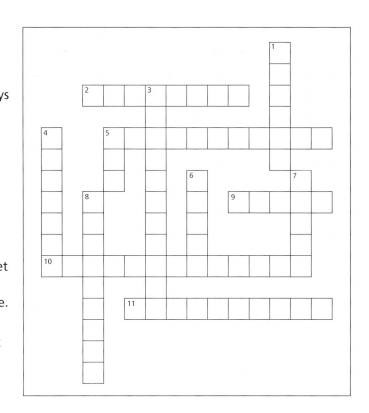

✔ LEARNING LOG

I know these words:

NOUNS
- □ black market
- □ budget
- □ budget deficit
- □ CD
- □ certificate of deposit
- □ crook
- □ fee
- □ individual retirement account

- □ inflation
- □ IRA
- □ minimum monthly payment
- □ penalty fee
- □ perk
- □ share (of a stock)
- □ stock
- □ telemarketer

VERBS
- □ activate
- □ guard
- □ invest
- □ max out
- □ set back
- □ tear up
- □ vary

ADJECTIVES
- □ bogus
- □ fixed
- □ secure
- □ specific

ADVERB
- □ fortunately

I practiced these skills, strategies, and grammar points:

- □ evaluating and planning a budget
- □ classifying words
- □ understanding financial terms
- □ summarizing
- □ listening and taking notes
- □ repeating information to confirm

- □ understanding credit cards
- □ using quoted and reported speech
- □ interviewing classmates
- □ understanding paycheck stubs
- □ understanding financial rates

Spotlight: Reading Strategy

COMPARING AND CONTRASTING

Writers often describe or explain something by comparing or contrasting it to something else. When writers compare two things, they emphasize the similarities. When they contrast two things, they emphasize the differences.

EXAMPLES: Both of my brothers are tall and thin. (Comparing)

CDs have higher interest rates than savings accounts. (Contrasting)

Writers often use the words below to show that they are comparing or contrasting two things.

Comparing		Contrasting	
both	similar to	but	in contrast
like	similarly	different from	neither . . . nor
in common		however	unlike

---

1 Follow the steps below to read the story on page 145.

Step 1: Read the title of the story. What do you think a king and a poor boy might have in common? Share ideas with your classmates.

Step 2: Skim the story. What do you think it is about?

Step 3: Scan the story. Circle the words in the story that show that the writer is comparing two things.

Step 4: Read the story to find words that describe the king and the boy. List them in the chart below.

The king	The boy

Step 5: Read the story again. How are the king and the boy similar and different? List your ideas in the Venn Diagram below. Then share ideas with your classmates.

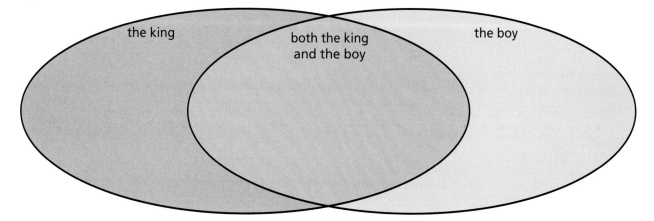

the king

both the king and the boy

the boy

The King and the Poor Boy
(A Cambodian Folk Tale)

In a small village near the edge of the forest, there once lived a boy who had no mother or father. His uncle, who was the chief cook for the king, was sorry for the poor boy, so he invited the boy to stay with him in the palace. The grateful boy worked hard to help his uncle. He washed the plates, polished the cups, cleaned the dining room tables, and mopped the floors. At the end of each month, his uncle gave him six *sen* as his wages.

Now, the king frequently inspected the palace. He often noticed the hardworking boy mopping the floors or polishing the cups. The king noticed the boy was always cheerful and in good humor, unlike the king.

One day the king asked the boy, "Do you receive wages for your hard work?"

The boy bowed and said, "Yes, I do, Your Majesty. I earn six *sen* every month."

Then the king asked, "Do you think you are rich or do you think you are poor?"

"Your Majesty," the boy replied, "I think that I am as rich as a king."

The king was taken by surprise. "Why is this poor boy talking such nonsense?" he said to himself.

Once more, the king spoke to the boy, "I am a king and I have all the power and riches of this country. But you earn only six *sen* a month. Why do you say you are as rich as I am?"

The boy put down his mop and slowly replied to the king, "Your Majesty, I may receive only six *sen* each month, but like you I eat from one plate. I sleep for one night and you also sleep for one night. We both eat and sleep the same. There is no difference. Now, Your Majesty, do you understand why I say that I am as rich as a king?"

The king understood and was satisfied.

Source: "The King and The Poor Boy" from *Cambodian Folk Tales* by Muriel Paskin

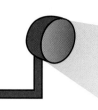

Spotlight: Writing Strategy

USING TRANSITION WORDS AND PHRASES

Writers use transition words and phrases to show how the ideas in a paragraph are related. On page 147, you learned some of the transition words you can use to compare and contrast things. Below are some other common transition words and phrases.

To add information	also	further	moreover
	and	furthermore	too
	besides	in addition	
To show the order of events or of importance	first	the most important	
	second	the second most important	
	third	the third most important	
To show cause and effect	as a result	due to	so
	because	for this reason	therefore
	consequently	since	thus
To give an example	for example	like	
	for instance	such as	
To show a contrast	but	however	on the other hand
	conversely	in spite of	though
	despite	instead of	whereas
	even though	nevertheless	yet

1 Circle the transition words in the paragraphs below. In the margin, identify the purpose of each transition word.

1.   Early Greek coins were both useful and beautiful, (and) many cities competed to produce the most beautiful coins. The city of Corinth, for example, made silver coins with a picture of the winged horse Pegasus. Athens, on the other hand, made coins with gold and silver decorated with a picture of the Athenian owl.

Word/Phrase	Purpose
and	*to add information*

2.   The rulers of countries quickly learned that having their faces on coins was a good form of advertising. The first ruler to do so was probably Ptolemy I of Egypt. Having their faces on coins, however, did not stop rulers from making the coins less valuable. The Roman emperor Nero, for instance, reduced the amount of silver in Roman coins and kept the money he saved for himself.

Word/Phrase	Purpose

3. Coins became impractical for trading because in large quantities they were very heavy. For this reason, paper money became common.

Word/Phrase	Purpose

4. Credit cards are useful for a number of reasons. Perhaps the most important reason is their convenience. When you have a credit card, you don't have to carry around cash. Despite their usefulness, credit cards can also cause problems. If you carry a balance on your credit card bill, you end up paying a very high interest rate.

Word/Phrase	Purpose

5. When I started working, I was able to save a little money even though I wasn't earning very much. This was probably due to the simple way I lived. I almost never spent money for entertainment, such as going to the movies or eating out. Instead, I spent time with my friends doing things that didn't cost anything.

Word/Phrase	Purpose

2 Complete the sentences with a transition word or phrase. More than one answer may be possible.

1. The most important thing you can do is pay off your debts. _The second most important thing_ is to start saving your money.

2. You should put your money in a savings account _____ don't touch it.

3. _____ to putting money into my bank account, I'm going to buy some stocks.

4. We stopped driving so much _____ the increase in gasoline prices.

5. When I was a teenager, I spent a lot of money on clothes. Nowadays, _____, I never buy expensive clothes.

6. My wife started investing her money when she was in her 20s and _____ she'll be able to retire by the time she is 50.

7. _____ eating out a lot, I try to save money by eating at home.

8. I never had any money when I was a child and _____ I worry a lot about money now.

3 Describe your spending habits in the past and today. Remember to collect ideas before writing and to write several drafts. Use transition words and phrases where appropriate.

A Irregular Verbs

Base Form	Simple Past	Past Participle	Base Form	Simple Past	Past Participle
be	was/were	been	keep	kept	kept
become	became	become	know	knew	known
begin	began	begun	leave	left	left
bleed	bled	bled	lend	lent	lent
break	broke	broken	lose	lost	lost
bring	brought	brought	make	made	made
buy	bought	bought	meet	met	met
choose	chose	chosen	pay	paid	paid
come	came	come	put	put	put
cost	cost	cost	read	read	read
cut	cut	cut	ring	rang	rung
do	did	done	run	ran	run
drink	drank	drunk	see	saw	seen
drive	drove	driven	sell	sold	sold
eat	ate	eaten	send	sent	sent
fall	fell	fallen	set	set	set
feel	felt	felt	shake	shook	shaken
fight	fought	fought	shut	shut	shut
find	found	found	sleep	slept	slept
forget	forgot	forgot	speak	spoke	spoken
fry	fried	fried	speed	sped	sped
get	got	gotten	spend	spent	spent
give	gave	given	take	took	taken
go	went	gone	teach	taught	taught
grow	grew	grown	tell	told	told
have/has	had	had	think	thought	thought
hear	heard	heard	wear	wore	worn
hold	held	held	write	wrote	written
hurt	hurt	hurt			

B Spelling Rules for Verbs

Spelling Rules for Verbs	
Spelling Rules	**Examples**

Verbs with One Syllable
 	
• If the verb ends in a consonant-vowel-consonant (*C-V-C*), double the final consonant and add *-ed* or *-ing*.
 	
• If the verb ends in a vowel-vowel-consonant pattern (*V-V-C*), add *-ed* or *-ing*.
	• stop—stopped
	  rub—rubbed
	
	• rain—rained
	  speak—speaking

Verbs with Two Syllables • If the first syllable is stressed, add the *-ed* or *-ing* ending. • For verbs in which the second syllable is stressed, double the final consonant.	• offer—offering • refer—referring
Verbs Ending in -*y* • If the verb ends in a consonant and *-y*, change the *-y* to *-i* and add *-ed* or *-ing*. • If the verb ends in a vowel and *-y*, add *-ed*, or *-ing*.	• study—studied • play—played
Verbs Ending in a Consonant and -*e* • If the verb ends in *-e*, just add *-d*. • If the verb ends in *-e*, drop the *-e* and add *-ing*.	• dance—danced • dance—dancing
Verbs Ending in -*ie* • If the verb ends in *-ie*, add *-d*. • If the verb ends in *-ie*, change the *-ie* to *-y*, and add *-ing*.	• die—died • die—dying

NOTE: Don't double the consonants for words ending in -*w*, -*x*, -*y*.	• fix—fixed
	  allow—allowing
	  enjoy—enjoying

C Simple Present Tense

Affirmative Statements		
I	like	
You	like	
He	likes	
She	likes	music.
It	likes	
We	like	
You	like	
They	like	

Negative Statements		
I	don't like	
You	don't like	
He	doesn't like	
She	doesn't like	tea.
It	doesn't like	
We	don't like	
You	don't like	
They	don't like	

D Present Continuous Tense

Affirmative Statements	
I	am working.
You	are working.
He	is working.
She	is working.
It	is working.
We	are working.
You	are working.
They	are working.

Negative Statements	
I	am not working.
You	aren't working.
He	isn't working.
She	isn't working.
It	isn't working.
We	aren't working.
You	aren't working.
They	aren't working.

E Present Perfect Tense

Affirmative Statements		
I	have	
You	have	
He	has	
She	has	been here for
It	has	3 hours.
We	have	
You	have	
They	have	

Negative Statements		
I	have not	
You	have not	
He	has not	
She	has not	left yet.
It	has not	
We	have not	
You	have not	
They	have not	

F Simple Past Tense

Affirmative Statements		
I		
You		
He		
She	worked	yesterday.
It		
We		
You		
They		

Negative Statements		
I		
You		
He		
She	didn't work	yesterday.
It		
We		
You		
They		

G Past Continuous Tense

Affirmative Statements		
I	was working	
You	were working	
He	was working	
She	was working	when the storm started.
It	was working	
We	were working	
You	were working	
They	were working	

Negative Statements		
I	wasn't sleeping	
You	weren't sleeping	
He	wasn't sleeping	
She	wasn't sleeping	when the storm started.
It	wasn't sleeping	
We	weren't sleeping	
You	weren't sleeping	
They	weren't sleeping	

Simple Past and Past Continuous

We often use the simple past and the past continuous in the same sentence. We use the simple past for a sudden action that interrupts the ongoing activity.

(sudden action)   (ongoing activity)

EXAMPLE: He <u>fell</u> while he <u>was climbing</u> up the ladder.

We often use the word "while" to introduce the ongoing activity. While means "during the time that." We often use the word "when" to introduce the sudden action.

EXAMPLES: The bell rang <u>while</u> I was sleeping.
I was sleeping <u>when</u> the bell rang.

H Past Perfect Tense

I You He She It We You They	**had**	already **left** work just **started** work already **eaten** lunch already **cleaned** the office	when the boss arrived.

Simple Past and Past Perfect

Use the simple past to tell about something that happened at a definite time in the past.

EXAMPLES: He **exercised** for an hour yesterday.
I **had** a fever last night.

Use the past perfect to show that one action happened before another in the past.

EXAMPLES: **I'd just gone** to bed when the phone rang.
I'd already made lunch when the kids got home.

I Simple Future Tense

Future with *Going to*					
I	am going to		I	am not going to	
You	are going to		You	are not going to	
He	is going to		He	is not going to	
She	is going to	leave tomorrow.	She	is not going to	be here tomorrow.
It	is going to		It	is not going to	
We	are going to		We	are not going to	
You	are going to		You	are not going to	
They	are going to		They	are not going to	

Future with *Will*			
I		I	
You		You	
He		He	
She	will come back soon.	She	won't be away for long.
It		It	
We		We	
You		You	
They		They	won't = will not

J Future Progressive Tense

I		I	
You		You	
He		He	
She	will be working when you come.	She	won't be working when you come.
It		It	
We		We	
You		You	
They		They	

K Active and Passive Verb Forms

In a sentence with an active verb, the subject does the action of the verb. In a sentence with a passive verb, the subject receives the action of the verb.

Active Verbs	Passive Verbs
They <u>lock</u> the building at night.	The building <u>is locked</u> at night.
The government <u>requires</u> you to register in order to vote.	You <u>are required</u> to register in order to vote.
The children <u>ate</u> the cake.	The cake <u>was eaten</u> by the children.
They <u>took</u> the dog for a walk.	The dog <u>was taken</u> for a walk.

L Present Real Conditionals

If Clause (present)			Result Clause (present or future)	
If	I	get a better offer,	I	will quit.
If	you	don't slow down,	you	are going to get a ticket.
If	he	is sick,	he	stays home.
If	she	doesn't leave soon,	she	won't be on time.
If	it	rains again,	it will	cause a flood.
If	we	get home late,	we are	going to eat out.
If	they	walk quickly,	they will	get there in 5 minutes.

M Present Unreal Conditionals

If Clause (simple past)			Result Clause (with *would, could*)	
If	I	got a better offer,	I	would quit.
If	you	were speeding,	you	could get a ticket.
If	he	were sick,	he	would stay home.
If	she	didn't leave at 8 every day,	she	wouldn't be on time.
If	you	turned It too hard,	it	would break.
If	we	had enough money,	we	could eat out.
If	they	didn't have a car,	they	would take the bus.

N Past Unreal Conditionals

If Clause (simple past perfect)			Result Clause (with *would have* plus past participle)
If	I	had gotten a better job,	I would have bought a house
If	you	had applied sooner,	you would have been accepted.
If	he	had been on time,	he would have caught the bus.
If	she	had wanted to come,	we would have waited.
If	you	had purchased the painting,	I would have hung it for you.
If	it	hadn't been so late,	we would have gone to dinner with you.
If	we	had moved to Boston,	we would never have met you.
If	they	had asked me,	I would have helped them.

O Questions

Direct and Indirect *Yes/No* Questions

Direct	Indirect
Is Sam a good driver?	⟶ Do you know if Sam is a good driver?
	Can you tell me if Sam is a good driver?
Do Mike and Laura live here?	⟶ Do you know if Mike and Laura live here?
Does Rita speak Spanish?	⟶ Do you know if Rita speaks Spanish?
Did Joe get the job?	⟶ Do you know if Joe got the job?
Can Mia speak English?	⟶ Do you know if Mia can speak English?

Direct and Indirect *Wh-* Questions

Direct	Indirect
What time is it?	⟶ Do you know what time it is?
	⟶ Can you tell me what time it is?
When does class start?	⟶ Do you know when class starts?
Where was the meeting?	⟶ Do you know where the meeting was?
What did she say?	⟶ Do you know what she said?
Why isn't Karen here?	⟶ Do you know why Karen isn't here?

Tag Questions

Question	Answer
This is a nice store, isn't it?	⟶ Yes, it is.
These are really cheap, aren't they?	⟶ Yes, they are.
This isn't very good, is it?	⟶ No, it isn't.
These aren't very well made, are they?	⟶ No, they aren't.
That wasn't a good movie, was it?	⟶ No, it wasn't.
They weren't very expensive, were they?	⟶ No, they weren't.
He won't be at work, will he?	⟶ No, he won't.

P Modals

Affirmative		Negative	
I		I	
You		You	
He	may be late.	He	may not be on time.
She	might leave early tomorrow.	She	might not leave until Wednesday.
It	should be here tonight.	It	shouldn't be here on Thursday.
We	can get there at 1:00.	We	can't get there until 1:00.
You	must get there early.	You	must not get there late.
They	had better be on time.	They	had better not be late.

Q Past Form of *Should* and *Could*

I You He/She/It We You They	should have slowed down. should have bought some insurance. shouldn't have gotten angry.

I You He/She/It We You They	could have taken the train instead of the bus. could have gotten a cheaper fare by booking early. couldn't have seen the accident because it was too dark.

R Adjective Clauses

An adjective clause is a dependent clause. It gives more information about a person, place, or thing in the main clause. Most adjective clauses begin with the pronoun *that, which,* or *who.*

EXAMPLES: I finished reading the book that my friend lent me.
Mike paid for the parking ticket which he got last week.
She went to Los Angeles with a friend who grew up there.
The city that I was born in now has over 10 million people!

S Adverb Clauses of Time, Reason, and Contrast

Time *(before, when, whenever, while, as soon as, since, until)*
You should eat something <u>before you take your medicine</u>.
She felt sick <u>when she woke up</u>.
<u>Whenever I drive long distances</u>, I get car sick.
He fell asleep <u>while he was reading</u>.

Reason *(because, since, now that)*
Margaret saw a doctor <u>because she had a high temperature</u>.
<u>Since she had to get up early</u>, she left the party at 11:00.

Contrast *(even though, although)*
<u>Although she felt sick yesterday</u>, she went to work.
He runs five miles a day <u>even though he has a bad knee</u>.

T Quoted and Reported Speech

When you write a person's exact words, you should use quotation marks around the words.
When you report what someone said by paraphrasing, you don't need quotation marks.

Quoted Speech	Reported Speech
Jamie said, "This is a great movie!" ⟶	Jamie said it was a great movie.
Lea asked, "Do you have my book?" ⟶	Lea asked if I had her book.
Roberta said, "I'm going to the store." ⟶	Roberta said that she was going to the store.
Chan reported, "I just got a raise!" ⟶	Chan reported that he had just gotten a raise.
"I shouldn't eat this cake," Maria said. ⟶	Maria said she shouldn't eat the cake.
I'll call you this evening," Karla said. ⟶	Karla said she would call me this evening.

Note: This audio script offers support for many of the activities in the Student Book. When the words on the student page are identical to those on the audio program, the script is not provided here.

UNIT ONE
Lesson 3.
2. Listen for General Information, page 8
Listen to 6 telephone calls and number them in order from first (1) to last (6).

Telephone call #1

A: You have reached the Smith residence. Please leave a message.

B: Hi, Pat. This is Leila calling. I just wanted to ask if you could give me a ride to the meeting tomorrow. My car isn't working again! Call when you can. 555-8724. Thanks. Bye.

Telephone call #2

Woman: You have reached the Continuing Education Office at Redwood High. Our office hours are Monday through Friday from 10:00 to 7:00 and on Saturday from 10:00 to 2:00. We are closed on Sunday. Please call during our business hours. Thank you for calling. Goodbye.

Telephone call #3

A: The Paper Shop.

B: Hi. Can I speak to Mr. Takase, please?

A: I'm sorry but Mr. Takase just left the office. Can I take a message?

B: Well, this is John Lee with Safe Software. I'm returning Mr. Takase's call.

A: I see. Do you want him to call you back?

B: Well, I'm going to be in and out today. Do you know when he'll be back in the office?

A: He should be here between 2:00 and 5:00 today.

B: Well, I'll try to call him back this afternoon then.

A: Okay. I'll tell him you called.

B: Thank you.

A: You're welcome. Goodbye.

B: Goodbye.

Telephone call #4

A: Hello.

B: Hi. Could I speak to Jan please?

A: I'm sorry but she's not at home right now.

B: Do you know when she'll be back?

A: No, I'm not sure.

B: Well, could you tell her that Maria called? I just wanted to apologize for missing the meeting today.

A: Okay. Do you want her to call you back?

B: No, that's not necessary. Tell her I'll see her next week.

A: Okay. Will do.

B: Thanks.

A: You're welcome. Bye.

B: Bye.

Telephone call #5

A: Metro Supply. This is Joe speaking.

B: Could I speak with Tom Field please?

A: I'm sorry but he's in a meeting now. Can I take a message?

B: Sure. Could you tell him that Betty Grand called to invite him to a lunch meeting next Wednesday at noon?

A: Could you spell your last name please?

B: Yes, that's G-r-a-n-d.

A: And you want to invite him to a lunch meeting next Tuesday at noon?

B: Ah, that was Wednesday not Tuesday.

A: Yes, of course. Next Wednesday at noon. Does Mr. Field have your phone number?

B: Well, I think so. But let me give it to you anyway. It's 555-3345.

A: Ah, sorry. Could you repeat that?

B: Sure. 555-3345.

A: Thanks. I'll give him your message, Ms. Grand.

B: Thank you. Bye bye.

A: Bye now.

Telephone call #6

A: Southwest Cartage. This is Ginger speaking.

B: Hello. My name is Sam Sellers and I'm calling about the sales job advertised in the newspaper.

A: Yes, you need to speak to Ms. Parker. Let me see if she's in her office. Can you hold for a second?

B: Sure.

A: I'm sorry but she isn't in her office. Can I have her call you back?

B: Sure, when it's convenient for her.

A: Your name again, please?

B: Sam Sellers. S-e-l-l-e-r-s.

A: Thanks. And you're calling about the sales job?

B: Yes, that's right. I've been in sales and marketing for over 7 years.

A: And your phone number?

B: It's 555-6688.

A: 555-6688.

B: Yes, that's right.

A: Okay. I'll have her call you back.

B: Thank you.

A: You're welcome. Goodbye.

B: Bye.

3. Listen for Specific Information, page 8
Read the telephone messages on page 9 and listen to the 6 telephone calls again. Add the missing information to the messages.

Lesson 7.

1. Listening Review, page 16

Listen and choose the statement that is closest in meaning to the statement you hear. Use the Answer Sheet.

1. Juanita did her share of the work.
2. Bill came up with a solution to the problem.
3. He is a proficient writer.
4. John returned my call.
5. I'm calling about the job in sales.

Listen to each conversation and choose the best answer to the question you hear. Use the Answer Sheet.

6.

A: How is your new employee?

B: Do you mean Sam?

A: Yes. Is he working out okay?

B: Yes, I think so. He seems to work well with everyone on the team.

Question: What does Sam's supervisor say about him?

7.

A: Do you need some help John?

B: Yes. I could use some help writing this report.

A: Let me ask Jane if she can help. She's a great writer.

B: Thanks.

Question: What is one of Jane's work skills?

8.

A: Johnson Wood Supply. Can I help you?

B: Yes. Is Mr. Taylor in?

A: He's in a meeting right now. Can I take a message?

B: Yes. Could you ask him to call Mike Jones?

A: Does he have your number Mr. Jones?

B: I think so, but let me give it to you just in case.

A: Okay.

B: It's 555-7993.

A: That's 555-7993.

B: That's right.

A: Okay. I'll give him the message.

B: Thank you.

A: Sure. Bye bye.

B: Bye.

Question: What message did the man leave for Mr. Taylor?

9.

A: Ashwood Town Hall.

B: Can I speak to Cindy Harris, please?

A: She's not in the office right now. Can I take a message?

B: Could you just tell her that Jan Smith called and I'll call back later.

A: Certainly.

B: Thanks, bye.

A: Bye.

Question: What telephone message did the woman leave?

10.

A: Excuse me.

B: Yes.

A: Do you know what time it is?

B: Sure, it's almost one.

A: Thanks.

Question: What did the man want to know?

2. Dictation, page 16

Listen and write the sentences you hear.

1. He expresses his ideas clearly.
2. Do you have good listening skills?
3. Bob called to get information.

UNIT TWO

Lesson 3.

2. Put in Sequence, page 26

Number the pictures about Tom and his accident in order from 1 to 5. Then listen to 5 conversations and check your guesses.

1.

Officer: Can I see your license and registration please?

Tom: My registration?

Officer: Yes. Your car registration. I need to see proof of insurance, too.

Tom: Yes, of course. Just a minute. Oh, good, yes, here they are.

Officer: Okay. Why don't you tell me what happened.

Tom: Well, I, uh, I was driving along, but I wasn't speeding or anything.

Officer: Of course.

Tom: And then suddenly the car in front of me stopped. I mean, it all happened in an instant. I slammed on my brakes, but there was nothing I could do.

Officer: I see. Good thing you were wearing your seatbelt.

Tom: Hmm. You're right. Oh, and officer?

Officer: Yes.

Tom: Could I get your name, please?

Officer: Yes, of course. I'm Officer Bee Goode.

Tom: Officer Bee Goode?

Officer: Yes, that's right.

Tom: Thank you for your help, Officer Goode.

2.

Recording: You have reached Unified Insurance Company. If you have a question about a bill, press 8. If you need to make a claim, press 7.

Recording: Please enter the 15-digit number of your policy, then press the pound key.

Agent: Hello. This is Yumiko Sazaki speaking. How can I help you?

Tom: I'm calling to report an accident.

Agent: Your name, please.

Tom: Tom. Tom Rideout.

Agent: Okay, Mr. Rideout. Could you please verify your policy number, address, and Social Security Number?

Tom: Yes, my policy number is 00044 44 244 4443 5. My address is 564 Philips Street in Miami, Florida, and my social security number is 123-45-6789.

Agent: First of all, I'm sorry to hear about your accident. Please tell me who was driving the car.

Tom: I was.

Agent: Were there any injuries?

Tom: No. Only damage to my car.

Agent: And this was your 2000 Porsche Boxster?

Tom: Yes.

Agent: Okay. And what day did the accident happen?

Tom: Today. This morning.

Agent: And where did the accident take place?

Tom: I was on Interstate 95 in Miami.

Agent: And the weather conditions when the accident happened?

Tom: The weather? Uhm, well, it was clear and sunny.

Agent: And how did the accident happen?

Tom: Well, I was driving along and suddenly the driver in the car in front of me slammed on his brakes.

Agent: I see.

Tom: Yes, and then my car hit the back of his car. It was terrible! The police came and I talked with Officer Bee Goode.

Agent: Okay, Mr. Rideout. Can you give me a number where I can reach you?

Tom: Yes. You can call my cell phone. The number is 555-3465.

Agent: Thank you, Mr. Rideout. I'll be back in touch with you within the next 24 hours.

Tom: Okay. Thanks.

Agent: You're welcome. Bye bye.

3.

Tom: So what do you think? Do you think you can fix it today?

Mechanic: Today? I don't think so.

Tom: I can't believe this. I just can't believe this. So how long *is* it going to take?

Mechanic: Well, it depends.

Tom: Depends! Depends on what?

Mechanic: Well, you're going to need a new bumper and two new headlights and then there's that crack in your windshield. It's really a question of how quickly I can get the parts.

Tom: So there's no chance it could be fixed by tomorrow?

Mechanic: Don't think so. But I might have it for you by next Tuesday.

Tom: Oh, but that's too late.

Mechanic: You have to be somewhere?

Tom: Yes, somewhere important. And it's a day's drive away—in Tampa.

Mechanic: Can't help you there, but I can take you to the bus station. It's just down the road.

Tom: Would you? Thank you so much.

4.

Ticket Agent: Next, please.

Tom: Yes, I need to get to Tampa as quickly as possible.

Agent: Let's see. Yes, the next bus to Tampa is at 4:10.

Tom: 4:10? But it's only 2 o'clock now.

Agent: Yes, well, I'm afraid you just missed the 1:45 bus to Tampa.

Tom: This is terrible. So when does that bus get into Tampa?

Agent: The 4:10?

Tom: Yes.

Agent: Hold on a minute. Okay, that bus gets into Tampa at 12:10.

Tom: 12:10 in the morning? Oh, boy. Great.

Agent: So do you want to buy a ticket?

Tom: Well, I, well, yes, I guess so.

Agent: One way or round trip?

Tom: Round trip.

5.

Bill: Hello.

Tom: Bill. It's Tom.

Bill: Tom? Where are you?

Tom: I'm in Miami.

Bill: You're in Miami? What are you doing there?

Tom: It's a long story. I'm at the bus station.

Bill: Where's your car?

Tom: It's a long story.

Bill: Are you okay?

Tom: Yes, I'm fine.

Bill: Are you going to get here in time?

Tom: Yeah, I think so. I was just wondering if I could ask three favors?

Bill: Whatever you want.

Tom: First, could you pick me up at the bus station at midnight tonight?

Bill: Yeah. Sure. No problem.

Tom: And can I borrow your car to get to the wedding tomorrow?

Bill: Anything you want brother.

Tom: And then could you drive Sara and me to the airport?

Bill: Of course. Boy, I can't wait to hear the whole story. Does Sara know?

Tom: Not yet. See you tonight.

Bill: Bye, Tom.

3. Listen for Specific Information, page 26
Read the statements below. Then listen to the conversations again and check (✓) True or False. Next, correct the false statements.

Lesson 7.
1. Listening Review, page 34
Listen to each conversation and choose the best answer to the question you hear. Use the Answer Sheet.

1.

A: Can you tell me when the next bus leaves for Miami?

B: Hmm. Let's see. Yes, there's a bus at 3:15.

A: There's nothing before that?

B: No, that's the next bus to Miami.

Question: Where does the man want to go?

2.

A: This is Aubrey Road Assistance. Can I help you?

B: Yes, I'm having a problem with my car.

A: Where are you now?

B: I'm on Route 19 just outside of Bedford.

A: What exactly is the problem?

B: I'm not sure. The engine just died and it won't start.

A: Okay. I should have a truck out there within 30 minutes.

Question: What did the man call to get?

3.

A: Unified Automobile Insurance. How can I direct your call?

B: I have a billing question.

A: Just a moment, please.

C: Billing Department. Can I have your policy number, please?

B: It's 45405504034004.

C: Your name, please.

B: Jane Tucker.

C: How can I help you, Ms. Tucker?

B: Yes, I'm calling about the insurance bill I just received.

C: Just a minute. Let me bring it up on my screen. Okay, I have it in front of me.

B: I usually get a discount for a good driving record, but I don't see it on my most recent bill.

C: Hmm. Yes, it looks as though it's missing from your bill. Let me correct that and we'll send you a new bill.

B: Thanks.

C: You're welcome. Bye now.

B: Bye.

Question: What did the woman call her insurance company to get?

4.

A: Hello.

B: Sandi. Hi. It's Joe.

A: Joe, Hi. So what did you decide to do?

B: I've decided to take the train instead of flying.

A: Really?

B: Well, I have the time. And I think it'll be interesting to see some of the country.

A: Makes sense. And it's cheaper than flying.

Question: Why does Joe decide to take the train?

5.

A: What happened to your car?

B: Oh, someone ran into me.

A: How fast were you going?

B: Well, actually, my car wasn't moving. I had to stop suddenly and the guy behind me couldn't stop in time.

A: Sounds like he was driving too close to you.

B: I'm not sure about that, but I know he was driving too fast.

Question: What does the woman think caused the accident?

Listen and choose the sentence that is closest in meaning to the sentence you hear. Use the Answer Sheet.

6. My car has depreciated a lot since I bought it.
7. My insurance policy is effective on August 1.
8. She bought her plane ticket seven days in advance.
9. She should have bought liability insurance.
10. I could have taken the train instead of the bus.

UNIT THREE
Lesson 3.
2. Listen and Take Notes, page 44

1. Listen to Conversation #1 and take notes in the chart.

Appointment Desk: Redfield Medical Clinic. How can I help you?

Male Patient: I'm calling to make an appointment with Dr. McCoy.

Desk: Do you need to see her right away?

Patient: No. I'm just making an appointment for my annual exam.

Desk: All right. Can you hold for a minute?

Patient: Sure.

Desk: OK, let's see, Dr. McCoy has an opening on November 15th at noon.

Patient: Uhm, the 15th will work, but 1:00 would be better. Do you have an opening then?

Desk: Yes, you're in luck. She does have an opening at 1:00. Your name please?

Patient: It's Jeff Bartell.

Desk: How do you spell that?

Patient: It's B-a-r-t-e-l-l.

Desk: Okay. And your telephone number Mr. Bartell?

Patient: It's 555-4834.

Desk: 555-4843.

Patient: Excuse me, but that's 4834.

Desk: Okay, 4834. Thank you. Well Mr. Bartell, we'll see you on the 15th.

Patient: Okay. See you then. Thank you very much.

Desk: You're welcome. Bye bye.

2. Listen to Conversation #2 and take notes in the chart.

Appointment Desk: Redfield Medical Clinic. Can I help you?

Patient: This is Shirley Bao calling. I have an appointment with Dr. McCoy on the 15th that I need to cancel.

Desk: Okay. Just a minute please. Yes, I see. Your appointment is at 2:30. Would you like to reschedule that?

Patient: No, not right now thank you. I'll call back next week.

Desk: Okay. I've canceled your appointment on the 15th. Anything else we can do for you?

Patient: No, that's it for now. Thank you.

Desk: Sure. Goodbye now.

3. Listen to Conversation #3 and take notes in the chart.

Appointment Desk: Redfield Medical Clinic. Can I help you?

Maria: Redfield Medical Clinic?

Desk: Yes, that's right.

Maria: I'm sorry. I must have dialed the wrong number. Is this 555-3312?

Desk: No, I'm sorry it's not. But you're close.

Maria: Okay. Sorry to bother you.

Desk: No problem. Bye bye.

Maria: Bye.

4. Listen to Conversation #4 and take notes in the chart.

Appointment Desk: Redfield Medical Clinic. How can I help you?

Patient: Yes, I need to change an appointment with Dr. McCoy.

Desk: And when's your appointment?

Patient: It's on the 12th at 2:30.

Desk: And your name?

Patient: Hong, Jim Hong. H-o-n-g.

Desk: Okay, Mr. Hong. When would you like to reschedule that for?

Patient: Anytime after the 14th would be fine.

Desk: Can you come in on the 15th at 9:00?

Patient: Hmm, that might be hard. Do you have anything later in the day?

Desk: What about 4:30?

Patient: Ah, yes. That would be great.

Desk: Okay, Mr. Hong. We'll see you on the 15th at 3:30.

Patient: Excuse me, but that should be 4:30. I can't come in at 3:30.

Desk: Yes, of course. I'm sorry Mr. Hong. We'll see you on the 15th at 4:30.

Patient: Okay. Goodbye now.

Desk: Goodbye.

5. Listen to Conversation #5 and take notes in the chart.

Appointment Desk: Redfield Medical Clinic. How can I help you?

Patient: I'm calling about a bill I just received from Dr. McCoy.

Desk: Can I have your name please?

Patient: It's June Waite.

Desk: White?

Patient: No, it's Waite. W-a-i-t-e. It rhymes with gate.

Desk: Okay, Ms. Waite. Thank you. And your date of birth?

Patient: 8-12-84.

Desk: 8-12-74.

Patient: Excuse me. That's 84 not 74.

Desk: Sorry. I'm having a little trouble hearing you. And you said there was a problem with your bill?

Patient: Yes, that's right. I just received a second bill for the checkup I had in August, but I already paid that bill. I paid it in September.

Desk: Well, it's probably just a mix up. Let me look into it and I'll get back to you.

Patient: Thank you. Bye bye.

6. Listen to Conversation #6 and take notes in the chart.

Appointment Desk: Redfield Medical Clinic. How can I help you?

Patient: I'm just calling to check on the time of my appointment with Dr. McCoy.

Desk: Your name please?

Patient: Coralia Torres. T-o-r-r-e-s

Desk: Do you know what day your appointment is?

Patient: Yes, it's on the 15th, sometime in the morning.

Desk: Just a minute please. Okay, Ms. Torres, you have a follow-up appointment at 11:30 on the 15th.

Patient: Seven-thirty? That can't be. I know I wouldn't make an appointment for 7:30.

Desk: I'm sorry Ms. Torres. I said 11:30 not 7:30.

Patient: Okay, that's much better. Sorry about that.

Desk: No problem. See you on the 15th.

Patient: See you then. Thanks.

Lesson 7.

1. Listening Review, page 52

Listen to each conversation and choose the best answer to the question you hear. Use the Answer Sheet.

1.

A: We're going out for lunch at one today, Silvia. Can you join us?

B: Thanks, Bob, but I can't. I have an appointment to get my eyes checked today.

A: You're having problems with your eyes?

B: Well, it's nothing unusual. I'm just getting older.

Question: Who does the woman have an appointment to see?

2.

A: Did you have a good day?

B: Yeah. Pretty good.

A: Did you see Dr. Heinsle?

B: Yeah.

A: Well, what did he say?

B: He doesn't think it's anything serious, but he wants me to see a dermatologist.

A: A dermatologist? Why?

B: She can do some tests just to be sure.

Question: What kind of exam does he need?

3.

A: Dr. Jones' office. Can I help you?

B: Yes. I'd like to make an appointment with Dr. Jones.

A: Are you a patient of Dr. Jones?

B: No, I'm not. But Dr. Smith said I needed to see a cardiologist. He referred me to Dr. Jones.

A: I see. Can you come in on March 16th at 2:00?

B: March 16th at 2:00?

A: Yes.

B: That would be fine.

Question: What kind of doctor is Dr. Jones?

4.

A: Dr. Jones' office. Can I help you?

B: Yes. I need to cancel my appointment on February 18th.

A: Your name, please?

B: Hernandez. Sandra Hernandez.

A: And what time was your appointment on the 18th?

B: At 10:00.

A: Okay. And do you want to reschedule that?

B: Ah, no. I'll call back later to reschedule.

A: Okay. Bye now.

B: Bye.

Question: Why did the woman call the doctor's office?

5.

A: Did you look at the label on this cereal?

B: No. Why?

A: It says it has 300 calories per serving.

B: Mmm. That's a lot.

A: Yeah. I don't think we should buy it.

B: Okay. Let's choose something different.

Question: What doesn't the man like about the cereal?

Listen and choose the statement that is closest in meaning to the statement you hear. Use the Answer Sheet.

6. A GP refers patients to specialists.
7. Your appointment is on Monday the 5th at 4:00 P.M.
8. She felt sick when she woke up in the morning.
9. John has high blood pressure even though he exercises a lot.
10. Sandra went to the doctor because she had a high fever.

2. Dictation, page 52

Listen and write the sentences you hear.

1. Do you know the name of a good pediatrician?
2. A cardiologist specializes in diseases of the heart.

UNIT FOUR
Lesson 3.
2. Listen and Take Notes, page 62

Listen to 6 peoples' opinions about education. Summarize each opinion.

1.

Woman: The biggest problem with schools today is that parents aren't involved. Maybe it's because they're too busy with work and other things, but the truth is, parents need to be more involved. I mean, they can volunteer and attend school meetings. And they can make sure their children do their school work. That's a parent's job.

2.

Man: I think students today spend too much time in extracurricular activities. When I was a child, we didn't have extracurricular activities. School was all about studying and learning. It wasn't about playing sports and having parties.

3.

Woman: I think children need to start school at a younger age. Why do we wait until they are 5 years old? A child's brain develops quickly from the time he or she is born. There are so many things they can learn before age 5.

4.

Man: I think it's a good thing that teachers can't physically punish their students. In the old days teachers could hit their students and maybe things were quieter in class, but I think students then were afraid to think for themselves and ask questions. And what's education if you can't think for yourself and ask questions?

5.

Woman: I really don't think schools should be coeducational, especially for teenagers. When girls and boys are together in class, they don't think about studying. And when girls study with boys, they don't talk as much. Well, that's my opinion anyway.

6.

Man: I just heard that students at the high school in my area can take dancing as an elective course. I think that's crazy. I mean, my tax money is paying for schools and I don't think I should be paying for young people to learn to dance. Their parents can pay for dance classes, not me.

3. Listen and Circle Your Answer, page 62

Listen to 5 conversations. Decide if the two people agree or disagree. Check (✓) the correct box.

1.

A: Do you think school should be compulsory?
B: Hmm. That's an interesting question. To be honest, I *don't* think it should be compulsory.
A: Yeah. Neither do I. I mean, when it's compulsory, kids don't value it.

2.

A: Do you think students should have more time for physical education?
B: Yes, yes, yes. It's not good for children to sit in a chair all day. They need exercise. They need to move around.
A: Why can't they get exercise after school? That would be better.
B: Well, they can do that too. But most kids are in school for at least 6 hours and that's too much time to be sitting.

3.

A: Do you think our high school should have a school newspaper?
B: Yes. That's a great idea.
A: Really? Why do you think so?
B: Well, it gives students a real purpose for writing. I think they learn a lot from putting out a newspaper.
A: Hmm.

4.

A: What's your opinion of the extracurricular activities at the high school? Do you think we have enough?
B: Yes, I guess so.
A: Hmm. Me too.

5.

A: What did you think of the PTA meeting last week?
B: Oh, I didn't go. I think it's a waste of time.
A: Why is that?
B: Oh, I don't know. Nothing important ever happens.
A: Well, next month we're going to discuss the new extracurricular activities. I think it should be interesting.
B: Hmm.

Lesson 7.

1. Listening Review, page 70

Listen and choose the statement that is closest in meaning to the statement you hear. Use the Answer Sheet.

1. Children are required to go to school.
2. People in the U.S. can follow any religious belief.
3. In public schools in the U.S., girls and boys study together.
4. It is necessary to register before you can vote.
5. People have different opinions about things.

Listen to each conversation and choose the best answer to the question you hear. Use the Answer Sheet.

6.
A: Are you going to vote in the election?
B: Of course.
A: Have you already registered?
B: Yes, I have. I did it last week.
Question: What has the woman already done?

7.
A: Are you going to the school meeting tonight?
B: I don't know. Do you think I should?
A: Yeah. I think it's really important. We need to know what's going on.
Question: What did the woman encourage the man to do?

8.
A: What does the FBI do?
B: The FBI? You know, it investigates crimes.
A: Is it a federal agency?
B: Yes, it is. It's the initials for the Federal Bureau of Investigation.
Question: What does the man ask about?

9.
A: What do you think about protest marches?
B: Well, they bring attention to social problems. So I think they're useful.
A: I do too.
Question: What do the man and woman agree about?

10.
A: Are you going to pay your taxes?
B: Do I have a choice? I have to pay taxes.
Question: What does the woman say about paying taxes?

Lesson 3.

2. Listen and Match, page 80

Listen to 5 conversations. Match each conversation to a picture. Write the number of the conversation in the circle next to the picture.

1.
Salesperson: Can I help you?
Customer: Yes. I'd like to buy these.
Salesperson: And how would you like to pay?
Customer: Do you take personal checks?
Salesperson: No, I'm sorry we don't. We only accept cash or credit cards.
Customer: Oh no. Really?
Salesperson: Yes. That's the store policy.
Customer: Oh boy. I don't have a credit card and I don't think I have enough cash on me.
Salesperson: Well, there's a ATM machine right over there.
Customer: Okay, good. I'll be right back.

2.
Salesperson: Can I help you?
Customer: Yes, I'd like to return these.
Salesperson: Do you have your receipt?
Customer: Yes. Uhm, here it is.
Salesperson: I'm sorry but these are nonreturnable.
Customer: Excuse me?
Salesperson: You can't return these pants. They were a final sale.
Customer: Are you sure?
Salesperson: I think so, but I'm not positive. I can check with the manager.
Customer: Would you please? Thank you.

3.
Salesperson: Can I help you?
Customer: Ah, no. No thank you.
Salesperson: Have you seen our new suits? They just arrived and they're on sale.
Customer: No, thank you. I don't need a suit.
Salesperson: Are you sure? These won't last long. I've already sold three of them today.
Customer: Ah, no thank you. I'm just looking. I'll let you know if I need help.
Salesperson: Okay.

4.

A: Can you tell me where the olive oil is?

B: Olive oil. Hmm. I'm pretty sure that it's at the end of Aisle 4, but I'm not absolutely certain. I'm new here.

A: Well, I'll look there. Thanks.

B: You're welcome.

A: Hmm. It's not in Aisle 4. I wonder where it is. Excuse me.

C: Yes?

A: Do you know where the olive oil is?

C: Hmm. It seems to me that I saw it in the next aisle, but I'm not sure.

A: You're not sure?

C: No, sorry. I don't work here.

A: Oh, sorry. I thought you were an employee. Hmm. It's not here either. Maybe they don't sell olive oil.

5.

Salesperson: Can I help you?

Customer: Yes, I'd like some information about computers.

Salesperson: Okay. Do you need a desktop or a laptop?

Customer: Well, it's possible that I'll need to travel with it, but I'm not sure. Right now I just work at home.

Salesperson: Well, we do have this light-weight, high-speed, wireless laptop. It's a great price!

Customer: Hmm. That looks pretty good. What's your return policy on this?

Salesperson: I'd have to check on that.

Customer: Could you please? I really don't want to buy this if I can't return it.

Salesperson: Sure. I'll check. Just a minute and I'll be right back.

Customer: Okay. Thanks.

3. Listen for Specific Information, page 80

Listen to the conversations again. What does each customer want? Take notes in the chart below.

Lesson 7.

1. Listening Review, page 88

Listen to each conversation and choose the best answer to the question you hear. Use the Answer Sheet.

1.

A: Excuse me. Can you help me?

B: Sure. What can I do for you?

A: I'd like to return this sweater.

B: No problem. The return counter is straight ahead. They can help you there.

A: Thanks.

Question: What does the man want?

2.

A: Excuse me.

B: Yes. Can I help you?

A: Yes, I'd like to buy one of these computers.

B: Okay. I'll have to get you one from out back. Uhm, do you want to get an extended warranty with that?

A: Well, it says here that it comes with a one-year warranty.

B: Yes, but for an extra 50 dollars you can buy an extended warranty. It's a good deal. It gives you an extra year of protection.

A: Well, thanks, but I don't think so. I'll just take the computer.

B: Okay.

Question: What does the woman buy?

3.

A: Excuse me.

B: Yes?

A: I think there's a mistake on my receipt.

B: Let me see.

A: On the receipt it says that milk costs two dollars a gallon, but the price in the store flyer is a dollar forty-nine.

B: Sorry about that. I'll correct that right away.

Question: What was the man's problem?

4.

A: How much is rice this week at the FoodBasket?

B: Hmm. Just a minute. Uhm, it's only $2.99 for a 5-pound bag.

A: That's a great price. Maybe we should get several bags.

B: Good idea.

Question: What are they going to buy in bulk?

5.

A: This is a really nice coat, isn't it?

B: Yeah, it sure is.

A: But it's kind of expensive, isn't it?

B: Well, actually, it's not a bad price.

Question: What do the man and the woman agree on?

Listen and choose the sentence that is closest in meaning to the sentence you hear. Use the Answer Sheet.

6. The warranty is included in the purchase price.

7. Can I get a cash refund if I return this?

8. I think you can return this, but I'm not certain.

9. This is delicious, isn't it?

10. Grapes aren't cheap, are they?

2. Dictation, page 88
Listen and write the questions you hear.
 1. What's your return policy?
 2. Do you have your receipt?
 3. Could I have a rain check, please?

UNIT SIX
Lesson 3.
2. Listen and Compare, page 98
Listen to a recorded message about getting a marriage license. Check the things you have to do in the After Listening column on page 99.

You have reached the County Clerk's Automated Information System.

For office hours and location, press 1.

For marriage license information, press 2.

For ceremony information, press 3.

For passport information, press 4.

As of Jan. 1, 1995, a blood test is no longer required to obtain a marriage license.

To obtain a public marriage license, the couple must appear together at the county clerk's office with picture identification. You can use a passport, driver's license, naturalization form, resident alien card, or military ID showing your full legal name. If the legal picture ID card does not contain your full legal name, you must also present a certified copy of your birth certificate or social security card, showing your full legal name.

If neither party speaks English, someone who can translate must accompany the couple. It usually takes about 30 minutes to issue a marriage license.

You do not need to be a California resident to marry in California. The same requirements apply whether you are a U.S. citizen or a tourist.

If either party has been married before, you will need to know the exact date of when the marriage was finalized. If the marriage was finalized within the last 90 days, we ask that a copy of the final judgment be brought—a certified copy of the divorce, annulment, or a death record.

The fee for a public marriage license is $83.00. It is effective the day it is issued. Your license is only valid for 90 days after it is issued, so a marriage ceremony must take place within 90 days after receiving your certificate.

To order a marriage license information sheet, press 1 now.

To order an application, press 2 now.

If you need additional information, press 3 now.

To hear this message again, press 9 now.

Listen to a recorded message about getting a driver's license. Check the things you have to do in the After Listening column on page 99.

Thank you for calling the Department of Motor Vehicles. There are 4 frequently asked questions about obtaining a new driver's license. The answer to each question is provided. To skip a question, press 9. To repeat the answer, press pound. To transfer to an agent, press 0.

 1. What is the fee to obtain an original CA license?
    The fee to obtain a new California license is $24.

 2. How do I obtain a new license?
    You will need to visit a DMV office. This process cannot be completed by mail or over the telephone. For your convenience, an appointment is recommended. You will need to complete an application for a new license. The application must be signed in person at the DMV office. You may request this form at the end of this message.

    You will need to provide evidence of your birth date, your valid social security card, which will be verified while you're in the DMV office, documents proving your true full name, such as an original certified copy of your birth certificate, an original passport, or a military ID or documents verifying proof of legal presence in the U.S.

 3. What is the process that will take place at the DMV office?
    You must take a vision and written test. Study the California driver handbook before you take the written exam. There are 36 questions about traffic laws and signs on the test. You have three chances to pass. Once you pass the written test, you may schedule an appointment for a behind-the-wheel driving test.

    You must supply proof of insurance and current registration for the vehicle used.

 4. What happens after I pass the written and behind-the-wheel test?
    Once all requirements are met and tests passed, you will be issued a 60-day temporary license until your new license is mailed to you. A fingerprint and photograph will be taken.

To hear frequently asked questions again, press 1.
To locate the nearest DMV office or schedule an appointment, press 2.
To request forms, press 3.
To repeat this information, press 4.
To transfer to an agent, press 0.

3. Listen for Specific Information, page 98
Read the questions in the Note-Taking Chart on page 99. Then listen again for the answers to the questions and take notes. Then get together with a classmate and take turns asking and answering the questions.

Lesson 7.

1. Listening Review, page 106

Listen and choose the sentence that is closest in meaning to the sentence you hear. Use the Answer Sheet.

1. A misdemeanor is more serious than an infraction.
2. If you commit an infraction, you will probably have to pay a fine.
3. A blood test is no longer required to obtain a marriage license.
4. You have 3 chances to pass the written test.
5. The defendant was accused of assault and burglary.

Listen to each conversation and choose the best answer to the question you hear. Use the Answer Sheet.

6.
   A: Did anyone witness the crime?
   B: Yes. I did.
Question: What did the woman do?

7.
   A: Do you have a picture ID with you?
   B: No, I don't. Do I need one?
   A: Yes, you do.
Question: What does the man need?

8.
   A: Do I need a blood test to get a marriage license?
   B: No, but you do have to fill out an application.
   A: Can I get one here?
   B: Sure. Just a minute and I'll get it for you.
Question: What does the man get from the woman?

9.
   A: Did you really get a traffic ticket?
   B: Yes. Can you believe it?
   A: What did you do?
   B: I went through a red light. Well, I thought it was yellow.
Question: What kind of traffic ticket did the woman get?

10.
   A: Did you see the book that was just here on the chair?
   B: No, I didn't. But there's a book on the dining room table.
   A: No. That's not the one I'm looking for.
Question: What is the woman looking for?

UNIT SEVEN

Lesson 3.

2. Listen for Specific Information, page 116

Listen to Roberta's interview and add the missing information to her job application on page 117.

   A: Can I help you?

   B: Yes. I have an appointment to see Mr. Harrison.

   A: And your name, please?

   B: Roberta Madera.

   A: Just a moment, Ms. Madera. I'll tell him you're here. He'll be with you in just a minute Ms. Madera. Won't you have a seat?

   B: Thanks.

   C: Ms. Madera?

   B: Yes.

   C: Hello. I'm Mr. Harrison.

   B: Hello, Mr. Harrison. It's nice to meet you.

   C: Please come in.

   B: Thank you.

   C: Have a seat.

   B: Thank you.

   C: I have your application here and I see here that you are applying for the assistant manager's position.

   B: Yes, that's right. I was very excited to find a job opening at Sayer's.

   C: And you'd be able to start on June 1st?

   B: Yes, that's right.

   C: I see that you went to Northeast Community College.

   B: Yes, I've completed two year's of work so far, and I hope to continue taking courses part time so I can get my degree.

   C: Yes, I see that your major is business administration.

   B: Yes. It's a good way to combine math and interpersonal skills.

   C: That's true. But tell me, do you find it difficult to work full time and take courses at the same time?

   B: It's challenging, but I just have to manage my time carefully.

   C: Yes, I see. Let's see, now, why don't you tell me a little about your last job. It says that you worked at Floormart until last April. That's when the store moved out of state, isn't it?

   B: Yes, that's right. They offered me a job if I was willing to move, but my family is here so I decided against moving.

   C: What was it like working at Floormart?

   B: Well, as the assistant manager, I was able to do a lot of different things, from working with customers to financial planning. I like that. And I had an excellent boss. He was always willing to teach me new things and give me more responsibility.

   C: Yes, I see. And uh what about your job at Reiko's?

   B: Yes. That was my first full-time job. I was a clerk, then a supervisor. I think it was that job that made me realize that I liked being in charge. I mean, I liked being responsible for the store and making decisions. And I enjoyed working with and training the salespeople. I would have stayed there but the job at Floormart came up and I couldn't refuse it.

   C: Yes, of course.

3. Listen and Evaluate, page 116

Read the questions below. Then look at the pictures and listen to the interview again. Check (✓) your answers.

Now listen to Richard's interview. On another piece of paper, answer questions 1–7 about him. Then compare each interview.

A: Can I help you?

B: Yeah. I want to see Ms. Michaels.

A: Do you have an appointment?

B: Yeah.

A: And your name, please?

B: Richard.

A: Uh, and your last name?

B: Smith. Richard Smith.

A: Just a moment, Mr. Smith. I'll tell her you're here. She'll be with you in just a minute, Mr. Smith. Why don't you have a seat?

B: Okay.

C: Mr. Smith?

B: Yeah, that's me.

C: Why don't you come in? Have a seat.

B: Yeah, okay.

C: I have your application here and I see that you worked for a travel agent for several years.

B: Yeah. It was so boring. And my boss was really mean. If I was even 10 minutes late in the morning, he'd yell at me. I was so glad when that place went out of business.

C: I see. Well, Mr. Smith. Thank you for coming in.

B: Is that all?

C: Yes.

Lesson 7.

1. Listening Review, page 124

Listen to each conversation and choose the best answer to the question you hear. Use the Answer Sheet.

1.

A: Sam, there are several customers waiting at the checkout.

B: Oh, okay. I didn't see them.

A: Sam, I don't want to find you loafing back here again. I don't want to have to tell you again.

B: Okay.

Question: What work rule did Sam break?

2.

A: Excuse me. Do you work here?

B: Yeah. What do you want?

A: Uhm, I'd like to pay for this.

B: Okay, okay. I'll be with you in a minute.

Question: How would you describe the salesclerk?

3.

A: Come in.

B: Am I interrupting?

A: No, come on in Tom.

B: I finished the report. You said you needed it by tomorrow, right?

A: Yes. Oh great. I knew I could count on you.

Question: How could you describe Tom?

4.

A: Ms. Smith?

B: Yes.

A: Please come in.

B: Thanks.

A: Have a seat.

B: Thank you.

A: I see on your résumé that you worked at Sayers Department Store for two years.

B: Yes, that's right.

A: Could you tell my why you left the company?

B: Yes, of course. I enjoyed the job, but I wanted a job with more responsibility. At the time, there weren't any other openings at Sayers.

A: I see.

B: When a better job came up at Reiko, I decided to apply for it. I didn't want to leave Sayers, but my supervisor there gave me a great recommendation and she understood why I wanted to leave.

Question: Why did the woman leave her job at Sayers Department Store?

5.

A: You look happy.

B: I am. I had my performance evaluation today.

A: So it went well?

B: Yes. He said my interpersonal skills are great. I work well with others.

Question: What is one of the man's strengths on the job?

Listen and choose the statement that is closest in meaning to the sentence you hear. Use the Answer Sheet.

6. Joshua is responsible for ordering merchandise.

7. Jill has two years of supervisory experience.

8. Bob can handle customer refunds and exchanges.

9. Tito had a good reason for leaving the job.

10. Noah is very cooperative and he works well with others.

UNIT 8
Lesson 3.
2. Listen and Check, page 134

Read questions 1 to 9 on page 135. Then listen to a conversation between a bank officer and a customer. Check 4 questions the customer asks.

A: Can I help you?

B: Yes. I'd like to speak to someone about opening a new checking account.

A: Can you have a seat and I'll see if Ms. Jeffries is available.

B: Sure. Thank you.

C: Hi. I'm Ms. Jeffries.

B: Hi Ms. Jeffries. I'm Sylvia Taylor.

C: Nice to meet you, Ms. Taylor. Why don't you come over to my desk and have a seat?

B: Thank you.

C: How can I help you today?

B: I just wanted to get some information about opening a checking account.

C: Sure. Which kind of account are you interested in?

B: Well, uhm, actually I'm not sure. I really don't know what your bank has to offer.

C: Well, we have 3 types of checking accounts. There's the Circle Checking Account, the Green Checking Account, and the Basic Checking Account.

B: I see. And, ah, how are they different?

C: Well, the Circle Account is the only one that earns interest.

B: That's nice.

C: And the Circle Account is the only one that *doesn't* charge a fee when you use an ATM at other banks.

B: I see.

C: Yes. And the Circle Account is the only one that gives you free checks. You don't have to pay for *any* of your checks.

B: That's great. So, uhm, how much money do you need to open a checking account?

C: Well, for the Circle Account, you need $50 and for the other two you just need $25.

B: That was 50 for the Circle Account and 25 for the Green Account and the Basic Account?

C: That's right.

B: And how much is the monthly maintenance fee?

C: Well, for the Circle Account it's fifteen dollars. But if you keep $5,000 in your account, you don't have to pay the monthly fee.

B: Not much chance of that.

C: Excuse me?

B: Oh, nothing.

C: And the Green Account is special because it's for online banking only so there is no monthly maintenance fee. And the Basic Account has a $2.50 monthly fee.

B: Does this account provide free online banking?

C: Yes, it does. In fact, all three types of accounts provide free online banking. Each account also provides an ATM and debit card at no additional charge.

B: I see. And I can pay my bills online free of charge?

C: Absolutely.

B: Well, I think that gives me the information I need. I thank you for your time.

C: Well, if there is anything else I can do for you, let me know. Here's my card.

B: Thanks.

C: Goodbye.

B: Goodbye.

3. Listen and Take Notes, page 134

Listen again and add the missing information to the chart on page 135.

Lesson 7.
1. Listening Review, page 142

Listen and choose the sentence that is closest in meaning to the sentence you hear. Use the Answer Sheet.

1. They spend 30 percent of their income on housing.
2. She pays an annual fee for her credit card.
3. John owns stock in a company that makes medicines.
4. Sue puts money in her IRA every year.
5. Carlos had to pay a penalty fee because he forgot to pay his credit card bill on time.

Listen to each conversation and choose the best answer to the question you hear. Use the Answer Sheet.

6.
A: What are you going to do with your money?
B: I think I'll buy a CD.
A: Are you sure you don't want to put it in your savings account?
B: No. I think a CD is better.
Question: What is the man going to do with his money?

7.
A: Does this account come with free checks?
B: No, it doesn't, but it does come with a free ATM card.
A: Well, I'm not really interested in that.
Question: What does the man want?

8.

A: How much money do I need to open a savings account?

B: A savings account?

A: Mmm-hm.

B: Fifty dollars.

A: Is that all?

B: Yes.

Question: What does the woman need to open a savings account?

9.

A: Hello?

B: Hello. May I speak to Mr. Delmotto please?

A: This is Mr. Delmotto.

B: Well, congratulations Mr. Delmotto. You have won a new TV set.

A: Really?

B: Yes. And I'm going to send it right out to you today.

A: Oh?

B: Yes. All I need is your credit card number. That's just for the shipping. So, what credit card do you want to put it on?

A: I'm not interested. Goodbye.

Question: What did the man refuse to do?

10.

A: What's the interest rate on a 6-month CD these days?

B: I think it's about two and a half percent.

A: Did you say two and a half?

B: Mmm-hm, yes.

A: That's not much.

Question: What did the woman want to know?

PRE-UNIT

UNIT 1

according to
accuracy
affect
assess
behavior
clarity
clearly
come up with
complex
comprehend
concentrate
concisely
cooperative
demand
distracted
diverse
encourage
essential
fulfilled
incredibly
interact
interpersonal
leave out
overcome
overview
personal responsibility
proficient
promotion
quote
resolve
share
sought after
speak softly
turn around
up to

UNIT 2

actual cash value
antenna
bumper
check into
claim
collision
comprehensive
coverage
deductible
depreciate
do your homework

effective
flat tire
hood
in advance
liability
nonrefundable
on a shoestring
oncoming
option
policy
policyholder
premium
reimbursement
rush hour
shoulder (of a road)
standard fare
trunk
uninsured
vehicle
warn
windshield
witness

UNIT 3

antiseptic wipe
blood vessel
calorie
cardiologist
cardiopulmonary
cardiovascular
container
cut back on
death
dental hygienist
depressed
dermatologist
diagnose
dietician
energy
FYI
general practitioner
gynecologist
immunization
immunize
measles
mumps
nutrition
nutritionist
obstetrician
optometrist
pass out

pediatrician
perform
physical therapist
preparation
procedure
psychiatrist
psychologist
recommend
refer
respiratory therapist
revive
serious reaction
side effect
specialize
specialty
susceptible
treat
vaccinate
vision
vital signs

UNIT 4

accountable
acronym
authorities
coeducational
compulsory
constitution
consumer
contact
crime
deserve
disaster
discriminate
elect
election
elective
enforce
extracurricular activity
federal
get together
harmful
honestly
initial
investigate
march (v.)
obey
participate
particularly
peaceful
physical punishment

protest
recall
register
religious
remedy
required
respect
say (n.)
security
spank
take advantage of
tolerant
work for a living

UNIT 5
brand
commission
comparison shopper
consignment shop
cover
end up
extended warranty
impulse buyer
in bulk
increase
keep in mind
merchandise
net weight
out of stock
policy
profitable
purchase (n.)
purchase (v.)
quality
rain check
ring up
scanner
selection
service contract
store credit
suspicious
thrift store
time limit
unit price
yard sale

UNIT 6
aggravated assault
assault
bailiff
battery

burglary
commit
court reporter
criminal
defendant
defense attorney
dismiss
fatal
felony
guilty
imprisonment
incite
infraction
innocent
jaywalking
judge
jury
lawyer
misdemeanor
murder
no big deal
offense
pay a fine
prison
probation
prosecutor
punishable
rape
summons
testimony
violation
witness (n.)
witness (v.)

UNIT 7
absenteeism
assist
attendance
courteous
creativity
deliver
disciplinary
discount
dismissal
disorderly
ensure
excessive
flooded
handle
ignore
independence

initiative
interfere with
loaf (v.)
oversee
performance
possess
prefer
prepare
previous
process
quarterly
recruitment
reprimand
retail
shipment
substantial
unacceptable
violate

UNIT 8
activate
black market
bogus
budget
budget deficit
CD
certificate of deposit
crook
fee
fixed
fortunately
guard
individual retirement account
inflation
invest
IRA
max out
minimum monthly payment
penalty fee
perk
secure
set back
share (of stock)
specific
stock
tear up
telemarketer
vary

A

absenteeism *n.* the state of not going to work when you are supposed to: *Lucia's absenteeism may get her fired.* **(7)**

according to *prep.* as stated by a person or other source of information: *According to the newspaper, the project will cost more than $1 million.* **(1)**

accountable *adj.* responsible for the effects of what you do: *After age 18, you're legally accountable for your actions.* **(4)**

accuracy *n.* the quality of not making or containing any mistakes: *The writer guaranteed the complete accuracy of the report.* **(1)**

acronym *n.* a word that is formed from the first letters of other words: *OPEC is an acronym for the Organization of Petroleum-Exporting Countries.* **(4)**

activate *v.* to make something start working: *You must call this number to activate your credit card.* **(8)**

actual cash value *n.* the cost to replace property (car, house, camera, etc.) minus the amount it has gone down in value since you bought it: *The car was so old, its actual cash value was only $300.* **(2)**

affect *v.* to have an effect on someone or something: *Ron's bad moods affect everyone around him.* **(1)**

aggravated assault *n.* the crime of attacking someone in a more serious way than regular assault: *It was considered aggravated assault because they were also trying to rob the bank.* **(6)**

antenna *n.* a piece of thin metal equipment on the outside of a car that helps your radio receive signals: *The antenna got bent in the carwash.* **(2)**

antiseptic wipe *n.* a small wet cloth that kills bacteria that can cause disease: *Clean the wound with an antiseptic wipe.* **(3)**

assault *n.* the crime of attacking someone: *Nearly 1 million people are arrested for assault every year.* **(6)**

assess *v.* to think about and judge someone or something: *How do you assess your employees' work performance?* **(1)**

assist *v.* to help someone do something: *Let me assist you with those bags, sir.* **(7)**

attendance *n.* the act of regularly going to work or a class: *Attendance makes up 10% of your grade.* **(7)**

authorities *n.* the people or organizations that are in charge of a particular place: *Report any illegal activity to the authorities.* **(4)**

B

bailiff *n.* someone whose job is to keep order in a court of law: *The bailiff took the protestors out of the courtroom.* **(6)**

battery *n.* the crime of hitting someone: *She accused her husband of battery.* **(6)**

behavior *n.* a particular way that a person or animal does things: *The animals were showing some strange behaviors before the earthquake.* **(1)**

black market *n.* the system by which things are sold illegally: *They tried to buy weapons on the black market.* **(8)**

blood vessel *n.* one of the narrow tubes that blood moves through in your body: *Too much cholesterol can block blood vessels.* **(3)**

bogus *adj.* fake and not real: *The phone number he gave us was bogus.* **(8)**

brand *n.* the name of a company that makes a particular product: *There are so many brands of sneakers that it's hard to choose.* **(5)**

budget *n.* an itemized plan of how a person or an organization will spend money for a given period of time: *Our household budget includes rent, utilities, and food.* **(8)**

budget deficit *n.* an amount of money that a person, organization, or government spends, that is more than what they earn or receive in taxes: *The government is trying to reduce the budget deficit.* **(8)**

bumper *n.* the piece of metal, rubber, or plastic on the front and back of a car that protects it when it hits something: *There's a new dent in the bumper.* **(2)**

burglary *n.* the crime of going into a building or car to steal things: *There was a burglary in the apartment building last night.* **(6)**

C

calorie *n.* a unit of measuring how much energy you get from food: *How many calories are there in a piece of chocolate cake?* **(3)**

cardiologist *n.* a heart doctor: *A team of cardiologists performed the open-heart surgery.* **(3)**

cardiopulmonary *adj.* relating to your heart and lungs: *The doctor specializes in cardiopulmonary disease.* **(3)**

cardiovascular *adj.* relating to your heart and blood vessels: *If you have cardiovascular disease, you should do things to take care of your heart.* **(3)**

CD *n.* certificate of deposit; a special kind of savings account that earns an unchanging interest rate for a specific period of time: *Why don't you put that extra money in a CD?* **(8)**

KEY: *abbr.* = abbreviation; *adj.* = adjective; *adv.* = adverb; *n.* = noun; *n. phr.* = noun phrase; *phr. v.* = phrasal verb; *prep.* = preposition; *prep. phr.* = prepositional phrase; *v.* = verb; *v. phr.* = verb phrase

certificate of deposit (CD) *n.* a special kind of savings account that earns an unchanging interest rate for a specific period of time: *Certificates of deposit usually pay better interest than regular savings accounts.* **(8)**

check into *phr. v.* to try to find out more information about something: *I'll check into the prices and let you know what I find out.* **(2)**

claim *n.* a policyholder's request to be paid back for a loss covered by their insurance policy: *We submitted an insurance claim right after the accident.* **(2)**

clarity *n.* the quality of being clear and easy to understand: *The clarity of her writing makes it very easy to follow.* **(1)**

clearly *adv.* in a way that is easy to understand: *The directions were very clearly written.* **(1)**

coeducational *adj.* including education for both males and females: *Most colleges today are coeducational.* **(4)**

collision *n.* a situation in which your car runs into another car, a wall, a tree, etc., or a type of insurance that covers damage to your car in this situation: *If you don't have collision coverage, you'll have to repair your car yourself.* **(2)**

come up with *phr. v.* to think of an idea or answer: *How did you come up with your team's name?* **(1)**

commission *n.* an amount of money that a salesperson is paid for selling something: *The sales staff are paid a basic salary plus commission.* **(5)**

commit *v.* to do something wrong or illegal: *I would never commit a crime.* **(6)**

comparison shopper *n.* someone who checks prices of different brands or at different stores before buying something: *Comparison shoppers can save a lot of money.* **(5)**

complex *adj.* having many complicated parts: *The problem is too complex for a quick solution.* **(1)**

comprehend *v.* to understand something difficult: *It took us a while to comprehend what she was saying.* **(1)**

comprehensive *adj.* used to describe a type of insurance that covers damage to your car from something other than another car, such as theft, fire, or earthquake: *I feel much less nervous with a good comprehensive policy.* **(2)**

compulsory *adj.* required by a rule or law: *Education is compulsory for the first 16 years.* **(4)**

concentrate *v.* to give all your attention to someone or something: *Turn off the TV so you can concentrate on your homework.* **(1)**

concisely *adv.* written or said without using more words than are necessary: *She told us concisely the main points of the meeting.* **(1)**

consignment shop *n.* a store that sells clothes you don't want anymore and gives you part of the money: *I'm going to take some of these old things to the consignment shop.* **(5)**

constitution *n.* the official document that lists the basic rules of a government: *The U.S. Constitution guarantees freedom of speech.* **(4)**

consumer *n.* someone who buys a product: *Consumers spent more money in December this year than last.* **(4)**

contact *v.* to write to someone or call them: *I contacted the office when I arrived at the airport.* **(4)**

container *n.* something that holds something else: *How many potato chips are in the container?* **(3)**

cooperative *adj.* willing to work with other people to do something: *I'm sure Jean will help us—she's very cooperative.* **(1)**

court reporter *n.* someone whose job is to type everything that people say during a court trial: *The lawyer asked the court reporter to read back what the witness just said.* **(6)**

courteous *adj.* polite and helpful: *All sales staff should be courteous to customers.* **(7)**

cover *v.* to be enough to pay for something: *Will $300 cover the price of the plane ticket?* **(5)**

coverage *n.* the amount of protection that an insurance policy gives you: *The coverage with this company is much better than with my old insurance.* **(2)**

cut back on *phr. v.* to do less of something: *I have to cut back on the amount of sugar that I eat.* **(3)**

creativity *n.* the ability to think of interesting and unusual ideas and make new things: *Roberto's paintings show a lot of creativity.* **(7)**

crime *n.* an illegal act or activity: *Shoplifting isn't a joke—it's a crime.* **(4)**

criminal *adj.* relating to crime and the laws that deal with it: *There was a criminal trial for the attack.* **(6)**

crook *n.* someone who does something dishonest to steal money: *The people in that store are just a bunch of crooks.* **(8)**

D

death *n.* the state of not being alive: *Doctors are still not sure what caused the woman's death.* **(3)**

deductible *n.* the part of the loss that you agree to pay before insurance pays the rest if you have an accident: *My insurance has a $500 deductible.* **(2)**

defendant *n.* the person in a court case who is accused of doing something illegal: *The defendant says she was nowhere near the fire.* **(6)**

defense attorney *n.* the lawyer in a court of law who represents the defendant: *The defense attorney gave a convincing argument.* **(6)**

deliver *v.* to bring or give something to someone: *The mail carrier usually delivers the mail around noon.* **(7)**

demand *n.* people's need or desire for something: *Demand for inexpensive housing will not go away.* **(1)**

dental hygienist *n.* someone who cleans your teeth and tells you how to keep your teeth healthy: *The dental hygienist cleans my teeth before the dentist comes in.* **(3)**

depreciate *v.* to go down in value over time: *Cars start depreciating as soon as you buy them.* **(2)**

depressed *adj.* feeling so sad that you lose interest in life: *If you're depressed, maybe you should see a psychologist.* **(3)**

dermatologist *n.* a skin doctor: *I went to a dermatologist for my acne when I was a kid.* **(3)**

deserve *v.* to be worthy of getting or having something because of what you have done: *After all Yuko's hard work, she deserves a raise.* **(4)**

diagnose *v.* to officially say what someone's medical problem is: *The doctors diagnosed him with cancer last year.* **(3)**

dietician *n.* someone whose job is to plan meals and programs for healthy eating: *The school dietician makes sure the meals we eat are healthy.* **(3)**

disaster *n.* a sudden accident or event that causes great destruction, damage, and loss: *Many people died from last year's natural disaster.* **(4)**

disciplinary *adj.* relating to methods of making people obey rules and laws and punishing them when they don't: *If he continues to be late, we'll have to take disciplinary action.* **(7)**

discount *n.* an amount by which a price is reduced: *You get a 5% discount if you pay with cash.* **(7)**

discriminate *v.* to treat someone unfairly because of his or her characteristics or qualities: *It is illegal to discriminate because of race.* **(4)**

dismiss *v.* to officially tell someone that he or she can leave: *The judge dismissed one possible juror because she knew the defendant.* **(6)**

dismissal *n.* the action of firing someone from his or her job: *Missing work too many times may result in dismissal.* **(7)**

disorderly *adj.* noisy and causing trouble: *Disorderly behavior is not allowed in the hospital.* **(7)**

distracted *adj.* not paying attention to what you are doing because you are thinking of something else: *It's easy to get distracted with so much activity going on.* **(1)**

diverse *adj.* including many different types of people or things: *The U.S. has a very diverse population.* **(1)**

do your homework *v. phr.* to find out all the necessary information before you do something: *Do your homework before you sign the contract to make sure you're getting a good deal.* **(2)**

E

effective *adj.* valid and being used now: *The rules will be effective for one year.* **(2)**

elect *v.* to vote to choose someone for a government job: *We elect a president every four years.* **(4)**

election *n.* an event in which people vote to choose someone for a government job: *Presidential elections are held every four years.* **(4)**

elective *adj.* not required and able to be chosen: *I can take two elective classes this semester.* **(4)**

encourage *v.* to try to give someone confidence to do something: *My parents always encouraged me to go to college.* **(1)**

end up *phr. v.* to come to be in a particular situation to do a particular thing, especially without planning to: *She ended up selling the car to her sister.* **(5)**

energy *n.* power that you use to move, make heat, etc.: *Eat more or you won't have any energy.* **(3)**

enforce *v.* to make sure that people obey a law: *The government has tried very hard to enforce drug laws.* **(4)**

ensure *v.* to make sure that something happens or is true: *Our goal is to ensure that everyone has a good time.* **(7)**

essential *adj.* necessary: *Good shoes are essential for the hiking trip.* **(1)**

excessive *adj.* too much: *Excessive drinking will damage your liver.* **(7)**

extended warranty *n.* a written promise from a company to fix a product you have bought after the end of the original warranty: *Extended warranties usually cost more than they're worth.* **(5)**

extracurricular activity *n.* something that you do at school in addition to your classes: *The kids are busy with sports and other extracurricular activities.* **(4)**

F

fatal *adj.* causing death: *She was involved in a fatal car crash.* **(6)**

federal *adj.* relating to the national government of a country like the U.S.: *Federal laws prohibit this kind of pollution.* **(4)**

KEY: *abbr.* = abbreviation; *adj.* = adjective; *adv.* = adverb; *n.* = noun; *n. phr.* = noun phrase; *phr. v.* = phrasal verb; *prep.* = preposition; *prep. phr.* = prepositional phrase; *v.* = verb; *v. phr.* = verb phrase

fee *n.* an amount of money that you have to pay to do or use something: *How much is the entrance fee?* **(8)**

felony *n.* a serious crime: *Drug possession is considered a felony.* **(6)**

fixed *adj.* not able to be changed: *Only a fixed number of users can use the computer system at one time.* **(8)**

flat tire *n.* a tire on the wheel of a car that has no air in it, especially because there is a hole in it: *We got a flat tire on the way home from the supermarket.* **(2)**

flooded *adj.* overflowing or excessive amount of something: *The post office is flooded with letters during the holidays.* **(7)**

fortunately *adv.* in a way that is lucky or good: *Fortunately, none of our stuff was damaged in the fire.* **(8)**

fulfilled *adj.* happy and satisfied with your life: *I love my family and my job is great—I feel very fulfilled.* **(1)**

FYI *abbr.* for your information; used before telling someone a piece of information you think they might need: *FYI: Terry is expecting everyone by 7:00.* **(3)**

G

general practitioner (GP) *n.* a medical doctor who treats common medical problems but does not have a specialty: *If you're not feeling well, make an appointment with your general practitioner.* **(3)**

get together *phr. v.* to come together or meet with someone: *I got together with some friends from work over the weekend.* **(4)**

guard *v.* to protect something and keep it safe: *A dog guards the building at night.* **(8)**

guilty *adj.* having done something illegal: *The man was found guilty of murder.* **(6)**

gynecologist *n.* a doctor who deals with women's health: *Lucy goes to see her gynecologist once a year.* **(3)**

H

handle *v.* to deal with something: *How do you plan to handle the problem?* **(7)**

harmful *adj.* causing or capable of causing damage, injury, or harm: *Cigarette smoke is harmful to your health.* **(4)**

honestly *adv.* in a way that does not involve lying or cheating: *Bob has always treated me honestly and fairly.* **(4)**

hood *n.* the large metal cover that goes over the engine of a car: *Open the hood so I can check the oil.* **(2)**

I

ignore *v.* to not pay attention to something: *Don't just ignore what I tell you.* **(7)**

immunization *n.* a shot with medicine that prevents you from getting a disease: *Have the kids had their immunizations yet?* **(3)**

immunize *v.* to give someone a shot with medicine to prevent them from getting a disease: *Children must be immunized before they start going to school.* **(3)**

imprisonment *n.* the situation of being forced to stay in a prison: *Her imprisonment lasted three years.* **(6)**

impulse buyer *n.* someone who buys something without planning and often without really needing it: *Gum and candy are near the checkout counters for impulse buyers.* **(5)**

in advance *prep. phr.* before something else happens: *Call at least three days in advance to make reservations.* **(2)**

in bulk *prep. phr.* in large amounts: *Because we have such a big family, we buy most of our food in bulk at warehouse stores.* **(5)**

incite *v.* to try to get someone to behave in a violent or criminal way: *It was clear that one man had incited the fight.* **(6)**

increase *v.* to make a price or amount higher or bigger: *All the gas stations in town have increased their prices.* **(5)**

incredibly *adv.* extremely, often in a way that is difficult to believe: *The test was incredibly easy! We all got A's.* **(1)**

independence *n.* the ability to make decisions and do things without help from others: *I have a lot of independence at my job.* **(7)**

individual retirement account (IRA) *n.* a savings or investment account with tax advantages where you can save money for when you retire (stop working): *An individual retirement account is a good way to plan for the future.* **(8)**

inflation *n.* the rise in prices over time: *Because of inflation, everything costs more today than ten years ago.* **(8)**

infraction *n.* an act of breaking a rule or law that is not considered serious: *I'm sure they won't do anything about it—it's just a minor infraction.* **(6)**

initial *n.* the first letter of a name or other word: *Her initials are E.J.S.—Ellen Jannette Sommers.* **(4)**

initiative *n.* the ability to do things and make decisions without being asked to do them first: *Lim has shown a lot of initiative in organizing the meetings.* **(7)**

innocent *adj.* having done nothing wrong and not guilty of a crime: *I swear I'm innocent!* **(6)**

interact *v.* to talk, work, and do things with other people: *We interact with family members, friends, coworkers, and strangers every day.* **(1)**

interfere with *phr. v.* to prevent something from happening or developing in the normal or planned way: *It looks like the class schedule might interfere with our vacation plans.* **(7)**

interpersonal *adj.* involving relationships between people: *If you improve your interpersonal skills, you will get along better with others.* **(1)**

invest *v.* to use money to buy something that is expected to make a profit: *She invested 10% of her income in stocks and CDs.* **(8)**

investigate *v.* to try to find out more information about something: *Police are investigating last night's robbery.* **(4)**

IRA *n.* individual retirement account; a savings or investment account with tax advantages where you can save money for when you retire (stop working): *I put as much as I can in my IRA every year.* **(8)**

J

jaywalking *n.* the illegal action of crossing a street where you are not supposed to cross: *I got a ticket for jaywalking downtown.* **(6)**

judge *n.* the person who is in control of a court of law and makes sure that the trial is fair: *The judge sent him to prison for 15 years.* **(6)**

jury *n.* the group of people in a court of law who decide if someone is guilty or not guilty: *The jury took only two hours to find the defendant not guilty.* **(6)**

K

keep in mind *v. phr.* to remember and consider something when you are doing or deciding somthing else: *I tried to keep in mind everything my mechanic told me about buying a car.* **(5)**

L

lawyer *n.* someone who is trained to work with the law and represent people in court: *You need a good lawyer to win the case.* **(6)**

leave out *phr. v.* to not include something: *Write your first name, but you can leave out your middle name.* **(1)**

liability *n.* your legal responsibility to pay for something: *Business owners usually have liability insurance in case anyone is injured at their business.* **(2)**

loaf *v.* to not do anything when you should be working: *Are you going to sit around loafing all day?* **(7)**

M

march *v.* to walk somewhere in a group in order to show your opinion about something: *Thousands marched in the streets against the war.* **(4)**

max out *phr v.* to reach the most, or the maximum amount, of something: *She maxed out her credit card during her shopping spree.* **(8)**

measles *n.* a disease in which you have a fever and get red spots all over your body: *My mother had measles as a child.* **(3)**

merchandise *n.* products that are meant to be sold: *Please be careful when you handle the merchandise.* **(5)**

minimum monthly payment *n.* the smallest amount that you can pay each month on money that you owe for a credit card: *If you only make the minimum monthly payment, it will take a long time to pay off that debt.* **(8)**

misdemeanor *n.* a crime that is not very serious: *For misdemeanors you usually spend less than a year in jail.* **(6)**

mumps *n.* a disease in which your neck and throat swells and hurts: *Many children in the U.S. used to get mumps.* **(3)**

murder *n.* the crime of killing someone: *He will spend life in prison for the murder.* **(6)**

N

net weight *n.* how much something weighs without its container: *The net weight is written on the outside of the package.* **(5)**

no big deal *n. phr.* used to say that something is not important or worth worrying about: *It's no big deal if you can't finish by Friday.* **(6)**

nonrefundable *adj.* used to describe something you buy for which you cannot get your money back if you decide you don't want it: *The tickets are nonrefundable.* **(2)**

nutrition *n.* the process of eating in a healthy way: *Nutrition is important for a healthy body.* **(3)**

nutritionist *n.* someone whose job is to plan meals and programs for healthy eating: *My nutritionist suggested that I eat more fruit and vegetables.* **(3)**

KEY: *abbr.* = abbreviation; *adj.* = adjective; *adv.* = adverb; *n.* = noun; *n. phr.* = noun phrase; *phr. v.* = phrasal verb; *prep.* = preposition; *prep. phr.* = prepositional phrase; *v.* = verb; *v. phr.* = verb phrase

O

obey *v.* to do what a person or law tells you to do: *If you don't obey the law, you might go to jail.* **(4)**

obstetrician *n.* a doctor who deals with pregnancy and the birth of children: *An obstetrician delivered the baby.* **(3)**

offense *n.* an action of breaking a rule or a law: *If it's a minor offense, it probably won't go to trial.* **(6)**

on a shoestring *prep. phr.* spending very little money: *Lora traveled all over Asia on a shoestring.* **(2)**

oncoming *adj.* coming toward you: *The truck crossed the center line and went into oncoming traffic.* **(2)**

option *n.* a choice about what you can do: *She likes to know all her options before she makes a decision.* **(2)**

optometrist *n.* a doctor who checks your eyes for problems and can order glasses for you: *It's about time to go to the optometrist and get a new pair of glasses.* **(3)**

out of stock *prep. phr.* not available to be bought: *The sweater I wanted was out of stock.* **(5)**

overcome *v.* to successfully deal with a problem that is stopping you from doing something: *She overcame her shyness and became very outgoing.* **(1)**

oversee *v.* to be in charge and make sure that work is done correctly: *The manager oversees all the work of the department.* **(7)**

overview *n.* a description of something big or complicated that includes just the most important parts: *There is a brief overview at the beginning of each chapter.* **(1)**

P

participate *v.* to do an activity with other people: *All team members need to participate in the decision making.* **(4)**

particularly *adv.* more than usual or than average; especially: *Jose is particularly good at math.* **(4)**

pass out *phr. v.* to become unconscious and not aware of anything around you: *It was so hot that several people passed out.* **(3)**

pay a fine *v. phr.* to pay money as punishment for something that you have done wrong: *I had to pay a $35 parking fine last week.* **(6)**

peaceful *adj.* quiet without any fighting: *The protests were very peaceful.* **(4)**

pediatrician *n.* a children's doctor: *Isn't he too old to still be going to a pediatrician?* **(3)**

penalty fee *n.* an amount of money you have to pay for doing something wrong: *I was late with my payment, so I had to pay an additional penalty fee.* **(8)**

perform *v.* to do a procedure or a piece of work: *Which doctor performed the operation?* **(3)**

performance *n.* how well someone does a job or activity: *My boss is very pleased with my work performance.* **(7)**

perk *n.* something good or special that you get in addition to the basic features of something: *Getting to travel is one of the perks of his job.* **(8)**

personal responsibility *n.* willingness to accept blame or praise for what you have done: *You should take personal responsibility for your actions and not blame others.* **(1)**

physical punishment *n.* the action of hitting or hurting someone's body because he or she has done something wrong: *Schools no longer allow physical punishment.* **(4)**

physical therapist (PT) *n.* someone who helps you use a part of your body after illness or an accident: *The physical therapist helped Magda learn to walk again.* **(3)**

policy *n.* 1. a contract you have with an insurance company: *The document lists the main features of your insurance policy.* **(2)**; 2. a set of rules or plans for doing something: *What is the company's policy for sick leave?* **(5)**

policyholder *n.* someone who has an insurance policy: *The insurance policy covers only policyholders—not their families.* **(2)**

possess *v.* to have something: *Does she possess the knowledge she needs for the job?* **(7)**

prefer *v.* to like something better than something else: *Do you prefer chocolate or vanilla?* **(7)**

premium *n.* the amount of money you pay for your insurance. The higher the deductible, the lower the premium: *My health insurance has a monthly premium of $200.* **(2)**

preparation *n.* the process of getting something ready: *Food preparation doesn't have to be boring or difficult.* **(3)**

prepare *v.* to get something ready: *Can someone help me prepare the decorations?* **(7)**

previous *adj.* before something else: *They met each other the previous week.* **(7)**

prison *n.* a building where criminals are sent to live as punishment for their crimes: *Joe spent six months in prison.* **(6)**

probation *n.* a period of time during which a criminal does not have to go to prison as long as he or she behaves well and follows particular rules: *He'll be on probation for the next six months.* **(6)**

procedure *n.* a particular method of medical treatment: *The procedure to fix your elbow will take several hours.* **(3)**

process *v.* to deal with something in an official step-by-step way: *How long does it take to process the application?* **(7)**

proficient *adj.* able to do something very well: *It took many years of study before I became a proficient speaker of English.* **(1)**

profitable *adj.* producing money for someone: *Inder's shoe store is very profitable.* **(5)**

promotion *n.* a move to a more important job within a company organization: *Ellen got a promotion. She's the manager now.* **(1)**

prosecutor *n.* the lawyer in a court of law who tries to show that someone did something illegal: *The prosecutor in the case is one of the best lawyers in the county.* **(6)**

protest *v.* to show disapproval of something through action or words: *Thousands of people protested the company's unfair policies.* **(4)**

psychiatrist *n.* a doctor who helps people with emotional problems: *The psychiatrist prescribed drugs for his depression.* **(3)**

psychologist *n.* someone who is trained to talk with people and help them with their emotional problems: *She saw a psychologist once a week after her mother died.* **(3)**

punishable *adj.* able to be punished in a particular way: *The misdemeanor is punishable by six months in jail.* **(6)**

purchase *n.* the action of buying something, or the thing you buy: *You can make your purchases at the front of the store.* **(5)**

purchase *v.* to buy something: *We purchased a new house in Miami.* **(5)**

Q

quality *n.* how good or bad something is: *The quality of the material is very good.* **(5)**

quarterly *adj.* happening every three months: *I have to give my boss four quarterly reports a year.* **(7)**

quote *v.* to write down or repeat the words that someone else has said: *He quoted Abraham Lincoln at the beginning of his speech.* **(1)**

R

rain check *n.* a written promise to let you buy something later at a special price because it is not available now: *We're out of that stereo, but I can give you a rain check.* **(5)**

rape *n.* the crime of forcing someone to have sex: *The three men were found guilty of rape.* **(6)**

recall *v.* to officially say that a product should be returned to the company that made it because something is wrong with it: *The cars were recalled because of a problem with the wheels.* **(4)**

recommend *v.* to say that it is a good idea to do or try something: *The doctor recommended that I get more exercise.* **(3)**

recruitment *n.* the process of finding people to work for you: *The company does a lot of recruitment at job fairs.* **(7)**

refer *v.* to tell someone to go to someone else who can help him or her: *My doctor referred me to an ear specialist.* **(3)**

register *v.* to put your name on an official list: *You have to register if you want to vote.* **(4)**

reimbursement *n.* repayment to you of money you have paid: *I still haven't gotten a reimbursement for the repairs I paid for.* **(2)**

religious *adj.* relating to religion and usually a belief in a god or gods: *People around the world have many different religious beliefs.* **(4)**

remedy *v.* to make a bad situation better or solve a problem: *Raising teachers' salaries could help remedy the teacher shortage.* **(4)**

reprimand *n.* the action of telling someone officially that he or she has done something wrong: *She was given a reprimand for breaking the safety rules.* **(7)**

required *adj.* necessary or needed because of a rule: *I took this required class in order to graduate.* **(4)**

resolve *v.* to find a solution or answer to a problem: *They were able to resolve their disagreement by themselves.* **(1)**

respect *v.* to consider someone important and treat him or her well: *It's important to respect everyone—even people you don't agree with.* **(4)**

respiratory therapist *n.* someone who treats you for breathing and lung problems: *Max worked with a respiratory therapist after his lung surgery.* **(3)**

retail *adj.* relating to selling things in a store: *How much retail experience have you had?* **(7)**

revive *v.* to make someone conscious again: *Doctors were able to revive her in the emergency room.* **(3)**

ring up *phr. v.* to total the amount of goods that someone is buying in a store using a cash register: *The clerk rang up the items and put them in a bag.* **(5)**

rush hour *n.* the time of day when people are going to or coming from work and there is a lot of traffic on the road: *It takes an extra half an hour to get there during rush hour.* **(2)**

KEY: *abbr.* = abbreviation; *adj.* = adjective; *adv.* = adverb; *n.* = noun; *n. phr.* = noun phrase; *phr. v.* = phrasal verb; *prep.* = preposition; *prep. phr.* = prepositional phrase; *v.* = verb; *v. phr.* = verb phrase

S

say *n.* an opportunity to take part in making decisions: *Workers want a say in how the company is run.* **(4)**

scanner *n.* a machine in a store that reads the price of a product by shining a light on it: *The supermarket uses a scanner at the checkout counter.* **(5)**

secure *adj.* safe and protected: *Secure websites protect your credit card information from being stolen.* **(8)**

security *n.* things that are done to keep a person or place safe, or how safe they are: *They've increased security at the building in the evenings.* **(4)**

selection *n.* a group of things that you can choose from: *The store has a great selection of jackets and coats.* **(5)**

serious reaction *n.* a strong response to a treatment, situation, or an event: *Michael had to go to the doctor because he had a serious reaction to his new medicine.* **(3)**

service contract *n.* an agreement with a company that they will repair any problems you have with its product: *The service contract costs an additional $50.* **(5)**

set back *phr. v.* to cost someone money: *The car set us back $12,000.* **(8)**

share *n.* 1. a part of something that belongs to you or you are responsible for: *Bob always does his share of the work.* **(1)**; 2. one of the equal parts of a company that you can buy for investment: *She bought 100 shares of her brother's new company.* **(8)**

shipment *n.* a product or group of products that is sent somewhere, or the process of sending them: *The shipment still hasn't arrived.* **(7)**

shoulder (of a road) *n.* the side of the road: *He drove the car onto the shoulder to change the tire.* **(2)**

side effect *n.* something bad that happens as a result of something else, but which is not the main intended effect: *Does the medicine have any side effects?* **(3)**

sought after *adj.* wanted by many people: *He is one of the most sought after directors in Hollywood.* **(1)**

spank *v.* to slap a child on the bottom as a punishment: *My parents never spanked us.* **(4)**

speak softly *v. phr.* to talk using a quiet voice: *Please speak softly to avoid disturbing other guests.* **(1)**

specialize *v.* to focus most of your work on one particular subject or activity: *Dr. Walters specializes in the treatment of childhood diseases.* **(3)**

specialty *n.* something that you know a lot about or do very well: *Dr. Smith's specialty is family medicine.* **(3)**

specific *adj.* clearly defined, explained, or understood: *Can you tell me a specific time that you will be available?* **(8)**

standard fare *n.* the regular or usual price for a ticket to go somewhere: *The special price is half the price of the standard fare.* **(2)**

stock *n.* shares in the ownership of a company: *I bought some stock in a small computer company last year.* **(8)**

store credit *n.* an amount of money that can be spent only in one particular store: *We can't refund your money but we can give you store credit.* **(5)**

substantial *adj.* large and important: *I'm hoping for a substantial raise at work this year.* **(7)**

summons *n.* an official legal document that says you have to go to court: *Nadia got a summons to appear at the trial.* **(6)**

susceptible *adj.* likely to get a disease: *Babies and older people are more susceptible to disease than young adults.* **(3)**

suspicious *adj.* thinking that something bad is probably true: *I was suspicious when she wouldn't give me a receipt.* **(5)**

T

take advantage of *v. phr.* to treat someone unfairly to get what you want, especially by tricking him or her: *I think the salesman took advantage of me.* **(4)**

tear up *phr. v.* to rip paper into small pieces: *She tore up the letter after she read it.* **(8)**

telemarketer *n.* someone whose job is to call people on the phone to sell something: *A telemarketer called just as we started eating dinner.* **(8)**

testimony *n.* the information someone knows about a crime that he or she gives in a court of law: *Her testimony surprised everyone in the courtroom.* **(6)**

thrift store *n.* a store where used items are sold at low prices: *You can get some good deals on furniture at a thrift store.* **(5)**

time limit *n.* a period of time during which something must happen: *There is a five-day time limit on all returns.* **(5)**

tolerant *adj.* willing to let different ideas or activities exist around you without becoming upset or criticizing them: *I always try to be tolerant of other people's beliefs even if I don't agree with them.* **(4)**

treat *v.* to give medical care to someone for a particular problem: *What is the best way to treat a burn?* **(3)**

trunk *n.* the space at the back of a car that you open from the outside, where you can store things: *Just put the suitcases in the trunk.* **(2)**

turn around *phr. v.* to change from being in a bad situation to being in a good situation: *After a couple of bad years, things turned around, and I found a great job.* **(1)**

U

unacceptable *adj.* not appropriate or good enough for a particular situation: *Fighting with coworkers is unacceptable.* **(7)**

uninsured *adj.* without insurance: *The other driver was uninsured so my insurance had to pay for all my repairs.* **(2)**

unit price *n.* the cost of a particular amount of a product: *It's a good idea to compare the unit price for different size packages.* **(5)**

up to *adj. phr.* physically or mentally able to do something: *I'm afraid I'm not up to a long bike ride tonight.* **(1)**

V

vaccinate *v.* to give someone a shot with medicine to prevent them from getting a disease: *The nurses vaccinated all the children against measles.* **(3)**

vary *v.* to change at different times and in different situations: *The price will vary depending on where you buy it.* **(8)**

vehicle *n.* something such as a car, truck, or bicycle that is used to move people from one place to another: *Motorized vehicles are not allowed on park trails.* **(2)**

violate *v.* to break a rule or law: *Anyone who violates these rules will be punished.* **(7)**

violation *n.* an action of breaking a rule or law: *I got three tickets for traffic violations.* **(6)**

vision *n.* your ability to see: *As Louise got older, her vision got worse.* **(3)**

vital signs *n.* measurements of your heart rate, breathing, temperature, etc. that show if you are healthy: *The patient was unconscious, but his vital signs were strong.* **(3)**

W

warn *v.* to tell someone about a bad or dangerous situation so that they are ready for it: *They warned us that the roads were icy.* **(2)**

windshield *n.* the large window on the front of a car: *You should clean the windshield so you can see better.* **(2)**

witness *n.* 1. someone who is present at or has personal knowledge of a crime or incident: *The police officer talked to the two witnesses who saw the car accident.* **(2)**; 2. someone who tells what he or she knows about a crime in a court of law: *The first witness explained how the weapon was used.* **(6)**

witness *v.* to be present or have personal knowledge of a crime or an incident that took place: *I witnessed a terrible car accident and don't want to drive anymore.* **(6)**

work for a living *v. phr.* to work at a job in order to earn money to live: *Jon's parents were poor, and he has to work for a living.* **(4)**

Y

yard sale *n.* an event in front of someone's house where he or she sells things that he or she doesn't need anymore: *Let's have a yard sale and get rid of the stuff we don't use anymore.* **(5)**

KEY: *abbr.* = abbreviation; *adj.* = adjective; *adv.* = adverb; *n.* = noun; *n. phr.* = noun phrase; *phr. v.* = phrasal verb; *prep.* = preposition; *prep. phr.* = prepositional phrase; *v.* = verb; *v. phr.* = verb phrase

ALL-STAR STUDENT BOOK 4 SKILLS INDEX

ACADEMIC SKILLS
Grammar
Active (vs. passive) verbs, 66–67
Adjective clauses, 102–103
Adverb clauses of time, 48
Adverb clauses of reason and contrast, 49
Clauses
    adjective, 102–103
    adverb (of time, reason, contrast), 48–49
Compound sentences, 38–39
Conditionals
    present real, Appendix L (153)
    present unreal, Appendix M (153)
    past unreal, 121, Appendix N (153)
could (past), 31, Appendix Q (155)
Modals, Appendix P (154)
    in past time, 30–31, Appendix Q (155)
Passive verbs, 66–67
Past perfect, 120–121, Appendix H (151)
Past time
    with could, 31, Appendix Q (155)
    with should, 30, Appendix Q (155)
Questions,
    indirect, 13, Appendix O (154)
    Wh-, 13, Appendix O (154)
    tag, 84–85, Appendix O (154)
    yes/no, 12–13, Appendix O (154)
Quoted speech, 138–139, Appendix T (156)
Reported speech, 138–139, Appendix T (156)
should (past), 30, Appendix Q (155)
Tag questions, 84–85, Appendix O (154)
Verbs
    Future progressive, Appendix J (152)
    Future tense, Appendix I (152)
    Irregular verbs, Appendix A (148)
    Past conditionals,
        unreal, Appendix N (153)
    Past continuous, Appendix G (151)
        versus simple past, Appendix G (151)
    Past perfect, Appendix H (152)
        versus simple past, Appendix H (151)
    Perfect tenses,
        past, Appendix H (151)
        present, Appendix E (150)
    Present conditional,
        real, Appendix L (153)
        unreal, Appendix M (153)
    Present continuous tense, Appendix D (150)
    Present perfect, Appendix E (150)
    Simple past tense, Appendix F (150)
        versus past continuous, Appendix G (151)
        versus past perfect, Appendix H (151)
    Simple present tense, Appendix C (149)
    Spelling, Appendix B (149)

Wh- questions, 13 (direct vs. indirect),
    Appendix O (154)
Yes/no questions, 12–13, Appendix O (154)

Listening
Comprehension, 16–17, 34–35, 52–53, 70–71, 88–89, 106–107,
    116–117, 124–125, 142–143
Conversations, 26–27, 44–45, 80–81
Dictation, 16–17, 52–53, 88–89
Interviews (job), 116–117
Introductions, 2–3
Opinions, 62–63
Personal information, 2–3
Telephone, 8–9 (messages), 98–99 (recordings)
Transactions, 80–81

Math
Averages, 123
Deductions (from salary), 140–141
Graphs, 68–69
Percentages, 50–51
Rates, 141

Pronunciation
Blending words (in questions with you), 15
Changing stress with that, 105
Intonation in tag questions, 87
Reduction of past modals, 33

Reading
Accident reports, 32–33
Advertisements, 82–83 (grocery stores), 86–87 (housing)
Advice, 78–79 (consumer), 82–83 (shopping)
Applications, 116–117 (job), Authentic Materials A
    (marriage license), Authentic Materials F (job)
Articles, 10–11, 14–15, 18–19, 58–59, 60–61, 72–3, 104–105,
    108–109, 122–123, 136–37
Biography, 126–127
Budgets, 130–131
Bus schedules, 26–27
Comprehension, 10–11, 32–33, 64–65, 68–69, 78–79, 82–83,
    104–105, 118–119, 122–123, 132–133, 136–137, 140–141
Crime reports, Authentic Materials E
Definitions, 6–7, 24–25, 42–43, 60–61, 64–65, 132–133
Description, 6–7, 42–43 (medical professions), 122–123
    (job benefits), 132–133 (spending habits)
Dictionaries, 24–25
Emails, 10–11, 28–29
Facts, 22–23
FAQs (Frequently Asked Questions), 50–51, 132–133
Food labels, 46–47
Forms, 118–119 (employee evaluation),
    Authentic Materials C (taxes)
Goals, 4, 22, 76

Graphs, charts, and maps, 26–27, 50–51, 62–63, 68–69, 96–97, 134–135, 136–137
Health care professions, 42–43
Immunizations, 50–51
Instructions, 8–9 (telephone), 32–33 (car accidents)
Insurance policies, 24–25
Interviews, 14–15
Job descriptions, 114–115
Journal entries, 94–95
Labels (food), 46–47
Laws, 66–67, 94–95, 96–97, 100–101, 102–103
Letters,
    Business, 20–21
    Complaint, 92–93
    to Government Representatives, 74–75
Licenses, 98–99
Messages (telephone), 8–9
Money, 132–133
Paragraphs, 6–7, 36–37, 57, 62–63, 78–79, 82–83, 108–109, 126–127
Parts of a book, 3
Pay stubs, 140–141, Authentic Materials D
Percentages, 130–131
Questions, 134–135
    frequently asked, 50–51, 132–133
Reports
    accident, 32–33
    crime, Authentic Materials E
Rules, 62–63, 112–113
Schedules (bus), 26–27
Signs (traffic), 100–101
Statements, 40–41
Strategies, 18–19, 36–37, 54–55, 72–73, 90–91, 108–109, 126–127, 144–145
Stories, 136–137, 144–145
Telephone messages, 8–9
Test (driver's), Authentic Materials B
Tickets (traffic), 100–101
Tips, 78–79 (consumer tips), 82–83 (shopping tips)
Vocabulary, 96–97
Want ads, 86–87
Warranties, 78–79
Websites, 68–69, 100–101, 114–115, 116–117

Speaking
Accidents, 32–33
Activities, 4–5
Advice, 136–137
Banking, 134–135
Calling 911, 40–41
Consumer issues, 76–77, 78–79
Conversations, 24–25
Courtrooms, 94–95
Description, 22–23

Disagreeing, 62
Education system, 62–63
Employment, 112–113, 116–117, 118–119
Finances, 130–131, 132–133
Food labels, 46–47
Giving opinions, 58–59
Health care professions, 42–43
Immunizations, 50–51
Insurance policies, 24–25
Interviews, 14–15 (business), 28–29, 60–61, 66–67, 76–77, 116–117, 138–139
Introductions, 2–3
Laws, 96–97
Licenses, 98–99
Making appointments, 44–45
Messages (telephone), 8–9
Money, 130–131, 132–133
Opinions, 58–59, 84–85
Personal information, 2–3
Rights, 58–59
Shopping, 76–77, 78–79, 80–81, 82–83
Skills, 6–7
    writing, 10–11
Stories, 94–95
Strategies (communication), 8, 26, 44, 62, 80, 98, 116, 134
Telephone,
    making appointments, 44–45
    messages, 8–9
Tickets (parking/traffic), 100–101
Transactions, 80–81
Transportation, 22–23, 24–25, 26–27, 28–29
Vocabulary, 78–79, 132–133

Strategies
Acronyms, 64
Asking questions, 100
Classifying, 130–131
Communication,
    Agreeing and disagreeing, 62
    Correcting someone, 44
    Expanding your answer, 116
    Expressing doubt, 80–81
    Paraphrasing, 98–99
    Pausing expressions, 26–27
    Polite disagreement, 62
    Repeating to confirm, 134–135
    Stating your purpose, 8
Compare/contrast, 144–145
Evaluating, 2–3, 6–7, 10–11, 58–59, 74–75, 116–117, 130–131, 132–133
Homonyms, 60
Prefixes, 112
Reading,
    Cause and effect, 108–109

Compare/contrast, 144–145
Context, 54–55, 78
Dictionaries, 90–91
Inferences, 18–19
Making inferences, 18–19
Main idea, 36–37
Reading speed, 72–73
Sequence of events, 126–127
Topic, 36–37
Using dictionaries, 90–91
Setting goals, 4, 22, 76
Synonyms, 24
Word forms, 42–43, 96–97, 114–115
Writing,
    Business letters (formatting), 20–21
    Cluster diagrams, 110–111
    Compound sentences, 38–39
    Graphic organizers, 110–111
    Letters of complaint, 92–93
    Organizing your ideas, 110–111
    Outlining, 110–111
    Punctuation, 56–57
    Purpose, 74–75
    Transition words and phrases, 146–147
    Writing Process, 128–129

Writing

Accident reports, 32–33
Activities, 4–5
Advertisements, 86–87
Advice, 30–31
Applications, 116–117 (job), Authentic Materials A
    (marriage license), Authentic Materials F (job)
Crime reports, Authentic Materials E
Definitions, 78–79
Description, 114 (job), 128–129 (friend), 146–147
    (spending habits)
Forms, 4–5 (registration)
Goals, 4, 22, 76
Graphs, charts, and maps, 14–15, 28–29, 60–61, 73, 78–79,
    80–81, 96–97, 110–111, 114–115, 118–119, 132–133,
    134–135, 144–145
Inferences, 22–23
Job descriptions, 114
Letters,
    Business, 20–21
    Complaint, 92–93
    to Government Representatives, 74–75
Notes, 28–29, 42–43, 80–81, 98–99, 100–101, 126–127, 134–135
Opinions, 84–85
Paragraphs, 20–21, 36–37, 74–75, 92–93, 110–111, 128–129,
    146–147
Personal information, 2–3
Punctuation, 56–57

Reports,
    accident, 32–33
    crime, Authentic Materials E
Registration forms, 4–5
Statements, 39, 48–49, 66–67, 102–103, 120–121, 138–139
Stories, 40–41
Strategies, 20–21, 38–39, 56–57, 74–75, 92–93, 110–111,
    128–129, 146–147
Summaries, 62–63, 100–101, 132–133
Telephone messages, 8–9
Tips (consumer), 78–79
Vocabulary, 40–41, 60–61, 78–79, 94–95, 96–97, 114–115
Want ads, 86–87

APPLICATION

Community, 32–33, 104–105
Family, 50–51, 86–87, 122–123
Work, 14–15, 68–69, 140–141

LEARNING LOGS

17, 35, 53, 71, 89, 107, 125, 143

LIFE SKILLS
Consumer Education

Advertisements (classifieds), 86–87
Automobiles, 22–23, 24–25, 26–27, 32–33
Banking, 134–135
Complaint letters, 92–93
Credit cards, 132–133, 136–137
Household/housing, 86–87
Insurance (automobile), 24–25
Letters of complaint, 92–93
Making transactions, 80–81
Money, 76–77, 132–133, 134–135, 136–137
Prices, 82–83
Product labels (food), 46–47
Receipts, 80–81
Sales, 82–83
Shopping, 76–77, 78–79 (impulse), 82–83
Taxes, Authentic Materials C
Tips (for consumers), 78–79
Transactions, 80–81
Warranties, 78–79
Weights and measures, 82–83

Environment and World

United States Map, 192

Family and Parenting

Household/ housing, 86–87
Marriage license, 98–99, Authentic Materials A
Setting goals, 4–5, 22–23, 76–77

Government and Community

Agencies, 64–65
Courtrooms, 94–95
Crime reports, Authentic Materials E
Education systems (United States), 62–63
Identification, 98–99
Laws, 66–67, 94–95, 96–97, 100–101, 102–103
Letters to representatives, 74–75
Licenses, 98–99, Authentic Materials A,
    Authentic Materials B
Neighborhood watch, 104–105
Protests, 58–59
Public services, 64–65
Reports,
    accident, 32–33
    crime, Authentic Materials E
Representatives, 74–75
Rights (Constitutional), 60–61
School systems, 62–63
Signs, 100–101
Taxes, Authentic Materials C
Tickets, 100–101
Traffic tickets, 100–101
Trials (legal), 94–95
Unions, 68–69
Washington, D.C., 58–59

Group Work

2–3, 4–5, 6–7, 8–9, 10–11, 14–15, 22–23, 24–25, 26–27, 28–29,
32–33, 36–37, 40–41, 42–43, 44–45, 46–47, 50–51, 54–55,
58–59, 60–61, 62–63, 72–73, 76–77, 78–79, 80–81, 82–83,
84–85, 86–87, 94–95, 96–97, 98–99, 100–101, 104–105,
112–113, 116–117, 118–119, 122–123, 130–131, 132–133,
134–135, 136–137, 140–141, 144–145

Health and Nutrition

Accidents, 32–33 (car), 40–41
Doctor's visit (making appointments), 44–45
Immunizations, 50–51
Medical professions, 42–43
Nutrition facts, 46–47

Interpersonal Communication

Agreeing and disagreeing, 62
Correcting someone, 44
Disagreeing, 62
Expanding your answer, 116
Expressing doubt, 80–81
Introductions, greetings, and farewells, 2–3
Making appointments, 44–45
Paraphrasing, 98–99
Pausing expressions, 26–27
Personal information, 2–3
Polite disagreement, 62
Repeating to confirm, 134–135
Stating your purpose, 8

Learning to Learn

Analysis, 22–23, 76–77, 112–113
Application, 24–25, 32–33, 42–43, 46–47, 68–69, 122–123,
    130–131, 140–141
Classification, 130–131
Evaluation, 2–3, 6–7, 10–11, 74–75, 116–117, 130–131, 132–133
Making comparisons, 28–29, 46–47, 82–83, 78–79
Making inferences, 18–19, 22–23, 118–119
Problem solving skills, 112–113
Sequencing, 26–27, 40–41, 94–95, 126–127
Summarizing, 62–63, 100–101, 108–109, 132–133
Thinking skills, 22–23, 32–33, 50–51, 64–65, 68–69, 78–79,
    87–88, 90–91, 104–105, 118–119, 122–123, 136–137,
    140–141

Pair Work

2–3, 4–5, 6–7, 10–11, 13–14, 15–16, 22–23, 26–27, 44–45,
46–47, 58–59, 67–68, 69–70, 76–77, 78–79, 80–81, 84–85,
94–95, 96–97, 98–99, 100–101, 112–113, 116–117, 132–133,
134–135, 138–139

Safety and Security

Accidents, 32–33 (car), 40–41
911 use, 40–41

Telephone Communication

Answering machine messages, 8–9
Making appointments, 44–45
Messages, 8–9
Telephone etiquette, 8–9
911 use, 40–41

Time and Money

Banking, 134–135
Budgets, 130–131
Credit cards, 132–133, 136–137
Investments, 132–133
Money, 132–133, 146–147
Pay stubs, 140–141, Authentic Materials D
Taxes, Authentic Materials C

Transportation and Travel

Automobile, 22–23, 24–25, 26–27
Accidents, 26–27, 32–33
Bus, 26–27
Highway maps, 27, 28–29
Insurance (automobile), 24–25, 26–27
Licenses, 36–37, 98–99, Authentic Materials B
Schedules, 26–27 (bus)
Travel, 28–29 (planning a trip)
Types, 22–23, 28–29

TOPICS

Accidents, 32–33, 40–41
Activities, 4–5
Automobiles, 22–23, 24–25, 26–27
Banking, 134–135
Consumer Issues, 76–77, 78–79, 80–81, 82–83, 84–85, 86–87, 92–93
Education, 4–5, 62–63
Employment, 10–11, 14–15
Government, 58–59, 60–61, 62–63, 64–65, 66–67, 68–69, 74–75, 94–95, Authentic Materials E
Health and lifestyle, 42–43, 44–45, 46–47, 48–49, 50–51
Household/housing, 86–87
Introductions, 2–3
Laws, 94–95, 96–97, 98–99, 100–101, 102–103
Letter writing, 20–21, 74–75, 92–93
Medical, 40–41, 42–43, 44–45, 46–47, 48–49, 50–51
Money, 76–77, 82–83, 130–131, 132–133, 134–135, 136–137, 138–139, 140–141, Authentic Materials C, Authentic Materials D
Occupations, 42–43
Personal Development, 4–5, 6–7, 10–11
Shopping, 76–77, 78–79, 80–81, 82–83, 84–85, 86–87
Skills, 4–5, 6–7, 10–11
Telephone, 8–9, 40–41, 44–45
Transportation, 22–23, 24–25, 26–27, 28–29, 30–31, 100–101
Travel, 28–29
Work, 112–113, 114–115, 116–117, 118–119, 120–121, 122–123, 124–125, 126–127, 140–141, Authentic Materials C, Authentic Materials D, Authentic Materials F

WORKFORCE SKILLS
Applied Technology

Telephone, 8–9, 44–45

Maintaining Employment

Evaluations (performance), 118–119
Pay stubs, 140–141, Authentic Materials D
Rules, 112–113
Setting goals, 6, 22–23, 76–77
Taxes, Authentic Materials C

Obtaining Employment

Applications and resumes, 116–117, Authentic Materials F
Business letters, 20–21
Choosing a job, 122–123
Experience, 114–115
Interviews, 14–15, 116–117
Job descriptions, 114–115
Job hunting, 114–115
Occupations, 42–43
Skills, 4–5, 6–7, 10–11, 114–115
Types of companies, 122–123
Work experience, 114–115

A Sample Online Marriage License Application (State of Ohio)

Marriage License Application

This is the basic information page and is required by all applicants. Other pages may be required if either the Bride or Groom has been previously married.

GROOM INFORMATION:

First Name: [   ]   Middle: [   ]   Last: [   ]

Date of Birth: (Month [▼] Day [   ] Year [   ]) Age in years: [   ]

Home Phone: ([   ]) [   ] - [   ]   Work Phone: ([   ]) [   ] - [   ]

Current Address: Number & Street: [   ]

City: [   ]   County: [   ]   State: Ohio [▼]   ZIP: [   ]

Place of Birth, State or Country: [   ]   Occupation: [   ]

Your Father's full name: First [   ]   Middle: [   ]   Last: [   ]

Your Mother's full name: First: [   ]   Middle: [   ]   Last: (Maiden): [   ]

Have you ever been married? No [▼]   If yes, how many times [0]

BRIDE INFORMATION:

First Name: [   ]   Middle: [   ]   Last: [   ]

Date of Birth: (Month [▼] Day [   ] Year [   ]) Age in years: [   ]

Home Phone: ([   ]) [   ] - [   ]   Work Phone: ([   ]) [   ] - [   ]

Current Address: Number & Street: [   ]

City: [   ]   County: [   ]   State: Ohio [▼]   ZIP: [   ]

Place of Birth, State or Country: [   ]   Occupation: [   ]

Your Father's full name: First: [   ]   Middle: [   ]   Last: [   ]

Your Mother's full name: First: [   ]   Middle: [   ]   Last: (Maiden): [   ]

Have you ever been married? No [▼]   If yes, how many times [0]

Name of the Clergy you expect to perform your marriage ceremony: [   ]

Source: http://www.co.franklin.oh.us

B Sample Driver Written Test (partial test)

Department of Motor Vehicles, California
Sample Driver Test

1. You may drive off of the paved roadway to pass another vehicle:

○ If the shoulder is wide enough to accommodate your vehicle.
○ If the vehicle ahead of you is turning left.
○ Under no circumstances.

2. You are approaching a railroad crossing with no warning devices and are unable to see 400 feet down the tracks in one direction. The speed limit is:

○ 15 mph
○ 20 mph
○ 25 mph

3. When parking your vehicle parallel to the curb on a level street:

○ Your front wheels must be turned toward the street.
○ Your wheels must be within 18 inches of the curb.
○ One of your rear wheels must touch the curb.

4. When you are merging onto the freeway, you should be driving:

○ At or near the same speed as the traffic on the freeway.
○ 5 to 10 MPH slower than the traffic on the freeway.
○ The posted speed limit for traffic on the freeway.

5. When driving in fog, you should use your:

○ Fog lights only.
○ High beams.
○ Low beams.

6. A white painted curb means:

○ Loading zone for freight or passengers.
○ Loading zone for passengers or mail only.
○ Loading zone for freight only.

7. A school bus ahead of you in your lane is stopped with red lights flashing. You should:

○ Stop, then proceed when you think all of the children have exited the bus.
○ Slow to 25 MPH and pass cautiously.
○ Stop as long as the red lights are flashing.

8. California's "Basic Speed Law" says:

○ You should never drive faster than posted speed limits.
○ You should never drive faster than is safe for current conditions.
○ The maximum speed limit in California is 70 mph on certain freeways.

9. You just sold your vehicle. You must notify the DMV within ____ days.

○ 5
○ 10
○ 15

10. To avoid last minute moves, you should be looking down the road to where your vehicle will be in about _____.

○ 5 to 10 seconds
○ 10 to 15 seconds
○ 15 to 20 seconds

Answers:

1. Under no circumstances.	6. Loading zone for passengers or mail only.
2. 15 mph	7. Stop as long as the red lights are flashing.
3. Your wheels must be within 18 inches of the curb.	8. You should never drive faster than is safe for current conditions.
4. At or near the same speed as the traffic on the freeway.	9. 5
5. Low beams.	10. 10 to 15 seconds

Source: http://www.dmv.ca.gov.

C Sample W-2 Form: Wage and Tax Statement

a Control number	22222	OMB No. 1545-0008		

b Employer identification number		**1** Wages, tips, other compensation	**2** Federal income tax withheld

c Employer's name, address, and ZIP code	**3** Social security wages	**4** Social security tax withheld
	5 Medicare wages and tips	**6** Medicare tax withheld
	7 Social security tips	**8** Allocated tips

d Employee's social security number	**9** Advance EIC payment	**10** Dependent care benefits

e Employee's first name and initial Last name	**11** Nonqualified plans	**12a** Code
	13 Statutory employee ☐ Retirement plan ☐ Third-party sick pay ☐	**12b** Code
	14 Other	**12c** Code
		12d Code

f Employee's address and ZIP code

15 State Employer's state ID number	**16** State wages, tips, etc.	**17** State income tax	**18** Local wages, tips, etc.	**19** Local income tax	**20** Locality name

Form **W-2** Wage and Tax Statement

2004

Department of the Treasury—Internal Revenue Service

Copy 1—For State, City, or Local Tax Department

D Sample Pay Stub

FASHION SOLUTIONS, INC.

Employee: Julia Smith

Check Number: **56499543**

Social Security Number: 123-45-6789

Pay Period Date: 10/01/05 to 10/15/05

Check Date: 10/20/05

EARNINGS	Rate	Hours	This Period	Year-to-Date
	15.00	80	1,200.00	22,800.00
GROSS PAY			1,200.00	22,800.00
DEDUCTIONS				
	Federal Income Tax		156.00	2,964.00
	Social Security		132.00	2,508.00
	Medicare		31.20	592.80
	CA Income Tax		36.13	684.47
	CA State Disability Ins.		16.80	319.20
Total Deductions			372.13	7,069.27
NET PAY			827.87	

E Sample Form to Report a Crime

Submit Crime Tips Online – Anonymously or Otherwise

In order to insure the usefulness of the tips, try and give the most information possible.
You DO NOT have to give your name, but it would be useful if we can contact you.
If you would like to talk to someone personally, call the department at 555-3322.
Anonymous tips may also be left by telephone at 555-4888.

Online Crime Tips Form:

What crime did you witness or have information about:

Who is/are the victim(s):

What is the suspect's name:

What is the suspect's address:

What is the phone number of the suspect:

How do you know this information:

Who were the other witnesses to this crime (if any):

What is/are the address/addresses of the other witness/witnesses:

What are the phone number/numbers of the other witness/witnesses:

Optional: What is your name:

Optional: What is your address:

Optional: What is your phone number:

Would you be willing to appear in court: ⦿ Yes
If so, please be sure to input your
name, address and phone number ◯ No
above.

Any additional information you'd like to include:

Click the SUBMIT button below to send your information to the Sheriff's department. **The information will be submitted anonymously unless you chose to enter your name and contact information.**

Submit | Reset

Source: http://www.co.monterey.ca.us

F Sample Job Application

APPLICATION FOR EMPLOYMENT

PERSONAL INFORMATION:

Date ....

☐ Full Time ☐ Part Time ☐ Temporary

Name ....

Street Address ....

City/State/Zip ....

Available Start Date ....

Referral Source ....

Phone ....

SSN ....

EDUCATION:

Schools Attended	# of Years	Year Grad	Degree

EMPLOYMENT/WORK EXPERIENCE:

Start with your present or most recent position. (Attach another sheet of paper for additional work experience.)

Employer	Job Title
Supervisor	Phone
Describe Duties/Responsibilities/Accomplishments	Reason for Leaving
Dates of Employment (Month/Year) From: To:	

Employer	Job Title
Supervisor	Phone
Describe Duties/Responsibilities/Accomplishments	Reason for Leaving
Dates of Employment (Month/Year) From: To:	

BUSINESS REFERENCE:

Please provide contact information for one or more business references. (Attach another sheet of paper for additional references.)

Name	Company
Position	Phone

SPECIAL SKILLS:

Describe any skills or qualifications you have for this work.

Map of the United States

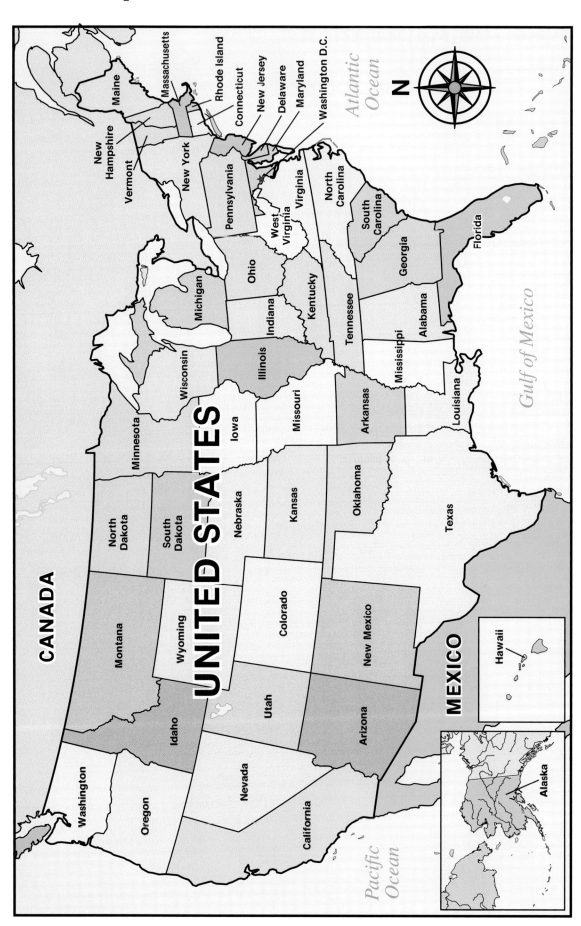

Photo Credits

From the CORBIS Royalty-Free Collection: p. 7 photo 2; **p. 43** photo 7; **p. 43** photo 8; **p. 47** top; **p. 62** top; **p. 62** bottom; **p. 63** photo 5; **p. 96** top, bottom; **p. 101** photo 10; **p. 134** middle, bottom **From the Getty Images Royalty-Free Collection: p. 6** photo 1; **p. 8; p. 38** left; **p. 43** photo 10, photo 11; **p. 47** middle; **p. 61** photo 2, photo 3, photo 6 top left, photo 6 bottom left, photo 6, right; **p. 63** photo 6; **p. 65** middle left, right; **p. 73; p. 83; p. 85** top left; **p. 96** second from top; **p. 98** top; **p. 100; p. 101** photo 1, photo 2, photo 3, photo 4, photo 5, photo 6, photo 7, photo 8, photo 9; **p. 104; p. 122** bottom; **p. 127** bottom; **p. 133** photo 9 **Other Images: p. 2** photo 1: Brand X Pictures/PictureQuest; **p. 2** photo 2: © Jeff Greenberg/PhotoEdit, Inc.; **p. 2** photo 3: © Michael Newman/PhotoEdit, Inc.; **p. 2,** photo 4: Color Day Production/Getty Images; **p. 3:** © Bonnie Kamin/PhotoEdit, Inc.; **p. 6** photo 4: Larry Dale Gordon/Getty Images; **p. 7** photo 3: Photodisc/PictureQuest; **p. 7,** photo 5: IT Stock Free/PictureQuest; **p. 7** photo 6: Stockbyte/PictureQuest; **p. 10** top: ImageState/ PictureQuest; **p. 10** middle: © Digital Vision; **p. 10** bottom: Photodisc/PictureQuest; **p. 28** top: Index Stock Imagery; **p. 28** second from top: John William Banagan/Getty Images; **p. 28** second from bottom: Sean Murphy/Getty Images; **p. 28** bottom: © James Leynse/CORBIS; **p. 32:** eStock Photo/PictureQuest; **p. 38** right: Pan America/PictureQuest; **p. 42** photo 1: David Joel/Getty Images; **p. 42** photo 5: Orion Press/PictureQuest; **p. 43** photo 2: Thinkstock/PictureQuest; **p. 43** photo 3: Thinkstock/PictureQuest; **p. 43** photo 4: © Bill Aron/PhotoEdit, Inc.; **p. 43** photo 6: Stockbyte/PictureQuest; **p. 43** photo 9: Creatas/PictureQuest; **p. 44:** Romilly Lockyer/Getty Images; **p. 46:** David N. Averbach; **p. 47** bottom: David N. Averbach; **p. 49:** Photodisc/PictureQuest; **p. 50:** ImageState/PictureQuest; **p. 60** photo 1: no credit needed; **p. 60** photo 4: David Averbach; **p. 61** photo 5: © Bettmann/ CORBIS; **p. 63** photo 1: © Michael Newman/PhotoEdit, Inc.;

p. 63 photo 2: © David Young-Wolff/PhotoEdit, Inc.; **p. 63** photo 3: Creatas/PictureQuest; **p. 63** photo 4: SuperStock/PictureQuest; **p. 64** top: Index Stock Imagery/PictureQuest; **p. 64** bottom: © David Young-Wolff/PhotoEdit, Inc.; **p. 65** top: Stockdisc/ PictureQuest; **p. 65** bottom left: Digital Vision/PictureQuest; **p. 78** photo 1: Gabor Geissler/Getty Images; **p. 78** photo 4: Stockbyte/ PictureQuest; **p. 79** photo 2: Holly Harris/Getty Images; **p. 79** photo 5: © Felicia Martinez/PhotoEdit, Inc.; **p. 79** photo 6: © Michael Newman/PhotoEdit, Inc.; **p. 79** photo 8: © Michael Newman/PhotoEdit, Inc.; **p. 79** photo 9: Blend Images/Picture Quest; **p. 80:** Digital Vision/PictureQuest; **p. 81** top: Greg Pease/ Getty Images; **p. 81** bottom left: Thinkstock/PictureQuest; **p. 81** bottom right: Digital Vision/PictureQuest; **p. 85** top right: Digital Vision/PictureQuest; **p. 85** middle left: Philip Habib/Getty Images; **p. 85** middle right: Photodisc/PictureQuest; **p. 85** bottom left: Dorling Kindersley/Getty Images; **p. 85** bottom right: McGraw-Hill Companies, Inc./Gary He, photographer; **p. 93:** Ryan McVay/ Getty Images; **p. 96** second from bottom: Thinkstock/PictureQuest; **p. 98** bottom: © Spencer Grant/PhotoEdit, Inc.; **p. 110:** © Fat Chance Productions/CORBIS; **p. 114** top: The McGraw-Hill Companies, Inc./ Christopher Kerrigan, photographer; **p. 114** bottom: © Spencer Grant/PhotoEdit, Inc.; **p. 116** top: © Tony Freeman/PhotoEdit, Inc.; **p. 116** bottom: Ed Honowitz/Getty Images; **p. 118** top: Timothy Shonnard/Getty Images; **p. 118** bottom: Chabruken/Getty Images; **p. 122** top: © Michael Newman/PhotoEdit, Inc.; **p. 127** top: AFP/Getty Images; **p. 132** photo 1: Digital Vision/PictureQuest; **p. 132** photo 4: Brand X Pictures/PictureQuest; **p. 132** photo 7: David N. Averbach; **p. 133** photo 5: © Jeff Greenberg/PhotoEdit, Inc.; **p. 133** photo 6: Stockbyte/PictureQuest; **p. 134** top: Image Source/PictureQuest; **p. 135:** Digital Vision/PictureQuest; **p. 136** top: Eric O'Connell/Getty Images; **p. 136** bottom: © Spencer Grant/PhotoEdit, Inc.

Text Credits

Used with permission: p. 11 From Netscape Network (http://channels.netscape.com). **p. 19** Adapted from Montgomery Advertiser Gannett Co., Inc. Copyright 2004. **p. 32** Adapted from AAA Insurance (http://www.ouraaa.com/ insurance/auto/accident.html). **p. 50, 51** Adapted from Centers for Disease Control and Prevention (www.cdc.gov/nip/recs/ adult-schedule.htm). **p. 68** Adapted from AFL-CIO Organization (http://www.aflcio.org/aboutunions/joinunions/). **p. 73** From AFL-CIO Workers' Rights in America survey (http://www.aflcio.org/ yourjobeconomy/rights/workersrights/upload/report.pdf).

p. 90, 91 From *Newbury House Dictionary,* Fourth Edition. **p. 101** From Self-Help Center: Traffic Information (www.courtinfo.ca.gov/selfhelp/traffic/info.htm). **p. 104** From *U.S. Express,* Vol. 1, No. 3, October 21, 1988, Scholastic, Inc. **p. 109** From *The Macmillan Book of Fascinating Facts,* by Ann Elwood and Carol Madigan. 1989. **p. 133** Graph from Bankrate.com Roper ASW poll. **p. 145** Adapted from "The King and The Poor Boy" from *Cambodian Folk Tales* by Muriel Paskin Carrison, Charles Tuttle Co, Inc, Japan.

We apologize for any apparent infringement of copyright and if notified, the publisher will be pleased to rectify any errors or omissions at the earliest opportunity.